Theology and Horror

Theology and Pop Culture

Series Editor: Matthew Brake

The *Theology and Pop Culture* series examines the intersection of theology, religion, and popular culture, including, but not limited to, television, movies, sequential art, and genre fiction. In a world plagued by rampant polarization of every kind and the decline of religious literacy in the public square, *Theology and Pop Culture* is uniquely poised to educate and entertain a diverse audience utilizing one of the few things society at large still holds in common: love for popular culture.

Titles in the Series

Theology and Horror: Explorations of the Dark Religious Imagination, edited by Brandon R. Grafius and John W. Morehead
Sports and Play in Christian Theology, edited by Philip Halstead and John Tucker
Theology and Prince, edited by Jonathan H. Harwell and Rev. Katrina E. Jenkins
Theology and the Marvel Universe, edited by Gregory Stevenson

Theology and Horror

*Explorations of the Dark
Religious Imagination*

Edited by Brandon R. Grafius
and John W. Morehead

LEXINGTON BOOKS/FORTRESS ACADEMIC
Lanham • Boulder • New York • London

Published by Lexington Books/Fortress Academic
Lexington Books is an imprint of The Rowman & Littlefield Publishing Group, Inc.
4501 Forbes Boulevard, Suite 200, Lanham, Maryland 20706
www.rowman.com

6 Tinworth Street, London SE11 5AL, United Kingdom

British Library Cataloguing in Publication Information Available

Library of Congress Cataloging-in-Publication Data

ISBN: 978-1-9787-0798-6 (cloth : alk. paper)
ISBN: 978-1-9787-0799-3 (electronic)
ISBN: 978-1-9787-0800-6 (pbk. : alk. paper)

∞™ The paper used in this publication meets the minimum requirements of American
National Standard for Information Sciences Permanence of Paper for Printed Library
Materials, ANSI/NISO Z39.48-1992.

Contents

Introduction

Theology and Horror

Brandon R. Grafius and John W. Morehead

Pointing out that horror and religion are connected is to risk stating the obvious. The black-and-white Universal classics from the 1930s are far from the earliest examples, but they are some of the best known. When Victor Frankenstein succeeds in giving life to his monster, he famously proclaims, "Now I know what it feels like to be God!" a line that was excised from many early prints of James Whale's 1931 film adaptation for its blasphemous overtones. The connections between *Dracula* (Tod Browning, 1931) and religion are also directly on that film's surface, with religious iconography such as the crucifix being one of the only effective weapons against this powerful monster. And the Universal version of *The Mummy* (Karl Freund, 1932) plays not only with the titular figure as an ethnic other but also as representative of frighteningly pagan religious practices.[1]

Scholars of horror and culture have been well aware of this, with Leo Braudy's monograph *Haunted* being only one of the more recent examples.[2] In Braudy's reading, the popular fascination with the supernatural emerged from the Enlightenment's attempt to remove the supernatural element from religion. But this attempt only served to chase the supernatural out of Protestant and Catholic religion and into the realm of folklore. The supernatural, in essence, becomes the repressed of religion. Robin Wood, in his seminal essay, "The American Nightmare," famously linked Freudian ideas of the "return of the repressed" to horror and the monstrous; in his analysis of American horror, in particular, he locates the repressed in the "Puritan consciousness," which makes a clear and inextricable link between "the Devil and sexuality."[3]

Similarly, theologians,[4] biblical scholars, and scholars of religion in general have long known that the biblical text and the Christian tradition in general are filled with monsters and fear. The literature on the monstrous Leviathan, most directly present in Psalm 104 and the divine speech which serves as the climax of the Book of Job, is voluminous, having expanded to proportions almost as chaotically monstrous as the sea creature they attempt to contain.[5] Several decades ago, Phyllis Trible noted how many biblical texts have served as "texts of terror" for female readers, working to threaten them with death, rape, or erasure of identity if they transgress the culturally approved boundaries.[6] Jon Levenson's fascinating work of theodicy, *Creation and the Persistence of Evil*, explores the Bible's use of Leviathan and other images of chaos to create a vision of a world where God is in control, a control which only seems tenuous from the limited perspective of humanity.[7] These works, along with many others in a similar vein, are thoughtful, frequently provocative, and shine an important light on aspects of our religious history and experiences.

But over the last several decades, and with an increasing acceleration in the last several years, something different has been happening. Scholars of religion, theologians, and biblical scholars have begun to explore these ideas not simply within the confines of the biblical text or the traditions of religion, but as they spill into popular culture, as represented in narratives, movies, and video games. Tina Pippin made some tentative steps in this direction with her 1999 monograph *Apocalyptic Bodies: The Biblical End of the World in Text and Image*, connecting the apocalyptic narratives of the Book of Revelation with contemporary film, television, and the landscape of the southern United States.[8] But perhaps the first full-blown work of such intention was Timothy Beal's *Religion and Its Monsters*, appearing at a time when the discipline of horror studies itself was still in its nascent stages.[9] In this oft-cited monograph, Beal connects the battle against chaos in the Bible and other Ancient Near Eastern literature with *Dracula* and *Nosferatu* (F. W. Murnau, 1922), with Lovecraft's Cthulu mythos, and with many other monsters which live in the more contemporary imagination.

The exploration of horror by scholars of religion, the Bible, and theology proceeded slowly over the next decade, with a few notable works appearing near the end of the millennium's first decade. Amy Kalmanofsky's *Terror All Around* is, in many ways, a work of traditional biblical scholarship, with its focus on close readings of Hebrew vocabulary and detailed exegesis of individual verses.[10] But she also interacts with scholarship such as Noël Carrol's *Philosophy of Horror* and, especially, Carol Clover's *Men, Women, and Chain Saws*.[11] In Kalmanofsky's imaginative interpretation, the city of Zion, frequently portrayed in the biblical text as a woman and always under threat from invading armies, is recast as the Bible's "final girl." And stepping into the world of religious scholarship more broadly, Douglas Cowan's *Sa-*

cred Terror makes the explicit connection between the horrors that are dramatized on screen in horror films and the fears that religion attempts to soothe.[12] In both cases, these fears are profoundly existential, asking us to confront the universal questions of our place in the universe and our relationship to the world around us. In Cowan's handling, horror movies do not simply use religious imagery; they are, themselves, religious texts. This is not to say that horror is itself a form of religion; rather, horror emerges from the same well of human imagination. Writing specifically about the horror stories of Stephen King, Cowan notes that they "emerge from the same place in the human imagination" as does religion, asking the same questions, wrestling with the same anxieties.[13]

In the last decade, the scholarly energy around these questions has continued to build, resulting in a series of monographs, articles, and edited volumes that have continued to move the fields of religion, theology, and biblical studies into deeper conversations with the traditions of horror literature, film, and scholarship. Brian R. Doak uses monster theory as a productive conversation partner to examine the book of Job's vision of the self in relation to the world.[14] In his revised dissertation, Safwat Marzouk proves himself to be fully conversant in traditional historical-critical scholarship and a wide range of Ancient Near Eastern texts from outside of the biblical corpus but also makes use of the theories of scholars such as Noël Carroll and Jeffrey Jerome Cohen to complicate the relationship between the hero and the monster in the mythological combat stories of these texts.[15] And one of the editors of this volume, Brandon R. Grafius, uses psychoanalytic theories of horror, including Wood, Kristeva, and Creed, to analyze the story of Phinehas (Numbers 25), reading the murderous priest through the lens of the socially conservative slasher films of the 1980s.[16] In the last several years, the field has grown large enough to accommodate a program unit on religion and monsters, several edited volumes and a monograph series have appeared on religion and horror,[17] and a number of survey articles have appeared to introduce readers to the field.[18] It's an exciting time to be engaged in horror and religion.

But behind all of this, there are some nagging questions. In a recent monograph, Robert Miller III uses traditional methodologies to trace the dragon-slayer myth through various traditions, into the Hebrew Bible, and through the New Testament.[19] It's a masterful work of scholarship, one borne of a deep knowledge of comparative mythology, linguistics, and a variety of textual traditions. Near the monograph's end, he briefly engages with monster theory, noting that not all of it is helpful; for Miller, a significant amount of monster-theory-inspired work is "common sense explanations" dressed up in theoretical language.[20] If this assessment is accurate and complete, then pursuing interdisciplinary work in areas of horror and religion could be an intellectual dead end.

Miller's critique is one we should take seriously. But we would also suggest it's incomplete; when it's not done well, introducing contemporary horror theory into the worlds of theology, Bible, or religious studies can be little more than an empty exercise. But the practice can generate much richer meaning. As some of the work in the last handful of years demonstrates, there are significant insights to be gained from the kind of interdisciplinary work being explored at the crossroads of religion and horror.[21] When Marzouk introduces monster theory into his discussion of the *Chaoskampf* motif from Ancient Near Eastern mythology, he is able to demonstrate that the texts frequently depict monsters such as Tiamat as more human (or heroic) than scholarship generally acknowledges, and heroes such as Marduk as more monstrous.[22] Rather than viewing binary oppositions between the forces of order and chaos,[23] as biblical scholarship has traditionally held, Marzouk is able to identify ways in which these identities are frequently blurred and always unstable.

Further development can be seen in the ways in which a conversation with horror allows scholars to open up questions of religion to an engagement with the contemporary world. Steve Wiggins's recent monograph, *Holy Horror*, has explored the ways in which the Bible itself is used in recent horror films and what this usage signifies for our culture's relationship to the Bible.[24] He notes its varied uses as a protective icon, as the source of salvific knowledge, and even as the potential source of misdirection. These are all attitudes toward the Bible which are present in the wider culture, but which often go unnoticed. And it took the attention of a biblical scholar to bring this consistent motif of horror to the surface.

Scholars of religion and its affiliated fields have the potential to bring new attention to these pervasive elements of horror narratives and the necessary background knowledge to provide a deep history of these ideas. Through this depth of historical knowledge, the potential exists to provide a richer understanding of the worldview portrayed in these horror films and the ways in which this worldview reflects, refracts, and shapes the worldviews of the culture as a whole. And in another potential avenue of exploration, we can take these learnings from horror films and smuggle them back into the realm of religion. After all, religion is in horror, but we also find plenty of horror in religion. The theoretical tools of horror studies offer the potential of rereading these horrific elements of the religious experience, whether they be passages of scripture, disturbing theological doctrines, religious rituals, religious adherents behaving and thinking monstrously in the name of their religion, or the exploration of the multifaceted ways in which the horrific contributes to the holistic experience of religion.

This exploration emerges from what has long been present in horror itself: an engagement with questions of spirituality and the nature of the divine. Horror attempts to wrestle with the same questions that animate religious thought—

questions about the nature of the divine, humanity's place in the universe, the distribution of justice, and what it means to live a good life, among many others. For decades, horror has been "doing" theology, even if it proceeds in a very different manner from the academic discipline of theology.

This is how we have attempted to use the word "theology" in the title of this volume. In line with the understanding of theology in this series ("Theology and Pop Culture"), we use "theology" to refer to the pursuit of questions regarding the nonphysical realities, spaces where both divinity and horror dwell. While from the standpoint of current academic divisions many of these essays might fit more comfortably within the discipline of "religious studies" than of "theology," our aim with this volume is somewhat different from either of these disciplines when narrowly understood. We aim to explore how questions of spirituality, divinity, and religious structures are lifted up, complicated, and even sometimes answered (at least partially) by works of horror. What we are most interested in is how the works under discussion in these chapters are "doing" theology through their narratives. This approach may seem foreign to those used to associating theology largely with the Christian tradition as expressed in works on biblical and systematic theology, but we are seeking to break new ground.

We believe the essays gathered in this volume make a vital contribution to our emerging understanding of horror's place in religion, just as they help us to understand more fully the role that religion plays in horror. We hope that these essays will not so much "reverse the hermeneutical flow"[25] as they interpret in multiple directions at once, from religion to horror to culture all at the same time. These essays affirm that the religious imagination remains a central part of our human experience and that texts of horror continue to be vital expressions of this imagination.

The organization of the essays in this volume is fourfold, with three chapters in each section. The first section provides the theoretical foundations for the book. Douglas E. Cowan explores the theological implications of various horrific depictions of hell. Through a depiction of fear about the dark side of the unseen order, Cowan argues that this exemplifies theology's central role in the human experience: to impose order on the seeming chaos. In the second chapter in this section, Steve A. Wiggins discusses horror's origins in relation to theology. While conventional treatments of the horror genre trace its origins to the Gothic novel, Wiggins argues that it goes back much further and that the Bible may be seen as the progenitor of horror, with horror comprising as an essential element of theological thought in the Western tradition that grew out of Judaism and Christianity. Jack Hunter provides the final chapter in this section. He explores Rudolf Otto's understanding of the numinous as the essence of religious experience, and how this is expressed through the writings of Bram Stoker, Arthur Machen, and H. P. Lovecraft.

The second section of this volume involves three chapters that explore different Christian theological readings of subject matter. Karrá Shimabuku-ro draws upon the lens of Roman Catholicism and analyzes the lessons presented by horror films on exorcism and demonic possession, the concept of hell, as well as priests and the institution of the Church. She focuses on how pop culture Catholicism is presented and shaped through the images presented in specific horror films. Kevin J. Wetmore, Jr., continues this section with a consideration of a Protestant apocalyptic. Wetmore examines how the adaptation of the images and theologies of the Book of Revelation subverts the Christian "original" meaning of the text, while also reinforcing the idea of a battle with evil. In this manner, pop Christian apocalyptic narratives are reinterpreted through the broader popular culture, with the meanings of the apocalyptic tradition being reconceived for a different time and audience. The final chapter in this section is an essay by Alyssa Beall that draws on the theological concept of Gnosticism or "secret knowledge." Beall argues that the surge in a particular type of horror narrative is an outcome of the growing heretical or heterodox religious climate of the United States. The framing narratives of particular films are placed in direct opposition to or directly challenge the orthodox worldview. In this way, these filmic texts can be read as reclaiming the theological power, and terror, of knowledge itself.

The third section of this volume explores various monstrous or paranormal elements in horror and theology. Joshua Wise argues that the traditional ghost story, involving the themes of unresolved injustice, strong personal moral evil, abiding terrestrial presence, and deep regret, fills the gap left by the promise and hope of the public, social, and terrestrial proclamation of good and evil. This section continues with Michael Asher Hammett's chapter that seeks to untangle the historical and theological issues connected to lycanthropy. Hammett begins with a consideration of theological treatments of lycanthropy, and then applies these divergent explanations to contemporary depictions of werewolves to help the reader understand the horror and appeal of werewolves as characters. This section is completed with a chapter by Jessi Knippel in an exploration of zombies. Knippel explores the ways in which the graphic novel series _iZombie_, read through the lens of theologian Marcella Altaus-Reid's _Indecent Theology_, acts as a counternarrative to the common constructions of community, gender, race, sexuality, and the end of the world as present in apocalyptic and zombie narratives.

The last section of this volume explores theological analyses of horror films. Mark Richard Adams looks at the _Hellraiser_ franchise as one that presents a conflicted narrative space, where ideas of religion, spirituality, and damnation, often contrast or even conflict with Lovecraftian themes of cosmic horror, explorations of sadomasochistic pleasure, and queer monstrosity. Adams explores the depictions of religion and the afterlife and representations of the demonic, in order to understand this franchise's ambiguity and contradictory approaches to its representation of theological concepts. Amy Beddows draws upon the psychological horror videogame and movie franchise *Silent Hill*. This chapter explores how the portrayal of theology in this franchise serves as a critical reflection of religious beliefs and practices as embodiment of social control, especially the silencing and discrediting of women. Beddows's analysis also explores the value of alternative theologies in horror as a challenge to the dominant power structures in nonsecular and secular society. This volume concludes with a chapter by Wickham Clayton in an analysis of three of the *Friday the 13th* films. Clayton explores the narrative, generic, and characterological functions of hell in the films, as well as the mythological conceptions and models of hell they present. He concludes that even with potentially failed entries in a popular franchise, theological conceptions of religion are central to the development of modern horror stories like these.

Individually, these chapters each offer new ways to understand how theology speaks through manifestations of horror in popular culture, as well as how horror influences our understanding of theological traditions. Taken together, the chapters in this volume speak to the continued vitality of this approach and point to the untapped potential that yet remains. When read individually as separate cultural spheres, theology and horror each speak to our culture's fears and hopes, and what it means to be human. When read together, this conversation only deepens, and we can begin to see the blurred boundaries, the shifting meanings, and the way that interpretation gets passed back and forth, with new insights added each time.

NOTES

1. An excellent overview of the cultural history of the mummy in horror films is found in Glynn, *The Mummy on Screen*. See also Day, *The Mummy's Curse: Mummymania in the English-Speaking World* (New York: Routledge, 2006).

2. Braudy, *Haunted*.

3. Wood, "The American Nightmare: Horror in the 70s," in *Hollywood from Vietnam to Reagan . . . and Beyond!*, 63–84, quotations from 66.

4. With the possible exception, perhaps, of conservative Christian theologians and biblical scholars.

5. Recently, see the volume *Playing with Leviathan*, eds. Koert van Bekkum et al.

6. Trible, *Texts of Terror*.

7. Levenson, *Creation and the Persistence of Evil*.

8. Pippin, *Apocalyptic Bodies*.

9. Beal, *Religion and Its Monsters*.

10. Kalmanofsky, *Terror All Around*.

11. Carroll, *The Philosophy of Horror*.

12. Cowan, *Sacred Terror*.

13. Cowan, *America's Dark Theologian*, 9.

14. Doak, *Consider Leviathan*.

15. Marzouk, *Egypt as a Monster in the Book of Ezekiel*.

16. Grafius, *Reading Phinehas, Watching Slashers.*

17. For example, Michael E. Heyes, ed., *Holy Monsters, Sacred Grotesques*; Beal and Greenaway, eds., *Horror and Religion*; the monograph series *Horror and Scripture* from Lexington Books/Fortress Academic.

18. Grafius, "Text and Terror"; Wiggins, "Good Book Gone Bad"; Murphy, "Leviathan to *Lucifer*." Also noteworthy is the 2019 "Gods and Monsters" conference, sponsored by Texas State University, out of which emerged both a forthcoming edited volume (Lexington Books, 2020) and the peer-reviewed, open access *Journal of Gods and Monsters.*

19. Miller, *The Dragon, the Mountain, and the Nations.*

20. Ibid., 286–87 n. 46.

21. Almost as if in answer to Miller's critique, much of this work was being done concurrently with Miller's monograph or has been published subsequently. We would like to think that Miller would agree with our assessment that much recent scholarship has contributed more than the "common-sense" reading that Miller rightly criticizes.

22. Marzouk, *Egypt as a Monster*, esp. 70–94.

23. Or even between authorized royal power and foreign power, as in Crouch, *War and Violence in the Ancient Near East.* The theoretical framework of *Chaoskampf* has become more strongly contested in recent biblical scholarship, with many scholars coming to believe that Gunkel's hypothesis, and its appropriation by other biblical scholars, has created a flatter picture of varied Ancient Near Eastern texts than is justified. See, for example, the essays gathered in Scurlock and Beal, eds., *Creation and Chaos.*

24. Wiggins, *Holy Horror.*

25. On the question of "reversing the hermeneutical flow," in which the movie under discussion "deconstructs the biblical text," rather than simply being held up as a normative standard by which to judge the film, see, for example, Aichele, "Film Theory and Biblical Studies."

WORKS CITED

Aichele, George. "Film Theory and Biblical Studies." In *Close Encounters between Bible and Film: An Interdisciplinary Engagement*, edited by Laura Copier and Caroline Vander Stichele, 11–26. Atlanta: SBL Press, 2016.

Bela, Eleanor, and Jonathan Greenaway, eds. *Horror and Religion: New Literary Approaches to Theology, Race, and Sexuality.* Cardiff, UK: University of Wales Press, 2019.

Beal, Timothy K. *Religion and Its Monsters.* New York: Routledge, 2002.

Bekkum, Kurt van, Jaap Dekker, Henk van de Kemp, and Eric Peels. *Playing with Leviathan: Interpretation and Reception of Monsters from the Biblical World.* Leiden, Netherlands: Brill, 2017.

Braudy, Leo. *Haunted: On Ghosts, Witches, Vampires, Zombies, and Other Monsters of the Natural and Supernatural Worlds.* New Haven, CT: Yale University Press, 2016.

Carroll, Noel. *The Philosophy of Horror: Or, Paradoxes of the Heart.* New York: Routledge, 1990.

Cowan, Douglas E. *Sacred Terror: Religion and Horror on the Silver Screen.* Waco, TX: Baylor University Press, 2008.

———. *America's Dark Theologian: The Religious Imagination of Stephen King.* New York: New York University Press, 2018.

Crouch, C. L. *War and Violence in the Ancient Near East: Military Violence in Light of Cosmology and History.* BZAW 407. Berlin: de Gruyter, 2009.

Doak, Brian R. *Consider Leviathan: Narratives of Nature and the Self in Job.* Minneapolis, MN: Fortress Press, 2014.

Glynn, Basil. *The Mummy on Screen: Orientalism and Monstrosity in the Horror Film.* London: Bloomsbury Academic, 2019.

Grafius, Brandon R. "Text and Terror: Monster Theory and the Hebrew Bible." *Currents in Biblical Research* 16, no. 1 (2017): 34–49.

———. *Reading Phinehas, Watching Slashers: Horror Theory and Numbers 25.* Lanham, MD: Lexington Books/Fortress Academic, 2018.

Heyes, Michael E., ed. *Holy Monsters, Sacred Grotesques: Monstrosity and Religion in Europe and the United States*. Lanham, MD: Lexington Books, 2018.

Kalmanofsky, Amy. *Terror All Around: The Rhetoric of Horror in the Book of Jeremiah*. New York: T&T Clark, 2008.

Levenson, Jon D. *Creation and the Persistence of Evil: The Jewish Drama of Divine Omnipotence*. Princeton, NJ: Princeton University Press, 1988.

Marzouk, Safwat. *Egypt as a Monster in the Book of Ezekiel*. FAT 2/76. Tübingen, Germany: Mohr Siebeck, 2015.

Miller, Robert D. II. *The Dragon, the Mountain, and the Nations: An Old Testament Myth, Its Origins, and Its Afterlives*. University Park, PA: Eisenbrauns, 2018.

Murphy, Kelly J. "Leviathan to *Lucifer*: What Biblical Monsters (Still) Reveal." *Interpretation* 74, no. 2 (2020): 146–58.

Pippin, Tina. *Apocalyptic Bodies: The Biblical End of the World in Text and Image*. New York: Routledge, 1999.

Scurlock, JoAnn, and Richard H. Beal, eds. *Creation and Chaos: A Reconsideration of Hermann Gunkel's* Chaoskampf *Hypothesis*. Winona Lake, IN: Eisenbrauns, 2013.

Trible, Phyllis. *Texts of Terror: Literary-Feminist Readings of Biblical Narratives*. Minneapolis, MN: Fortress Press, 1984.

Wiggins, Steve A. "Good Book Gone Bad: Reading Phinehas and Watching Horror." *Horizons in Biblical Theology* 41, no. 1 (2019): 93–103.

———. *Holy Horror: The Bible and Fear in Movies*. Jefferson, NC: McFarland, 2018.

Wood, Robin. *Hollywood from Vietnam to Reagan . . . and Beyond!* New York: Columbia University Press, 2003.

FILMOGRAPHY

Dracula. Directed by Tod Browning. Universal City, CA: Universal Pictures, 1931.

Frankenstein. Directed by James Whale. Universal City, CA: Universal Pictures, 1931.

The Mummy. Directed by Karl Freund. Universal City, CA: Universal Pictures, 1932.

Nosferatu. Directed by F. W. Murnau. Berlin: Jofa-Atelier Berlin-Johannisthal, 1922.

Part I

Horrifying Foundations

Chapter One

Consider the Yattering

The Infernal Order and the Religious Imagination in Real Time

Douglas E. Cowan

VIOLET

No! That can't be real!

CONSTANCE

You're a smart girl. How can you be so arrogant to think that there is only one reality that you're able to see?

(*American Horror Story: Murder House*)

. . . there stretches beyond this visible world an unseen world of which we now know nothing positive, but in its relation to which the true significance of our present mundane life consists.

(William James, "Is Life Worth Living?")

Three common problems tend to plague discussions of religion and horror, not to mention religion and science fiction, and all their various hybrids: (a) dismissing the appearance or use of religion as little more than a snide attempt at discrediting the faithful; (b) ignoring any aspect or implication of religion that does not accurately reflect one's own ideological commitment to whatever one considers sacred; and (c) explaining away the horrific in religion (or vice versa) as nothing more than a metaphor for something else.[1] This chapter proposes a somewhat different approach, one that takes both the power of storytelling in human experience seriously and, more importantly, the place of religion in horror at its word.

So, to that end, I invite you to consider the Yattering.

"Why the powers (long may they hold court; long may they shit light on the heads of the damned) had sent it out from Hell to stalk Jack Polo, the Yattering couldn't discover."[2] Here, the minor inconvenience that is the demon's parenthetical comments read almost as a form of ritual invocation, Hell's version of "Praise the Lord" or "Peace be upon him," and its way of ensuring that imps like the Yattering remember their place in the infernal order. Indeed, from the opening lines of his rules-based comedy-horror "The Yattering and Jack," published first in *Books of Blood*, Clive Barker establishes the framework of an unambiguously religious universe. It may not be one that believers among us recognize readily, but it is one nonetheless. The very possibility of hell (in whatever form), of demons (whether major or minor), and of diabolical persecution (and the statutes by which it is governed) exist only within the context of the religious imagination. Like the concept of a soul, *hell* is an explicitly theological idea, and makes no sense apart from the religious storyworld (whatever the religion and however the storyworld is imagined) in which it comes embedded. Whether it's a gloomy land of shadows where the dead pass their endless days (à la Homer), the classic Christian image of a lake of fire and eternal torment, or something far more baroque (à la Hieronymus Bosch), a great, terraced pit with different levels of punishment reserved for this or that class of sinner (à la Dante's *Inferno*), or the Buddhist concept of a long, but ultimately finite round of suffering based on one's particular attachments in life (and imagined most viscerally, perhaps, in the Hell Gardens of Wang Saen Suk) makes no difference. Call it Hell, Hades, Tartarus, Erebus, the Narakas, or any of its other myriad names, the idea of a place of eternal, postmortem punishment is the infernal love-child forever born from the union of fear and the religious imagination.

While that may seem a bit obvious, it's a point worth remembering, if for no other reason than the number of times in popular culture it appears either forgotten or ignored, or else the notion of hell itself is deployed as a kind of free-floating signifier for "many bad things happen here." Some commentators, for example, consider the most remarkable thing about Barker's best-known characters, the *Hellraiser* Cenobites, to be their "S&M black-leather garb," their body-horror aesthetic, and little else.[3] Only one seems to have noticed that "cenobite" is a religious term.[4] As I point out in *Sacred Terror*, though, the Roman Catholic Church recognizes two different types of monastic order: "the eremitic (those who live as hermits) and the cenobitic (those who live in religious community). The *Hellraiser* Cenobites invert a number of the characteristics of the latter. Pinhead's costume resembles a medieval cassock. An initial draft of the screenplay includes a scene in which the Cenobites are seen in something resembling medieval monastic cells. Indeed, in Barker's novella, the Cenobites are introduced as 'theologians of the Order of the Gash. Summoned from their experiments in the higher reaches of pleasure, to bring their ageless heads into a world of rain and failure.'"[5] While *The Scarlet Gospels*, Barker's sequel to *The Hellbound Heart*, fills in considerable backstory on the Cenobite Hell Priest, the infernal religious order to which he belongs, and the almost mundane bureaucracy of Hell, little in that book rises to the atmospheric majesty of Barker's original story.[6] Though devoted fans of the Hellraiser mythos awaited *The Scarlet Gospels* breathlessly, as I pointed out elsewhere, unfortunately it "reads at times like a *Dungeons & Dragons* campaign with Barker acting as Dungeon Master for the Hell realm."[7]

To return to the Yattering, though, not unlike Wormwood, the unfortunate junior devil in C. S. Lewis's *The Screwtape Letters*, Barker's little annoyance demon has been assigned to ensure the damnation of Jack Polo, "a gherkin importer," whose "family was dull, his politics were simple-minded and his theology non-existent."[8] From low-level poltergeist activity to more intimate temptations to anything else permitted within the rules of his class, the Yattering has a simple job to do: get Jack Polo. It "would even share the shower with Jack," Barker tells us, "hanging unseen from the rail that held up the shower curtain and whispering obscene suggestions in his ear. That was always successful the demons were taught at the Academy. The obscenities in the ear routine never failed to distress clients, making them think they were conceiving of these pernicious acts themselves."[9] Here, the Yattering has been trained to leverage what is arguably the most insidious of Christian theological dicta: that believers are just as surely convicted by the whisper of erotic thought-crime as by the actual violation of whatever sexual standards and statutes have been set by their God. Obviously, readers recognize this as the Yattering's (dis)embodiment of Matthew 5:28, Jesus's warning against looking at a woman with lust in your heart. Although to many, this may appear the horror story equivalent of a flip, "devil made me do it" defense, conjuring up legions of Bob Larson followers wailing and gnashing their collective teeth over their temptation by the demon-of-this or the demon-of-that, it's actually much more.

Jack Polo's theology may appear "nonexistent" to the Yattering, but it isn't to Barker, and it isn't to millions of the people who will take up the *Books of Blood* as a bit of prebedtime scariness. This is an infernal framework with an order, a logic, a structured way of doing things, both in this world and the world unseen. Indeed, as "Law One stated"—and made the Yattering's job that much more difficult—"Thou shalt not lay palm upon thy victims."[10] Whatever temptations are offered, this version of Hell's organizational theology requires that souls damn themselves. They cannot *be* damned, as it were. All of this is to say, Hell has rules, tenets and canons intended both to guide its various demonic personnel and by which they themselves are eternally bound.

For example, the Yattering's lengthy attempts to interest Jack in the woman across the street, a "young widow [who] seemed to spend most of her life parading around the house stark naked," have backfired in the most spectacular way possible.[11] Not only has Jack *not* "developed a passion" for her, but the Yattering *has*! Because the rules explicitly forbid the demon from doing anything except watch her, however, longingly and perhaps painfully ithyphallic, the fulfillment of its own desire is forever denied. Obviously, it's torment for the Yattering, because "it could never cross the threshold of Polo's house. This was the Law, and the Yattering was a minor demon, and his soul-catching was strictly confined to the perimeters of his victim's house. To step outside was to relinquish all powers over the victim: to put itself at the mercy of humanity."[12]

Even the demons, that is, are in hell.

Born in the early 1950s, not surprisingly Barker was brought up, at least nominally, in the Church of England—though he is quick to write even that bit of business into his own horrorography. "I went to church once when I was baptized," he told Douglas Winter in an interview shortly after *Hellraiser* was released in theaters, "but the font water boiled. They took me out and decided never to take me again."[13] A generation ago, when this interview took place, Barker told Winter that he believed "in system." That is, "I believe in life after death. I absolutely assume the continuity, in some form or another, of mind after bodily corruption. I certainly don't believe in any patriarchal god—I don't believe in Yahweh, the vengeful Lord of the Old Testament. But I don't think we live in a universe in which anything's ever lost. Transformed, maybe, but never lost. I think that may be the bottom line of any religious belief."[14] I would like to suggest in this chapter—and I think Barker would likely agree—that this is less *religion*, per se, than it is an example of the *religious imagination*, something that has been at work in us from the moment our proto-hominin ancestors first wondered if there might be something *more* and began to tell stories that grew in complexity until they ranged from Roman Catholic dogmatic theology to the multivariate Buddhist heavens, hells, and infinite worlds, and from the new religious nursery of the New Age movement to the conflicting theologies implicated in *Deities and Demigods*, *Dungeons & Dragons*'s venerable handbook of all things divine.[15]

That is, Barker may not be a believer in any traditional sense, but he is as captive to the religious imagination as any of us. Again, this is not to say religious belief, let alone any form of organizational adherence or participation, but simply the ability to imagine compelling storyworlds woven from the skeins of myth, ritual, doctrine, and practice—as well as the tenebrous spaces between them—that have haunted humankind for millennia. Rather than religious questions, as they are so often and incorrectly called, stories such as these inevitably interrogate the "properly human questions" that bind horror to religion, not as its narrative servant or literary beard but as its cultural sibling.[16]

This brief consideration of Barker's story raises three issues of particular interest for anyone concerned with the various intersections of religion and horror: (a) the general problem of how we define religion (and the ongoing relevance of William James); (b) the more detailed matter of how we envision the infernal (as an active exercise of the religious imagination); and (c) the specific purpose of hell as a function of our craving for natural justice (plus the problem of Father Brown). Put differently, imagining the infernal allows us to interrogate and extrapolate three central theological concerns: cosmology, theology, and theodicy. All of which point to some of the reasons why, as a species, we appear to be obsessed with the supernaturally scary.

IMAGINING THE UNSEEN ORDER: WHY WILLIAM JAMES STILL MATTERS

Undoubtedly, many readers would argue that the implications of Barker's darkly comedic vision in "The Yattering and Jack" do *not* reflect what Hell looks like: believers because they have their own ideas about the infernal regions, nonbelievers because they find the whole thing just a bit silly. However, his storyworld invokes one of the most basic principles required to understand the relationship between theology and horror: that is, all religions are aspects of the religious imagination, but not all aspects of the religious imagination ultimately take shape in the real world as religions. Far more of these are displayed through short stories and novels, others find expression in movies and television, while still others enact themselves through roleplaying games and the myriad shared universe of fiction that emerges from and contributes to them.[17] This does not make them any less important, and all of them eagerly await the scholar's attention—a fact we ignore to our detriment. Because, ask yourself this: How many conversations have you ever been in that began, in one way or another, "Say, what did you think about that awesome position paper the Doctrine Commission just released on hell?"[18] Now ask yourself how many conversations you've been in that began something like "Did you see last night's *Supernatural*? Dean goes to Hell . . . again!" or "Have you read the latest Stephen King novel?" or "I can't wait for the new *insert-supernatural-horror-movie-title-here* to come out!" The particulars don't matter so much as the fact that we are far more immersed in popular culture than we are the traditional dictates and mandates of organizational religion—however much we might want to protest otherwise. These popular exercises of the religious imagination—from horror stories about

annoyance demons to blockbuster films supposedly based on real supernatural events, from binge-television like *American Horror Story* to a dungeon-
crawl through the *Temple of Elemental Evil*—have at least as much effect on
our own religious imaginations as the official pronouncements of ecclesial
councils or doctrinal conclaves.[19]

If we think back a few pages, each of the problems I enunciated at the
beginning—dismissing religion in horror, ignoring it, or explaining it away
as something else—is grounded in a more basic problem: *definition*. How we
define religion determines what we are willing to count *as* religion. Now,
definitions, it needs be said, are neither good nor bad. They are simply useful
or not useful for their particular purpose. They either help us accurately
distinguish what we're talking about, or they don't. And, if they don't, they
can artificially limit what we think of as religion. Which is to say, definitions
often serve an ideological function as much as anything else. Yet, the number
of times this fundamental fact is forgotten is roughly equal to the number of
essays, articles, and books that begin with "Such-and-such dictionary defines
'religion' as . . ."[20]

For most of our history, humans have had neither word nor concept for
"religion" per se. Although, writes historian Jonathan Z. Smith, our species
has imagined its various "deities and modes of interaction with them" for as
long as we have records, we have "had only the last few centuries in which to
imagine religion."[21] "While there is a staggering amount of data" for what
we might consider "*religious*," he continues, or in the language I am using
here, the *religious imagination*, "*there is no data for religion*."[22] Indeed, in a
passage worth tacking up on the wall above one's desk, he argues that "religion is solely the creation of the scholar's study. It is created for the scholar's
analytic purposes by his imaginative acts of comparison and generalization.
Religion has no independent existence apart from the academy. For this
reason, the student of religion, and most particularly the historian of religion,
must be relentlessly self-conscious. Indeed, this self-consciousness constitutes his primary expertise, his foremost object of study."[23]

Because it seems so profoundly counterintuitive, if not entirely wrong-
headed, his first claim, that "religion is solely the creation of the scholar's
study," never fails to confuse, confront, and occasionally scandalize students
when I assign it in class. What on earth could he possibly mean by that? No
such thing as religion? Absurd! Although it might not seem so at first, and it
is obscured somewhat by the nature of his prose, he actually answers this
objection in the next paragraph. "For the self-conscious student of religion,"
he writes, "no datum possesses intrinsic interest. It is of value only insofar as
it can serve as *exempli gratia* of some fundamental issue in the imagination
of religion."[24]

Read that again, because that's the key: *no datum possesses intrinsic
interest*.

Put differently, as I try to teach my own students, whether first-year undergraduate or doctoral candidate, *nothing is inherently sacred, but is so only by the consent of, and agreement among, those who regard it as sacred.* Which is to say, whatever *it* is—a well in the woods, a building high on the cliff, a book kept hidden from the plebes—it is sacred because it is defined as sacred. It is sacred because a particular group of people agree on its sacrality. Put simply, it's sacred because we say so. The implications of this are all the more important for the scholar who, as Smith notes, "accepts neither the boundaries of canon nor of community in constituting his intellectual domain, in providing his range of exempla"—words that should inspire anyone interested in the intersections of religion and horror explored in this volume.[25] All that said, then, is there a way of defining religion that allows us to demonstrate why scary stories and monster movies should be of interest—not only to horror nerds like us—but to anyone interested in the religious imagination and impulse?

As it happens, there is.

More than a century ago, psychologist and philosopher William James proposed not one, but two definitions of religion. Unfortunately, only one of these is indexed in *The Varieties of Religious Experience*, the published version of his 1902 Gifford Lectures, so that tends to be the one with which people are familiar. In the second lecture, James defines religion—"arbitrarily," he admits—as "the feelings, acts, and experiences of individual [persons] in their solitude, so far as they apprehend themselves to stand in relation to whatever they may consider the divine."[26] Keep in mind the important point here: "whatever they may consider the divine"—or, if you prefer, whatever they *define as sacred.* The main problem here is that religion is not, principally, an individual or solitary pursuit. It is far more both social process and cultural phenomenon and is all but entirely influenced by both. That is, it takes place in the context of a community; it is shaped and corrected by that community; it extrudes from the religious imagination into consensus reality only and always as a function of that community. Thus, we take also James's second definition, which is harder to find, but far more useful for our purposes. That is, in lecture three, he writes that "the life of religion," conceived in "the broadest and most general terms possible . . . consists of the belief that there is an unseen order, and that our supreme good lies in harmonious adjustment thereto."[27] As I have argued elsewhere, both definitions actually offer scholars a number of significant advantages, improvements that are especially apparent when considering the various intersections of religion and popular culture.

First, whether it's the notion of an "unseen order" or "whatever they may consider the divine," both obviate the need for specific gods, let alone *a* god or some form of supreme god, or even the notion of gods at all. There is simply communal recognition that the material universe as we so narrowly apprehend it is not all that there is. The "belief that there is an unseen order" says nothing more than that *something else* exists beyond, above, beside, or behind the reality that we accept by consensus, if not necessarily certitude.

Second, because of this, these definitions preclude the need for discussion of authenticity, historical or otherwise, especially when that authenticity is ideologically motivated or deployed in support of a supernormal "truth" that believers consider self-evident, but nonbelievers regard as fantasy or delusion. Which is to say, we don't need to get into endless rounds of debate over whose invisible super-friends are real and whose aren't. Religion is no longer limited to a particular agenda, as though what counts as "religion" is what people most readily recognize as religion—which, not surprisingly, is usually their own. James proposes that we set aside issues of authenticity, and resist "the temptation to establish whether something is 'true' or not."[28]

Following from this, then, to take just one example, our use of James exposes the false dichotomy between religion and magic, an artificial separation which is usually intended to privilege the former at the expense of the latter. Ever since Émile Durkheim declared rather dogmatically that "there is no Church of Magic," theologically motivated distinctions between the two have been almost de rigueur, and pursued primarily for the purpose of religious legitimation, and, thus, of authority.[29] Divorced from this false dichotomy, though, the unseen order could as reasonably be populated by the hierarchy of spirits of which someone like occultist Lon Milo DuQuette claims to live, as it is the pecking order of saints, angels, and demons cataloged by legions of Catholic dogmatic theologians.[30]

Fourth, and I think that this is one of the principal benefits for anyone who wants to interrogate the relationship between religion and horror, James's definitions allow us to liberate religion from the good, moral, and decent fallacy. Also known as approbation bias, this is the specious and self-serving position that if something evil or violent is done by religious believers, either through their own interpretation of the faith or at the explicit command of their god, it cannot be religion. Religion is, by definition, a good thing. It's difficult to imagine a more erroneous position from which to view the world around us or cast our eyes over the vault of history. Absent the good, moral, and decent fallacy, however, Charles Wesley's "gentle Jesus, meek and mild" has no more intrinsic hold on the religious imagination than, say, the "grinning, vulpine" Christ of "He Who Walks Behind the Rows," and the orthodox god of a small fishing village is no more intrinsically reasonable than the "debased quasi-pagan thing imported from the East a century before."[31] The utility of this in terms of the many crossroads between religion and the horror mode should be obvious.

Fifth, James's definitions open up conceptualization of the religious imagination apart from either reflecting or depending upon religions as they exist—or are imagined to exist—at this moment in the real world. Of course, in many, perhaps even most cases, one will be a refraction of the other. The horror mode will reveal facets of real-world religion that we might rather not face or accept. One could hardly imagine *The Exorcist* apart from its Roman Catholic underpinning or *The Omen* from its reliance on aspects of Protestant dispensationalism. But, that doesn't mean that the horror mode must correlate in some way to religion in the real world, as though religion as we commonly encounter it on the street or in the pew provides a necessary limit-case for consideration of the religious imagination. Once freed from the demands of such spurious correlation, we can more easily avoid the kind of superficial this-looks-like-that comparison that litters so much of the scholar-ship on religion and horror. Because James's definitions defy limitation to what is conventionally or doctrinally regarded as "religion," they open up vistas of the religious imagination that are contained in such products of the human imagination as horror, science fiction, fantasy, and the web of hybrids between them.

Finally, taken together, James's definitions allow us to investigate the double helix of human religiosity: the social and the personal. "Religion" is a social phenomenon, though exercises of the "religious imagination" need be neither a product of the one, nor confined to the other. While there cannot be a religion of one—at least, we could argue not—nothing precludes the soli-tary exercise of the religious imagination, whether one actually believes in the object of those exercises or not. Don't believe me? Ask H. P. Lovecraft. He left a legacy of horror fiction from August Derleth to Caitlín Kiernan. Derleth was one of the first to give shape to what is known as the Cthulhu Mythos, and Kiernam is a modern writer of weird fiction who is often re-ferred to as Lovecraft's literary granddaughter. Yet, despite the efforts of some to demonstrate that Lovecraft really was a believer, that the mythos really does describe an unseen order he considered real, the fact is that he was a thoroughgoing materialist and made no bones about it.[32] Like Barker, his was an exercise in the religious imagination, not religious profession or commitment, but it should be of no less interest to us for that. The ambiguity of James's definitions lets the storytelling power of the horror mode take a legitimate place in our ongoing attempts to understand the properly human questions that have driven our species for millennia and from which both religious practice and horror culture emerge, rather than remain bound to the answers we struggle weakly to convince ourselves are true.

IMAGINING THE INFERNAL:
THE RELIGIOUS IMAGINATION IN REAL TIME

"The teaching of the Church," reads the Catechism, "affirms the existence of hell and its eternity," and "immediately after death, the souls of those who die in a state of mortal sin descend into hell, where they suffer the punishments of hell, 'eternal fire.'" Although the Catechism adds that "the chief punishment of hell is eternal separation from God," one has to think that conscious, eternal torment ranks at least a close second.[33] It's important to remember, though, that, at one time, a time that lasted for centuries and could not but have haunted the nightmares of parents without number, babies born without the dubious benefit of baptism were consigned to limbo, an eternal destination hung, literally, between Heaven and Hell. While Purgatory—a place where "for certain lesser faults, we must believe, before the Final Judgement, there is a purifying fire"—is still catechistically in place, the concept of limbo was officially abandoned only little more than a decade ago.[34] Similarly, the Southern Baptist Convention (SBC), the largest Protestant denomination in the United States (for which it arguably warrants the title "mainstream") reaffirmed its commitment to belief in a literal hell less than a decade ago. In direct response to the suggestion that salvation is not exclusively the province of those who profess "faith alone, in Jesus Christ alone," hundreds of delegates to the SBC's annual meeting in Phoenix, Arizona, considered a resolution entitled "On the Reality of Hell."[35] Following a number of preambulatory remarks, the last of which stated unequivocally that "the unrighteous will be consigned to Hell, the place of everlasting punishment," the motion concluded that the messengers of the Convention "do hereby affirm our belief in the biblical teaching on eternal, conscious punishment of the unregenerate in Hell."[36]

Both of these statements demonstrate the religious imagination at work in historical perspective, as it were. One way in which the horror mode shows us the religious imagination working in real time, however, is to take religious doctrines such as these at their word. Put differently, what does Hell *look* like, anyway?

As it turns out, "Hell is a city."[37]

"It stretches, literally, without end—a labyrinth of smoke and waking nightmare. Just as endlessly, sewer grates belch flame from the sulphur fires that have raged beneath the streets for millennia. Clock towers spire in every district, by public law, but their faces have no hands; time is not measured here in seconds or hours but in atrocity and despair."[38] That said, though, it's a lot like any other big city. Although "screams rip down streets and through alleys," still "the people of this place trudge the sidewalks back and forth, to home, to work, to stores, etc., just as they do in any city. There's only one dissimilarity. In *this* city, the people are all dead."[39]

In his *City Infernal* novels, Edward Lee takes extraordinary delight in imagining the excesses of "Mephistopolis."[40] Literally powered by terror, in the vast city that Hell became, "suffering serves as convertible energy," while "barges manned by Golems float atop the brown, lump-ridden surface of a river called Styx, pumping raw sewage *into* the city's domestic reservoirs."[41] The city has all the landmarks associated with any great metropolis, though these Lee presents as a kind of "who's who" treasure hunt of historical allusion and cultural critique. "De Rais University extended over countless acres and appeared almost campus-like in its layout. Here, the finest Warlocks in the land taught their pupils in the blackest arts."[42] "The Rockefeller Mint provided the city with all its currency," while "Osiris Heights stood proud and posh," its luxury apartments equipped with "the latest conveniences: harlot cages, skull-presses, iron-maidens, and neat personal-sized crematoriums."[43] "Boniface Square," named for the notorious tenth-century antipope, "encompassed whole city blocks in its leisure services," and "all manner of abyssal entertainment." As far as law enforcement goes, "the J. Edgar Hoover Building existed in the Living World as it did in Lucifer's."[44] The "sick" were treated at "Tojo Memorial Hospital," while scholars could browse the stacks at "the John Dee Library and Infernal Archives," and the more spiritually minded find inspiration at "St. Iscariot Abbey."[45] For all this, "the city of Hell" presents a fairly conventional view, the fiendish delights and unending torments reflecting little more than the nightmares of conservative Christians everywhere—not least of which, the fact that the vast majority of punishments are meted out for sexual offenses.

An important question for the religious studies scholar—or scholars of popular culture—to ask is why any of these hellish imaginings seem more or less reasonable than any others, why some should be of less intrinsic interest simply because they make no secret of the fact that they're fictional and don't pretend otherwise. Without exception, and whether canonical or literary, all are examples of the religious imagination at work, precisely because they pose questions rather than provide answers. For example, what happens when the Lord of Hell decides he's had enough and abandons the infernal regions for a chic Los Angeles piano bar (Mike Carey's *Lucifer*)? What happens when an unlikely mating of heaven and hell leads to an unholy power unleashed, and the literal abdication of God (Garth Ennis and Steve Dillon's *Preacher*)? All these beg the question why we imagine Hell at all, which brings us to the issue of natural justice, the problem of Father Brown, and the unending human need for questions.

"Hell's Event" is another short story from Clive Barker's *Books of Blood*, one that also presents the domain of the damned as a municipality with its own complex and entrenched bureaucracy as well as its own institutional structure. In London, every hundred years, two champions race from St. Paul's Cathedral, along the north bank of the Thames, down past the iconic London Eye, to the Palace of Westminster, the seat of British democracy. "Often," said the "goat-coated man," the race "has been run in the dead of night, unheralded, unapplauded," but, regardless of who is watching, "it is always the same race. Your athletes, against one of ours. If you win, another hundred years of democracy. If we win . . . as we will . . . the end of the world as you know it."[46] Here, rather than the splatter-horror hero's journey of the *City Infernal* novels, the relationship between the seen and the unseen orders comes down to a contest, an updated version of the wager between Yahweh and Satan that played out between them in the misery of an unsuspecting man named Job. Learning the exact nature of this relationship, though, can be more than a little unsettling.

"'Hell,' said Cameron again," still not certain he had heard the other man correctly.

"You believe, don't you?" asks the man known in this world as Burgess.[47] Indeed, it's not an unreasonable assumption, since at the time Barker wrote the story roughly a third of Britons still believed in Hell, a percentage that has been marginally increasing ever since.[48] Had he asked Americans, the number would have been significantly higher, nearly double on average, and triple among those who attend church more than once a week.[49] "You're a good church-goer," Burgess continues. "Still pray before you eat, like any God-fearing soul. Afraid of choking on your dinner."[50] That is, afraid of dying unshriven, absent the last rites intended to secure passage to an eternity with the Divine. "How do you know I pray?" Cameron demands.[51] I mean, how could he possibly know? We can almost imagine Burgess picking a piece of nonexistent lint from the lapel of his goat-hair coat as he explains nonchalantly: "Your wife told me. Oh, your wife was very informative about you, Mr. Cameron, she really opened up to me. Very accommodating. A confirmed analist, after my attentions. She gave me so much . . . information."[52]

It's one thing to sit in the pew every Sunday, dutifully repeating the words, the prayers and antiphons, singing the hymns, surrounded on all sides by those who believe, but have no more idea what's actually going on than you do. It's quite another to be confronted with a situation that takes the religion in which you profess to believe at its word. "Politics is the hub of the issue, Mr. Cameron," Burgess continues, implicitly invoking Dante. "Without politics we're lost in the wilderness, aren't we? Even Hell needs order. Nine great circles: a pecking order of punishments. . . . We stand for order, you know. Not chaos. That's just heavenly propaganda."[53]

As much as anything, this seems considerably more rational than many more liberal notions of Christian salvation, and for one simple reason: It satisfies our need of natural justice. Like many other animals, humans have evolved with a highly developed sense of inequity aversion. We simply don't want people to get away with bad things. Those who hurt us, or hurt those we love, deserve to be punished. In terms of "criminal justice," we may make culturally appropriate noises about rehabilitation and reform, but, for most of our history, what we're really into as a species is seeing the guilty punished—and, more often than not, punished *hard*.

This is one of the central issues of theodicy, the conceptual process by which we attempt to understand the nature of suffering and the divine's problematic place within it. The paradox of theodicy is highlighted by what we might call *the Father Brown problem*: that is, no one is beyond salvation, and no matter how heinous the offence, no matter what kind of suffering the perpetrator has visited upon others, God will forgive. Repentance assures entrance, as it were, and, theoretically at least, eternity in heaven awaits the criminal, while many of his or her nameless and numberless victims find themselves stuck somewhere considerably less pleasant.

In the latest television adaptation of the adventures of G. K. Chesterton's famous cleric-detective, no matter how vile the offender, no matter how repulsive the offense, whatever they have done in this life pales to insignificance in the face of Father Brown's relentless concern for their eternal soul. Consider this brief vignette: in the logic of Roman Catholic systematic theology, an ordinary man, devout in his way, no better or worse than his fellows, is still subject to the allegedly immutable theological law of original sin—and that regardless of whether he happens to be Jewish, or a communist, or Catholic, or a gypsy, or a Jehovah's Witness, or any of the other "undesirables" rounded up during the horror of the Nazi regime. Almost immediately gassed upon entry into this or that death camp, he dies in the showers, unconfessed and unshriven, unable to avail himself of whatever antemortem rites are prescribed to ensure passage to the afterlife. Surrounded by thousands of weeping, screaming, crying others, he slips into the darkness reserved for those who die outside of grace. On the other hand, decades later perhaps, stricken with horror in the final moments of life, the very death-camp guard who presided over the slaughter seeks God's forgiveness and, at least according to the Catholic logic of salvation, presumably spends eternity in heaven—perhaps watching the suffering of her victims in hell. Precisely here is the horror mode, the religious imagination that pushes us to imagine things that disturb us, scare us, and repel us beyond imagining.

If theology recapitulates cosmology—that is, if the way we imagine the gods shapes the way we see the world—and the Roman Catholic understanding of both the creation story and of postmortem consequences is correct, then it matters little whether the person is actually a Catholic or not. According to dogma, we are all inescapably sinners, but God wants all sinners, no matter how loathsome, to be brought to salvation. No one is to be left behind. This, however, is a complete reversal of what we think should happen, a sort of "Hitler in heaven" problem that profoundly offends our sense of natural justice, and that led at least in part to the Catholic religious imagination coming up with the concept of purgatory in the fifteenth century: an intermediate postmortem state though which the guilty must pass in order that their sins be cleansed with an appropriate length and degree of punishment. (A similar department presumably arrived at the slightly more problematic notion of Limbo, since even they could not see their way clear to worshiping a god who was content to condemn babies to Hell).

This entire discussion, which seems incredibly abstract and abstruse centuries later (though still a live issue for tens of millions of fundamentalist Protestants), underpins among other things the notion of the monstrosity of the gods, and of those who seek cover for their own monstrosity under the mantle of the divine. It seems we cannot stop interrogating the problem of evil. "Did Eva Braun hold Hitler's hand as she slept?" wonders P. K. Tyler, for example, in her introduction to the short story collection *UnCommon Evil*. "Was her existence good or intrinsically tied to the evil her partner imparted upon the world? Is there an excuse for her loving him? Or was loving him in itself perhaps evil in nature? Would he have become the man he was without her or did she gentle him in some unknowable way?"[54] How things could have been worse is anyone's guess, but Tyler follows this immediately with what is arguably the seminal insight into the appeal of both religion and horror: "Questions like this will never be answered, but the exploration of them is the writer's dream, the fodder upon which we feed."[55]

IN CASE YOU'RE WONDERING WHY ANY OF THIS MATTERS

Horror, as any number of critics and commentators will tell you, is less often about *transcendence*, and far more often about *trespass* and *transgression*. Even the former, however, is not out of the question, as the inimitable Pinhead tells the terrified Kirsty Cotton in the 1984 classic, *Hellraiser*. Asked desperately who—or what—the Cenobites are, the Hell Priest intones simply that they are "explorers, in the further regions of experience. Demons to some, angels to others."[56] While this might pass as little more than a cool bit of dialogue—and it is, make no mistake—far more is going on here than mere theatrics. The Hell Priest's answer points us to the *sine qua non* of the horror mode: the reality that things might not be as we imagine, or as we have told ourselves for countless generations that they are, or as we have believed when we cast our cosmic lots. Things may, in fact, be fantastically different, and the very existence of the Cenobites asks how we can be so arrogant as to believe that what we think we see around us is the only reality.

"Each answer remains in force as an answer," wrote philosopher Martin Heidegger in "The Origins of the Work of Art," only as long as it is rooted in questioning."[57] That is, an answer is only an answer so long as we continue to ask the questions. The moment we proclaim an answer, we're dead in the water, especially if we declare it the answer for everyone. Indeed, as Stephen King points out, when it comes to questions of the unseen order, of ultimate meaning, of "life, the universe, and everything," "only fiction can approach answers to those questions. Only *through* fiction can we think about the unthinkable, and perhaps obtain some kind of closure."[58]

As though presaging Constance Donovan from the first season of *American Horror Story*, it seems appropriate to give the last word to H. P. Lovecraft, who epitomizes the importance of the religious imagination in the opening words of one of his best-known works, words that any of us who profess to know the nature of reality ignore at our peril. "What do we know about the world and the universe about us?" Lovecraft writes in "From Beyond." "Our means of receiving impressions are absurdly few, and our notions of surrounding objects infinitely narrow. We see things only as we are constructed to see them, and gain no idea of their absolute nature."[59]

NOTES

1. For examples of each, respectively, see Stone, "The Sanctification of Fear"; Grigg, *Science Fiction and the Imitation of the Sacred*; and Clasen, *Why Horror Seduces*. For my own counterarguments to each, see, respectively, Cowan, *Sacred Terror*, 43–46; "Review of *Science Fiction and the Imitation of the Sacred*"; *Bodies Out of Place*, forthcoming.

2. Barker, "The Yattering and Jack," 1: 37.

3. Freeland, *The Naked and the Undead*, 253.

4. See Kane, *The* Hellraiser *Films and Their Legacy*.

5. Cowan, *Sacred Terror*, 85; Barker, *The Hellbound Heart*, 4.

6. See Barker, *The Scarlet Gospels*; Cowan, "The Crack in the World: New Thoughts on Religion and Horror."

7. Cowan, "The Crack in the World," 137.

8. Barker, "The Yattering and Jack," 1: 37.

9. Barker, "The Yattering and Jack," 1: 39.

10. Barker, "The Yattering and Jack," 1: 41.

11. Barker, "The Yattering and Jack," 1: 39.

12. Barker, "The Yattering and Jack," 1: 39–40.

13. Winter, *Faces of Fear*, 209.

14. Winter, *Faces of Fear*, 209.

15. Ward and Kuntz, *Deities and Demigods*. For an amusing look at the problem of trying to serve too many gods, see Zombie Orpheus Entertainment, "Pantheist Cleric."

16. On the concept of "properly human questions," see Cowan, *America's Dark Theologian*, 5–9.

17. See Cowan, *Magic, Monsters, and Make-Believe Heroes*, 166–76.

18. If you're interested, see Doctrine Commission of the Church of England, *The Mystery of Salvation*.

19. See Gygax and Mentzer, *The Temple of Elemental Evil*.

20. For one of the most egregious misuses of this, see Elkins, *On the Strange Place of Religion in Contemporary Art*, x–xi.

21. Smith, *Imagining Religion*, xi. In an endnote, Smith points out that "the history of the imagination of religion has yet to be written," but, sadly, declines to say what, precisely, he means by this (135, n. 1).

22. Smith, *Imagining Religion*, xi; emphasis in the original.

23. Smith, *Imagining Religion*, xi.

24. Smith, *Imagining Religion*, xi.

25. Smith, *Imagining Religion*, xi.

26. James, *Varieties of Religious Experience*, 36.

27. James, *Varieties of Religious Experience*, 61.

28. Cowan and Bromley, *Cults and New Religions*, 8.

29. Durkheim, *The Elementary Forms of Religious Life*, 42; see Cowan, *Magic, Monsters, and Make-Believe Heroes*, 64–66.

30. See DuQuette, *My Life with the Spirits.*
31. Stephen King, "Children of the Corn," in *Night Shift*, 265; Lovecraft, "The Shadow over Innsmouth," 277.
32. The most prominent exponent of the Lovecraft-as-Believer hypothesis is Canadian occultist and writer Donald Tyson, who has crafted an entire magical belief system based on the Cthulhu Mythos and written an alternative biography of Lovecraft that presents the Prophet of Providence as a channel for elder gods that actually exist. See, for example, Tyson, *Secrets of the Necronomicon*; *Grimoire of the Necronomicon*; *13 Gates of the Necronomicon*; *The Dream-World of H. P. Lovecraft*; cf. Cowan, "Dealing a New Religion," 256–62. For a splatter-horror homage to the theory that Lovecraft's imaginings were real, see Lee, *The Innswich Horror.*
33. Catholic Church, "Hell," *Catechism of the Catholic Church*, 1035.
34. Pullella, "Catholic Church Buries Limbo after Centuries."
35. http://www.sbc.net/resolutions/1214/on-the-reality-of-hell.
36. http://www.sbc.net/resolutions/1214/on-the-reality-of-hell.
37. Lee, *Infernal Angel*, 10.
38. Lee, *Infernal Angel*, 10.
39. Lee, *Infernal Angel*, 1.
40. See, in order, Lee, *City Infernal*; *Infernal Angel*; *House Infernal*; and *Lucifer's Lottery.*
41. Lee, *City Infernal*, 8.
42. Lee, *City Infernal*, 106.
43. Lee, *City Infernal*, 107.
44. Lee, *City Infernal*, 107.
45. Lee, *City Infernal*, 107.
46. Barker, "Hell's Event," 2: 46.
47. Barker, "Hell's Event," 2: 46.
48. See www.brin.ac.uk/figures/belief-in-britain-1939-2009/conventional-belief/belief-in-the-devil-1957-2006.
49. See https://news.gallup.com/poll/11770/eternal-destinations-americans-believe-heaven-hell.aspx.
50. Barker, "Hell's Event," 2: 46.
51. Barker, "Hell's Event," 2: 46.
52. Barker, "Hell's Event," 2: 46.
53. Barker, "Hell's Event," 2: 46.
54. Tyler, "The Nature of Evil," 2
55. Tyler, "The Nature of Evil," 2.
56. Barker, dir. *Hellraiser.*
57. Heidegger, "The Origins of the Work of Art," in *Basic Writings*, 195.
58. King, *The Bazaar of Bad Dreams*, 268.
59. Lovecraft, "From Beyond," 23.

WORKS CITED

Barker, Clive. *The Hellbound Heart.* New York: Harper Paperbacks, 1986.
———. "Hell's Event." In *Books of Blood, Volumes 1–3*, vol. 2, 35–57. London: Warner Books, 1998.
———. "The Yattering and Jack." In *Books of Blood, Volumes 1–3*, vol. 1, 37–56. London: Warner Books, 1998.
———. *The Scarlet Gospels.* New York: St. Martin's Press, 2015.
Catholic Church. "Hell." In *Catechism of the Catholic Church*, 2nd ed. New York: Doubleday, 1994.
Clasen, Mathias. *Why Horror Seduces.* New York: Oxford University Press, 2017.
Cowan, Douglas E. *Sacred Terror: Religion and Horror on the Silver Screen.* Waco, TX: Baylor University Press, 2008.

―――. "Dealing a New Religion: Material Culture, Divination, and Hyper-Religious Innovation." In *Handbook of Hyper-Real Religions*. Edited by Adam Possamai, 247–66. Leiden: Brill, 2012.

―――. "The Crack in the World: New Thoughts on Religion and Horror." *Religious Studies Review* 42, no. 4 (2015): 133–39.

―――. *America's Dark Theologian: The Religious Imagination of Stephen King*. New York: New York University Press, 2018.

―――. *Magic, Monsters, and Make-Believe Heroes: How Myth and Religion Shape Fantasy Culture*. Los Angeles: University of California Press, 2019.

―――. Review of *Science Fiction and the Imitation of the Sacred*, by Richard Grigg. *Journal of Contemporary Religion* 34, no. 2 (2019): 386–88.

―――. *Bodies Out of Place: Sex, Horror, and the Religious Imagination*. New York: New York University Press, forthcoming.

Cowan, Douglas E., and David G. Bromley. *Cults and New Religions: A Brief History*. 2nd ed. Oxford: Wiley Blackwell, 2015.

Doctrine Commission of the Church of England. *The Mystery of Salvation*. New York: Morehouse Publishing, 1996.

DuQuette, Lon Milo. *My Life with the Spirits: The Adventures of a Modern Magician*. York Beach, ME: Red Wheel/Weiser.

Durkheim, Émile. *The Elementary Forms of Religious Life*. 1912. Translated by Karen E. Fields. New York: Free Press, 1995.

Elkins, James. *On the Strange Place of Religion in Contemporary Art*. New York: Routledge, 2004.

Freeland, Cynthia A. *The Naked and the Undead: Evil and the Appeal of Horror*. Boulder, CO: Westview Press, 2000.

Grigg, Richard. *Science Fiction and the Imitation of the Sacred*. London: Bloomsbury Academic, 2018.

Gygax, Gary, and Frank Mentzer. *The Temple of Elemental Evil*. Lake Geneva, WI: TSR Inc., 1985.

Heidegger, Martin. *Heidegger: Basic Writings from "Being and Time" (1927) to "The Task of Thinking" (1964)*. Edited by David Farrell Krell. Rev. ed. New York: HarperSanFrancisco, 1993.

Hellraiser. Written and directed by Clive Barker. Cinemarque Entertainment BV, 1987.

James, William. *The Varieties of Religious Experience: A Study in Human Nature*. 1902. Reprint. New York: Modern Library, 1999.

Kane, Paul. *The* Hellraiser *Films and Their Legacy*. Jefferson, NC: McFarland, 2006.

Kane, Paul, and Marie O'Regan, eds. *Hellbound Hearts*. New York: Pocket Books, 2009.

King, Stephen. *Night Shift*. New York: Doubleday, 1978.

―――. *The Bazaar of Bad Dreams*. New York: Scribner, 2015.

Lee, Edward. *City Infernal*. 2001. Sanford, FL: Necro Publications, 2012.

―――. *Infernal Angel*. New York: Leisure Books, 2003.

―――. *House Infernal*. New York: Leisure Books, 2007.

―――. *The Innswich Horror*. Portland, OR: Deadite Press, 2010.

―――. *Lucifer's Lottery*. Sanford, FL: Necro Publications, 2013.

Lewis, C. S. *The Screwtape Letters*. London: Collins, 1942.

Lovecraft, H. P. "From Beyond." 1934. In *The Dreams in the Witch House and Other Weird Stories*, by H. P. Lovecraft. Edited by S. T. Joshi, 23–29. New York: Penguin Books, 2004.

―――. "The Shadow Over Innsmouth." 1936. In *The Call of Cthulhu and Other Weird Stories*, by H. P. Lovecraft. Edited by S. T. Joshi, 268–335. New York: Penguin Books, 1999.

"Pantheist Cleric." YouTube video, 6:31, posted by Zombie Orpheus Entertainment. October 8, 2015; https://www.youtube.com/watch?v=Xu8rR5EQvDc (accessed October 29, 2019).

Platt, Richard. *As One Devil to Another: A Fiendish Correspondence in the Tradition of C. S. Lewis*. Wheaton, IL: Tyndale, 2012.

Pullella, Philip. "Catholic Church Buries Limbo after Centuries." *Reuters*. (April 20, 2007); http://www.reuters.com/article/us-pope-limbo/catholic-church-buries-limbo-after-centuries-idUSL2028721620070420.

Smith, Jonathan Z. *Imagining Religion: From Babylon to Jonestown*. Chicago: University of Chicago Press, 1982.

Stone, Bryan. "The Sanctification of Fear: Images of the Religious in Horror Films." *Journal of Religion and Film* 5, no. 2 (2001): https://digitalcommons.unomaha.edu/jrf/vol5/iss2/7.

Tyler, P. K. "The Nature of Evil." In *UnCommon Evil*. Edited by Jessica West, 1–2. N.P.: Fighting Monkey Press, 2018.

Tyson, Donald. *Secrets of the Necronomicon*. Woodbury, MN: Llewellyn Publications, 2007.

———. *Grimoire of the Necronomicon*. Woodbury, MN: Llewellyn Publications, 2008.

———. *13 Gates of the Necronomicon: A Workbook of Magic*. Woodbury, MN: Llewellyn Publications, 2010.

———. *The Dream-World of H. P. Lovecraft: His Life, His Demons, His Universe*. Woodbury, MN: Llewellyn Publications, 2010.

Ward, James M., and Robert J. Kuntz. *Deities and Demigods: Cyclopedia of Gods and Heroes from Myth and Legend*. Edited by Lawrence Schick. Lake Geneva, WI: TSR Games, 1980.

Winter, Douglas E. *Faces of Fear: Encounters with the Creators of Modern Horror*. New York: Berkeley Books, 1985.

Chapter Two

The Theological Origins of Horror

Steve A. Wiggins

This chapter takes a broad sweep of literature to suggest that the Bible may be considered the basis of Western literature. By extension, the Bible is also the origin of horror fiction. This suggestion is made by sketching a history of horror back to the Bible and then forward again through spiritual writing. It suggests that, like the poor, horror has always been with us.

Horror, as a genre, bears an implicit suggestion of fiction. Given that the classification of horror as a genre became widespread only after the publication of Mary Shelley's *Frankenstein*,[1] this should not be surprising. This chapter suggests, however, that the classification of the Bible as "nonfiction" has prevented it from rightfully being considered as containing the early roots of horror. Somewhat subversively, the revisionist suggestion is made here that when the Bible—as well as the spiritual classics—are allowed to participate in fiction, the backstory of horror fits quite easily at the origins of the Western literary tradition. To make this case, horror, as used in this paper, has to be defined. This has, of course, been done many times—books on the genre abound, and many of them attempt definitions.[2]

What is horror? Leaving aside the question of the origin of fiction, the *Oxford English Dictionary* (*OED*) defines horror as "a literary or film genre concerned with arousing feelings of horror." The *OED* has much more to say, of course, but the essential primary summation does not specify fiction. Over time as literary genres grew more refined, the tendency to rank horror as fiction became predominant. Consider for a moment Truman Capote's nonfiction novel of multiple murder, *In Cold Blood*.[3] Is this horror? It is often found on that shelf. The question of fiction hangs in the air around it without ever settling. Fiction, for this discussion, must remain an open definition. The line between fact and fiction has become so effectively effaced that horror, which delights in violating boundaries, can be addressed in either category.

GOTHIC ORIGINS

Horror, as a genre, is traditionally traced to shadowy origins in the Gothic novel.[4] As in most historical sleuthing, there is sound reasoning in this. The Gothic, although an offshoot of Romanticism, is distinguished by a focus on the macabre and dalliance with the supernatural. These elements were picked up by writers such as Mary Shelley and Edgar Allan Poe and, with the expansion of publication, a host of more recent horror writers. Horror depicts images, plots, and themes that people prefer to avoid rather than confront. Literature in the nineteenth century (since more modern forms of popular media such as cinema did not yet exist) tended not to linger in the dark before the Gothic novel.[5] Negative themes and plots could be addressed, but the atmosphere that came to be associated with horror required some further basic cultural developments before it could become a distinct genre.

One of those necessary cultural elements finds reflection in Romanticism, the context in which Gothic sensibilities were conceived.[6] Beginning in the late eighteenth century, Romanticism represented a reaction against industrialization and the growing sense of materialism. The composers, artists, and authors of the movement all participated in a renewal of interest in nature, splendor, and human grandeur. Think of Beethoven's symphonies. Or the paintings of J. M. W. Turner. The sketches and poetry of William Blake. The novels of Sir Walter Scott. Celebrating the nonmechanized aspects of life, the Romantics condemned the human transformation from pastoral workers of the land into bits of industrial hardware, as represented by the life of the factory worker. There was a strong element of nostalgia involved.[7]

Human experience, however, is not always positive. Tragedies occur, even within the Romantic vision. Some Romantics came to see the melancholy appeal of negative emotions. Horace Walpole, born into the English aristocracy of the eighteenth century, is widely considered the author of the first Gothic novel, *The Castle of Otranto*. Borrowing freely from Romantic themes, and mixing in gloomier elements that would later become the hackneyed tropes of the genre, his 1764 story opened the portcullis to other writers poised between nostalgia and fear. The Middle Ages had been dark with dragons, witches, and the Black Death. The burgeoning Romantic movement thus allowed for a tenebrous side that had great appeal.

A list of Gothic authors and their works is not necessary to make the point that such moody, mysterious works led directly to the cultural phenomenon of the literary horror genre. This territory has already been well explored. Mary Shelley, although as yet not married to the Romantic poet Percy Bysshe Shelley, published perhaps the most famous horror novel of all time, *Frankenstein*, in 1818. The influence of *Frankenstein* would be difficult to overestimate.[8] Any successful literary feat attracts imitators, and the horror genre was soon in full swing. In America, Edgar Allan Poe would leave an indelible imprint on what was becoming considered a lower form of artistic literary expression. By the time of H. P. Lovecraft, a devoted acolyte of Poe, horror had been relegated to the status of pulp fiction and for all of his current-day popularity, Lovecraft had difficulty finding willing publishers.[9] In an era in which Stephen King novels have sold over 350 million copies, such a pedigree of penniless progenitors seems curiously counterintuitive.[10] Horror had to gain respectability by growing into a genre impossible to ignore (even if only for the potential revenue generated).

BIBLICAL ROOTS

The point of this chapter is to suggest that all of this horror should be considered an extension of a literary tradition that began with the Bible. There have been analyses of the theology of modern horror,[11] but scholars of the genre trace it back to the Gothic novel and tend not to probe its earlier, and unlikely, origins.[12] To get at this revisionist history of horror it is necessary to consider that the Bible was, and in many respects had to be, the progenitor of European literature.

This is not to suggest that an unbroken continuity existed in the sense that each author knew the history of horror prior to her or his own. The continuity posited here is that conveyed by a theology which encouraged horror that began in the Bible. The authors of most of the pieces examined did know the Good Book.[13] It provided a touchstone for the European mindset that would eventually give birth to horror as we know it. It also helped to establish the theology that supported it. Horror and religion have a long association.[14] This chapter simply attempts to make that obvious across Western literary history.

The darkness of the Middle Ages has already been mentioned. In the broad sweep of history, this medieval melancholy was part of the fallout of the "globalizing" effect of the Roman Empire. Extending its hegemony over the western continental parameters of Europe, Rome brought disparate cultures into contact. It is sometimes difficult to realize from our current globalizing context that travel was rare, dangerous, and expensive in antiquity. Interaction with those different than one's local community would have been in some sense shocking. The *pax romana*, as well as its military conquests, brought diverse cultures into contact.[15]

The Roman Empire also contributed to what would become the tragic side of the Middle Ages by becoming Christianized. When Emperor Constantine made Christianity the imperial religion after 313 CE, he not only put an end to Christian persecution but also supplied a vehicle to preserve its stories. Modern scholars of early Christianity have repeatedly demonstrated that Roman persecution was not as widespread or as vehement as the dominant narrative suggests.[16] Like the witch hunts of medieval Europe, the numbers were exaggerated with the telling.[17] By Christianizing the empire, Constantine had, perhaps unwittingly, cobbled a road by which those stories could be spread. The lives of saints and martyrs were among the relatively few books in wide circulation in the Middle Ages. So was the Bible.

At this point a caveat is necessary. Rates of literacy are difficult to assess prior to modernity. The consensus is that they were relatively low, no matter how they are counted.[18] This chapter is not suggesting that individuals consumed books as a commodity and read them like a modern shopper might do by picking up a Dean Koontz novel. What it does suggest, however, is that the impact of those books that were available was somewhat outsized, at least among the literate. Our medieval reader could not buy a book by E. L. James either. In such circumstances preserved books that contained the horrific demonstrate that the tendency toward scary writing was already present well before the Gothic novel. Religious literature had long used a tactic of fear in the service of theology.

ROMAN LATE ANTIQUITY

Books portraying the extreme trials undergone by the faithful, in addition to spiritual edification, perhaps provided the frisson that modern horror offers to a very different culture with different needs. Martyrdom stories are gruesome to read even in the present. The morals that such accounts provide are what we would likely call "conservative values" today.[19] They support the church and its symbolic righteousness against the wiles of those with differing value systems. Those tortured are enduring it for righteousness's sake.[20] The theology of the somewhat unified Catholic Christendom of the period, in regards to sexual relations, obedience to authority, and adherence to Christian teachings, all fit into what we would still recognize as conservative thinking. What happened to the martyrs, in other words, instead of demonstrating the cost of Christianity, transformed into stories warning of what could happen should Christendom collapse. It is less *The Cost of Discipleship* and more *Left Behind*. Such tales resemble horror and hover between fiction and nonfiction. Miracles are common, along with graphic cruelty.

The Roman Empire, which had enforced civility to some extent, had lasted into late antiquity. (History, of course, does not fall into neatly defined stages. The conventional periods, however, do help to see the general trends.) Rome prided itself on being a superior civilization. The excesses of the emperors indicate that such civilization often covered a darker reality. The treatment of perceived enemies of the empire, for instance, played to the strange spectacle that is horror. Violent contests pitting gladiators against one another, or even having Christians and other heathens torn apart by wild animals hardly seems a model of civilized behavior. It does look a lot like horror, however. Such events found their way into saints' lives. Examples are numerous, but one story will illustrate the point.[21]

The Acts of Saint Agnes dates from the fifth century, late in the Roman hegemony. In this account, Agnes, at the age of only thirteen or fourteen, caught the eye of Procopius, the son of a noble. From the beginning the fuzziness between fact and fiction becomes apparent. Being chaste, and determined to remain a virgin, Agnes refused to accept his proposal. She was sentenced to be hauled naked to a brothel where she might be publicly raped. Now, this is the territory of horror: a minor sentenced to gang rape would also fit into the horror genre today. She was rescued, as might be expected, by divine intervention. Nevertheless, she was destined to be a martyr. Sentenced to be burned alive, she was again put into a horror situation, but the wood would not ignite. Finally, she was gruesomely beheaded. Considered from the point of view of what is considered horror in the modern era, this tale qualifies.[22] Would it not have inspired horror as well as piety in late antiquity? Did it not uphold conservative social values as well as provide frissons of fear?

Accounts of cruelty at the hands of non-Christians clearly intended both to horrify and instill devotion. The accounts that were left of early saints and martyrs contain many scenes that are truly horrific. These lives of saints and martyrs display fabulist elements and had conservative social values as a goal. Remaining steadfast to one's faith, despite horrendous torture, led to divine approval and eternal reward. Not only does this blending of horror images and piety reflect the underlying conservatism of much of modern horror,[23] it goes back to even earlier roots in the Second Temple Period literature of Jewish writers. It would also continue into late antiquity.[24]

Also, during the period of late antiquity, monastic movements grew in the deserts of Egypt. The literature produced—to name just one example, *The Life of Antony*—highlighted the monster-fighter aspect of horror. We will come back to Antony momentarily, but both martyrs and monastics were reacting to what they believed fulfilled the dictates of Scripture.

THE BIBLE AND HORROR

This brings us to the theological starting point of horror: the Bible. Many centuries of study of the Good Book transpired before the question of its participation in horror ever was, or even could be, raised. The crux of this chapter highlights the aura of sanctity that grew to surround Scripture. This concept that the book itself was holy bore such theological weight that any recognition of the obvious—that the Bible contains much that qualifies as horror, as well as fiction—could not be properly addressed. Tracing respect for Holy Writ from the first century to the present could be done, but there really is no question about it.[25] For our purposes it is sufficient to recognize that it took feminist readings of the twentieth century to unlock the horror, to rupture the aura of accumulated sanctity.

In 1984, Phylis Trible published her influential study *Texts of Terror*.[26] Although it had long been known that horrific stories were embedded in the Bible, its perceived sanctity had prevented open discussion of the fact. Instead of dwelling on the terrifying aspects of many stories—the gang rape and dismemberment of the Levite's concubine in Judges 19, for example— theological explanations and discussions were offered. This is clearly evident in the early allegorical schools of interpretation and the later male-dominated developments of conventional theology. Not that women were the only victims of horror in the Good Book. Many other stories such as the slaying of Saul's family in 2 Samuel 21 surely qualify. Still, it took feminist sensibilities to bring this horror clearly into focus for what it is. Women have long been the victims in the horror genre.[27]

A second element adding to the avoidance of the horror label is the fact that the sanctity of Scripture precluded fiction. Fiction has never commanded the respect of nonfiction in the context of Holy Writ. The easy equation of "true" and "nonfiction" assured readers that even fantastic elements in the Good Book could be explained as miracles. When comparable stories, such as the flood account in the Gilgamesh Epic, were discovered, a crisis of credibility arose.[28] How could it be fiction in one telling and fact in another? Indeed, historical criticism was as much anathema as was Charles Darwin's *On the Origin of Species* for those who admitted no fictional elements in Scripture. The Bible was holy and no hint of fiction could be permitted.

Historically, the morality of the Bible was considered pure enough to uphold that aura of sanctity that had been growing around the very concept of sacred Scripture. This theological development clouded the obvious point that much in the Good Book is quite horrifying.[29] This was the genius of Trible's approach—she used literary theory to expose literalism's moral dilemma. The contents of the Bible present horror to readers, no matter what gender. Mel Gibson's *The Passion of the Christ*, for example while not Scripture, could well be considered a horror film.[30] Were it not for the theological freight the story of Jesus bears, the presentation in that movie could easily fall into the horror genre. Any suggestion of fiction in this episode lances at the heart of Christian theology. Once again, theology masks the horror that lies plainly in the open.

Clearly the Bible is not the earliest literature in the world. Nor is it the first that could be considered a participant in what would later become known as horror. The Gilgamesh Epic from ancient Mesopotamia, for example, features battles with monsters, a horrific and slow death scene, and the population of the world being drowned.[31] Also prior to the Bible, the Ugaritic texts of northern Syria portrayed the goddess Anat, bedecked with severed heads and hands, plunging her legs into blood and gore in the context of battle.[32] These kinds of disturbing images would also qualify as early horror. No analysts have insisted that they be classified as nonfiction. They lack the theological aura, however, that surrounds Scripture.

Another vital difference between these tales and the Bible is that other ancient stories fell out of circulation. Apart from the echoes that survived to be preserved in the Good Book, these literary pieces were buried and forgotten, only to be recovered in modernity. The Bible, however, never went out of circulation. Its influence continues to the present in an unbroken chain stretching back to the first century and beyond. Protected by the theological understanding that this text had somehow come from God, it preserved what would otherwise be considered horror in a baptized form. This book was sacred. When the study of horror began some two millennia later, horror was about as opposite from sacred as a literary scholar could get. Lowbrow, debased, and disgusting,[33] how could horror have anything to do with the Good Book? How could a genre based on fear and repulsion interact in any way with Scripture bearing the divine message of love? More importantly, theologically the Bible was holy.

While the message of love is obviously present, consider the broad parameters of the scriptural story. In the beginning God created, but the first human being born is the first murderer. Just ten generations after the world is created, an extinction event that outdoes even that of the Permian Period wipes out all but eight human beings and two of each animal on the planet. The reason for this is that wickedness is so rife among humanity that only eight people could be spared. God then chooses a nation that is given a divine genocidal command in order to inherit its land. Its leaders occasionally indulge in unsavory activities. A queen is thrown from a tower, trampled to death by horses, and eaten by dogs for worshipping the wrong god. Foreign armies frequently invade, and the horrors of war are nearly constant. The nation is destroyed and exiled. After a modest restoration under Persian hegemony came the rule of the Roman Empire (continuing the Christian narrative). In this period God sends his son to receive the Mel Gibson treatment—he dies a brutal death. Rome begins to persecute those who believe in this God and his plan, and the corpus ends with Revelation. Although Revelation might somewhat safely be categorized as apocalyptic literature, its vivid symbolism is the stuff of horror.[34] Massive numbers of deaths, blood flowing through the streets, incredible monsters, and terror permeate the book. Yes, it ends with a vision of heaven, but the reader has to go through a kind of hell to get there. Naming it apocalyptic also allows a masking of the fictional elements.

The Second Temple Period, during which much of the New Testament was written, also witnessed a florescence of early Jewish writing. Some of this is reflected in the Apocrypha, or deuterocanonical books of the Bible, and in the pseudepigrapha. Among them accounts of horror, often fictionalized, continue. The tales of the persecutions dreamed up by the invaders would still be worthy of cinematic horror. 3 Maccabees, for just one example, tells of how Ptolemy, wanting to massacre Jews unwilling to accommodate to foreign ways, attempted to unleash a herd of drunken elephants among groups of captives. This was clearly intended to be a horror spectacle, whether it actually happened or not. Among at least some groups of early Christians these stories were often part of the Holy Scriptures.

Quite apart from the horror action of many biblical stories, the Good Book also features monsters.[35] Leviathan—the sea serpent who later lends his name to demons, behemoth, night hags, and the fantastic beasts of Daniel and Revelation roam its pages. Demons appear, and there are giants and at least one ghost. Modern analysts tend to define horror as literature or cinema that contains monsters.[36] Since the Good Book fits that description, the only factors that prevent it from claiming the name are theological, especially its aura of sanctity and the reluctance to admit fictional content to Holy Writ.

The Bible nevertheless continued to influence other aspects of literature which, ironically, came to be considered lowbrow over time. Due to these literary works sharing a measure of the Bible's quality of sanctity, they were considered worthy reading for the faithful. In the Western canon, a high, if not the highest, form of philosophical thought was at one time considered to be theology. These concepts and their initial execution, it was believed, appeared in Scripture. Theology had trumped the obvious. And Holy Writ was behind it. Surveying the whole of Western literature is not necessary to substantiate this claim. Few would doubt that the Bible has been a major driving force behind Western culture up to the present. Stopping at pertinent examples along the way will illustrate the continuity of horror, mediated by following the Good Book in some way.

If the objection is raised that not all literature of any given period (including the Bible) falls into the horror category, it is essential to remember that is not the claim being made here. The genre—and even the concept of genre—developed over time.[37] What is being suggested here is that due to its preservation and cultural stature the Bible was the progenitor of horror but could not be recognized as such. It participates in some forms of fiction. Before moving forward from the Good Book back to the present, a slight diversion into the classics is necessary.

Darryl Jones has recently suggested that the Greek and Roman classics could be considered the ancestors of horror.[38] Rivaling the Bible for antiquity, the mythology we often see presented in action films could easily be cast in these terms. This is a valid point. We are far more comfortable classifying the classics as fictional. The classics, historically, have also had a tremendous influence on Western thought. There are undoubtedly horror stories here as well. The difference, however, is that the classics do not share the aura of sanctity that Scripture bears. The classics were the preserve of those with formal educations that included instruction in Greek and Latin, from the beginning of modern education. The Bible, on the other hand, was a resource commonly found in early modern houses even of the uneducated. The Good Book was ubiquitous and considered qualitatively different from the classics, no matter how noble the latter might be. Classics were not the "Word of God."

The classics contributed to the blend of sacred (the gods) and secular (their behavior), as well as fact and fiction, that characterize ancient writing. We do a disservice when we treat the Bible (or other ancient literature) as modern. Our categories often simply do not apply.[39] They are nevertheless the ancestors to modern genre fiction.

It is possible, even likely, that more than one tributary contributed to the river that would eventually become the horror genre. Ultimately, this multiplicity of sources does not weaken the premise being presented here. The suggestion that the Bible contributed to horror is not gainsaid by the contribution of the classics. The Good Book, however, baptizes the subject in a way that the classics cannot. They were not holy books even for the Greeks. They did not contribute substantially to the Christian theology that formed the cultural matrix in which they were often read, beyond fostering a decided fondness for Plato's philosophy. So we begin with Scripture.

To get a better sense of this, beginning with the Bible a few landmarks of the developing Western theological and literary tradition will serve as islands for our seven-league boots' tour through horror history.[40] This journey does not pretend to be comprehensive. It is a necessarily selective sampling and many other examples could be adduced.

BACK TO LATE ANTIQUITY

Our first stop beyond the Bible itself is with the early monks of late antiquity. Leading contemplative lives, they wrote mainly to offer spiritual advice to other seekers. Those who chronicle the monks often wrote horrific accounts of their struggles with demons.[41] The theological pedigree of demons may seem to suggest they are of a different class than garden-variety monsters, but in the context of horror, where one religion is not privileged, they should be considered one species of the genus Monster. Demons still serve to classify movies as part of the horror genre, after all. One of the early anchorites, sometimes inaccurately claimed to be the first solitary monk, Antony of Egypt became famous in his own lifetime. Athanasius of Alexandria wrote the *Life of Antony* to encourage future hermits as well as to promote Christianity.[42]

The *Life of Antony* itself, which could in no way be considered horror in the modern mindset, has to be imagined in its original context. Demons were taken with all seriousness up until, and even into, the Enlightenment.[43] Belief in a literal Hell below and a difficult to attain Heaven above combined to promote an atmosphere of earnest fear. According to Athanasius's text, demons physically beat Antony so severely that he could not even stand on his own and the other monks believed him to be dead. Put that into cinematic form and it would be horror. Consider, for example, *The Conjuring* (2013). Demons coming at night and leaving physical bruises on mortals constitutes horror. Demons attack Antony both physically and spiritually. Antony fends them off with Scripture. This puts the *Life of Antony* in direct theological succession of the horror the Bible initially offers. Antony's vision of the Devil swatting at souls trying to escape to Heaven could well fit into the image of early horror cinema such as *King Kong*, or even the providentially named Godzilla of the 1950s.

The writings of ante-Nicene Fathers such as Athanasius share a bit of Scripture's glow. Antony, in a long sermonic letter in the middle of the book, adjures Christians to maintain conservative values. Antony nevertheless struggles physically with demons his entire life. It is not as dramatically written as *The Exorcist*, but given its time and purpose, it is not so very different.[44] Although written with sincerity, the accounts of such attacks would be considered fictional by most modern standards.

Horror, as noted at the outset, defies easy definition. Since modern analysts consider monsters of some kind to be a necessary component and since demons are monsters, there is a tangible connection here. Demons are monsters with a prebiblical pedigree; ancient Mesopotamians believed in them.[45] For the monks, however, the main source of authoritative teaching on demons had to be the Bible. Although accounts of demons would fade after the Enlightenment, up until that time they were monsters to be exorcised or even fought physically as well as spiritually. The *Life of Antony* is but one example of this. It demonstrates that biblical horror continued into late antiquity. The sanctity of Scripture frightened off demons, and this narrative shares some of the holiness of its urtext.

It is certainly understandable that most literary treatments of horror do not go back as far as late antiquity looking for its roots. They are, however, clearly there in theological form. Religion and horror go naturally together, so why not theology?[46] Other examples from this period could be presented, but we still have far to go. The next league-step on this journey takes us to the European Medieval Period. In a world where war was common and plagues were a very real source of fear, a stable church served as a bastion of security. From what we know of culture at the time, even simply going out at night was potentially dangerous.[47] Violence was not uncommon. Horror, in other words, would have been quite familiar. It would be surprising if it did not appear in the writing of the time.

EARLY-TO-HIGH MIDDLE AGES

The Middle Ages likewise are seldom referenced as being a direct source of the horror genre, although they provide the necessary background for the early Gothic novels.[48] The usual image of the Middle Ages as a period of ignorance and suffering is certainly overblown. The large-scale picture that emerges from the surviving sources, however, documents wars and violence—not least of which involved the Crusades—and beliefs that included monsters, dragons, and witches. These are the raw elements of horror. Periodic plagues decimated the population, adding a fear of contagion that also appeared supernatural.[49] Surveying medieval literature as a whole is beyond the scope of this essay, but we find a convenient example in *Beowulf*.

The dating of *Beowulf* is debated, but it was likely composed between 700 and 1000.[50] As such, it is a useful stepping-stone across the centuries from the *Life of Antony*. Whether considered pagan or Christian, the story clearly draws on religious themes and is influenced by Christianity. Although theology does not play a major role in it, this tale continues the intersection of both horror and theology that brings the late antique horror into a new era.

Beowulf, in part because it has managed to survive from this period, is an important exemplar of medieval writing. It is a monster story. Not only does the protagonist have to fight Grendel, and then the monster's mother, he ends the epic poem facing a dragon. The overnight scene in Hrothgar's mead hall could have been taken from a modern horror film. Surviving in only a single exemplar, *Beowulf* cannot be claimed to be widely influential in itself, but it does demonstrate that an interest in telling frightening tales participates in religious contexts. Other stories from its time might reasonably be inferred to have done the same. Grendel is a descendent of Cain. Monsters descend from the Bible.

There is also a theology in *Beowulf*, an epic never denied the label "fiction." Sin is the source of the monsters—they are Cain's progeny. Hrothgar delivers a lengthy sermonic speech about the dangers of pride. Although Scripture is not directly cited, it is alluded to. In that sense it is Bible-inspired horror. It is clear that *Beowulf* participates in the lineage of horror, even as it does of fantasy.

Planting our next seven-league footstep toward the end of the Middle Ages, we can observe some of the theological visual precursors to horror as a medium that will be well adapted to cinema. During the Medieval Period horror themes also took on a striking visual aspect that might be seen as anticipating the horror film. This is most clearly observed late in the period as thinkers began to grapple with concepts that would later become known as the Reformation and the Enlightenment.[51] A few examples will demonstrate how aspects of horror became performative at this time. Visual representations reached viewers, even if they were comparatively few before travel became widespread, in a way that was perhaps more publicly available than written accounts.

EARLY MODERN ART

The artwork of Hieronymus Bosch (1450s–1516) has become synonymous with medieval horror.[52] His images of Hell, in particular, involve the monstrous and macabre. Shortly after Bosch's lifetime, Hans Holbein the Younger's woodcuts of the Danse Macabre were published (1526).[53] Both Bosch and Holbein suggested movement in their works that would prefigure horror's natural transition to film. Indeed, among the earliest film subjects were Frankenstein—a short film based on Mary Shelley's novel was made of this at Thomas Edison's studio shortly after the cinematic process was invented—and Dracula—in the form of F. W. Murnau's silent *Nosferatu, eine Symphonie des Grauens* in 1922. Horror set in motion helped capture the stereotype of a macabre Medieval Period, but there can be no question of the theological motivation of Bosch and Holbein.

Late medieval horror often incorporated biblical elements. The paintings of Bosch, remember, depicted the fallen nature of humans and suffering in Hell with its demons. Matthias Grünewald's "Isenheim Altarpiece" (1510–1515) was more directly Christianized. Featuring Jesus, this famous scene represented the horror of the physical torture involved in crucifixion in a way that anticipates Mel Gibson's *The Passion of the Christ*. Such visual representations, which could be multiplied, illustrate that the background to horror included the development of theologically inspired visual fear of the Middle Ages. Bosch, Holbein, and Grünewald worked in forms based on imagination rather than on fact.

It would be simplistic to suggest that the Middle Ages were unremitting misery and darkness.[54] Historically they were unsettled times, but science continued its progress—the engineering of medieval clocks alone indicates that the age was not as backward as it is often portrayed. Living conditions for many, however, and the realities of wars and plagues, create an overall impression of troubled times. Lifespans were not to the standard enjoyed today in most developed nations, and death was an eminently practical fascination. These circumstances led early Gothic-novel writers to look toward this time for settings that fit the mood of their work.

EARLY MODERN HORROR WRITING

As the Reformation took hold and divided European Christianity, open conflict erupted. Written horror continued in the realm of what was considered nonfiction at the time. John Foxe's *Actes and Monuments*, popularly known as *Foxe's Book of Martyrs* (1563), was a Protestant condemnation of religious persecution.[55] The treatment accorded heretics easily classifies as horror. Indeed, the premise of torture during the Inquisition counted on horror to obtain confessions. Not only that, but these factors also tie directly to the early Christian martyr tales such as that of Saint Agnes, already mentioned. The tradition continued into the Catholic counterexample, Alban Butler's *Lives of the Saints* (1756–1759).

Space limitations do not permit a thorough exploration of the many branches of horror's Medieval and Early Modern roots.[56] Toward the end of what is traditionally thought of as the Middle Ages, witch hunts, for example, once again brought horror themes to life. Never easily summarized, these real-life horrors also participated in the fiction of witches' Sabbats, intercourse with the Devil, and astral projection. These concepts, perhaps best symbolized as Heinrich Kramer's *Malleus Maleficarum*, "the hammer of witches," are a species of theological horror.[57] First published in 1487, *Malleus Maleficarum* falls into early modernity. It clearly continues the mix of theology, monsters, and fiction that had existed since the Bible concocted this world. Kramer drew his hatred of witches at least partially from Scripture. Although completely discredited, *Malleus Maleficarum* is recognized as "made up" with alternative facts and a truly horrific misogyny. It would also contribute to themes that would appear one last league-boot step away in the Gothic novel.

Such a long and sketchy view of Western literature is necessarily an oversimplification. Each of these eras had what we through our modern lenses see as horror, even if they did not recognize that genre classification. Horror is a more complex genre than generally supposed, and it has a long history in religious literature. The point of this chapter is not to suggest that this is *the* single way that the horror genre developed. As mentioned with regard to the classics, there were many tributaries contributing to this stream. One major and generally overlooked source, however, was the Bible.

Reluctance to address religion on the part of some horror analysts, it would seem, has foreshortened the view of horror's very deep roots in theology. An increasingly secular society that has a persistent interest in horror suggests that a longer view might help to explain how this "lowbrow" form of entertainment trades in the currency of a theology with biblical roots. The thread, or perhaps chain, that holds all of these disparate stops in history together is the Bible. Scripture was never coy about horror. The themes of that horror often reflected daily realities in a world under the sway of military might and very real violence. Some of the Psalms that illustrate this are difficult to read even today. The horrors of being on the receiving end of the Assyrian, Babylonian, Persian, Hellenistic, and Roman Empires were real enough. Crucifixion was intended to induce terror. Taking this idea as a central tenet of Christianity led to an acceptance of horror that would seem counterintuitive to a religion putatively based on love.

The desert monks and their demons both knew the Bible. In fact, the best means of driving demons away was often considered to be the recitation of Scripture.[58] The demons themselves, however, laid the groundwork of horror, and they continue to have the power to frighten. The entire diegesis of *The Conjuring* is based on demons. Mere mention of *The Exorcist* is enough to cause shivers of fear among many viewers. The early literature of the Western canon participates in generating that frisson as well. It is theological horror.

CONCLUSION

This chapter takes a broad view of historical developments that show horror as an essential element of theological thought in the Western tradition that grew out of Judaism and Christianity. The Bible, viewed from this perspective, is the progenitor of horror. This is not to suggest that other ancient writings did not contain horror elements—Gilgamesh had monsters, after all—but the Bible alone survived from this time period throughout Western culture where the horror genre developed. Moving forward from the Good Book, the lives of the saints and martyrs led to a medieval fascination with death, terror, and Christianity. Reasonable parallels could be drawn between Beowulf and Gilgamesh. Not only did Grünewald's "Isenheim Altarpiece" and the art of Bosch elicit horror, Holbein's danse macabre placed horror in a performative role—a moving picture, as it were, anticipating the horror film. This theological fascination with suffering and death lingered on until the Enlightenment led to a sublimation of spiritual concerns to the rational. Romanticism, with its attendant Gothic subculture, reacted by reintroducing elements of the supernatural. One of those elements was, and continues to be, the horror genre. This genre has been an integral part of the Western canon, disregarding the label of fiction, all the way back to the Bible.

NOTES

1. The importance of *Frankenstein* for the genre is widely recognized. See Mary Shelley, *Frankenstein: Annotated for Scientists, Engineers, and Creators of All Kinds*, David H. Guston, Ed Finn, and Jason Scott Robert, eds. (Cambridge, MA: MIT Press, 2017). See also the sources in note 8.

2. In the case of Peter Hutchings, *The Horror Film* (Harlow: Pearson, 2004), that definition can take a full chapter.

3. (New York: Random House, 1966).

4. Some standard histories of horror are Wheeler Winston Dixon, *A History of Horror* (New Brunswick, NJ: Rutgers University Press, 2010) and David J. Skal's *The Monster Show: A Cultural History of Horror*, 2nd edition (New York: Faber and Faber, 1993). Many more could be listed. Dixon does note that horror goes back as far as Gilgamesh, but then begins his analysis in the nineteenth century (CE).

5. Even a glimpse at the Wikipedia entry on "Horror fiction" (https://en.wikipedia.org/wiki/Horror_fiction, accessed 3/15/2019) indicates a broad awareness that horror has roots long before the Gothic.

6. *The Gothic World*, Glennis Byron and Dale Townshend, eds. (London: Routledge, 2014), contains ample historical background for its origins in Romanticism.

7. For an application of Romanticism that shows this, see Richard Holmes, *The Age of Wonder: How the Romantic Generation Discovered the Beauty and Terror of Science* (New York: Vintage Books, 2008).

8. Susan Tyler Hitchcock, *Frankenstein: A Cultural History* (New York: Norton, 2007); Roseanne Montillo, *The Lady and Her Monsters: A Tale of Dissections, Real-Life Dr. Frankensteins, and the Creation of Mary Shelley's Masterpiece* (New York: William Morrow, 2013); and Lester D. Friedman and Allison B. Kavey, *Monstrous Progeny: A History of the Frankenstein Narratives* (New Brunswick: Rutgers University Press, 2016). Once cinema developed, horror was one of the earliest topics explored as Thomas Edison's firm produced a short film of *Frankenstein*. The Universal monsters appeared beginning in the Depression, always casting an eye back to Gothic sensibilities. *Frankenstein* was the second Universal horror film, released shortly after *Dracula*, in 1931.

9. Several books by S. T. Joshi address Lovecraft's situation in life. See Don G. Smith, *H. P. Lovecraft in Popular Culture: The Works and Their Adaptions in Film, Television, Comics, Music and Games* (Jefferson, NC: McFarland, 2006) for his afterlife.

10. The figure of Stephen King books is from 2006: http://news.bbc.co.uk/2/hi/programmes/newsnight/6174256.stm (accessed 2/10/19).

11. For example, Douglas L. Cowan, *Sacred Terror: Religion and Horror on the Silver Screen* (Waco, TX: Baylor University Press, 2008). More recently, see his *America's Dark Theologian: The Religious Imagination of Stephen King* (New York: New York University Press, 2018).

12. After the proposal for this chapter had been submitted, Darryl Jones's most recent book, *Sleeping with the Lights On* (Oxford: Oxford University Press, 2018), arrived. Jones had made a similar point, suggesting that horror had its roots in the classics of Greek antiquity. His instincts seem correct, but do not reach back far enough. The Bible is arguably the very root of Western literature.

13. I used this colloquialism in *Holy Horror: The Bible and Fear in Movies* (Jefferson, NC: McFarland Books, 2018) for regularizing the Bible as literature, a practice I continue here.

14. This fact has long been noted by authors of books on horror, whether they play it down, as does Noël Carroll in his *The Philosophy of Horror, or Paradoxes of the Heart* (New York: Routledge, 1990), or if they are more accepting of it, as are Edward J. Ingebretsen, S. J. *Maps of Heaven, Maps of Hell: Religious Terror as Memory from the Puritans to Stephen King* (Armonk, NY: M. E. Sharpe, 1996); Kendell R. Phillips, *Projected Fears: Horror Films and American Culture* (Westport, CT: Praeger, 2005); Cynthia J. Miller and A. Bowdoin Van Riper, *Divine Horror: Essays on the Cinematic Battle between the Sacred and the Diabolical* (Jefferson, NC: McFarland, 2017); and Mathias Clasen, *Why Horror Seduces* (New York:

Oxford University Press, 2017). Clasen could claim to go back even earlier than the Bible as he considers horror's evolutionary utility.

15. See, for example, Peter Temin, *The Roman Market Economy* (Princeton, NJ: Princeton University Press, 2013).

16. Candida Moss, *The Myth of Persecution: How Early Christians Invented a Story of Martyrdom* (New York: HarperOne, 2013).

17. Lyndal Roper, *Witch Craze: Terror and Fantasy in Baroque Germany* (New Haven, CT: Yale University Press, 2006).

18. This is most thoroughly covered in William V. Harris, *Ancient Literacy* (Cambridge, MA: Harvard University Press, 1991).

19. "Conservative values" is a term frequently used in the "culture wars" to point toward traditional, "biblical" morality. It has been occasionally applied to the horror genre as well.

20. For a sense of this, see Thomas Williams, ed. *The Cambridge Companion to Medieval Ethics*, Cambridge Companions to Philosophy (Cambridge and New York: Cambridge University Press, 2019), especially the essay "Virtue" by Thomas M. Osborne, Jr.

21. For Christianity in a Roman context, see Harry O. Maier, *New Testament Christianity in the Roman World* (New York: Oxford University Press, 2019).

22. *The Acts of Saint Agnes* can be found in translation published in 1856 by P. F. Cunningham in New York. (The translator's name is not explicitly given in this edition.)

23. The conservative elements of horror are brought out in Carol J. Clover, *Men, Women, and Chain Saws* (Princeton, NJ: Princeton University Press, 1992).

24. Many pieces of literature from the period are now classified as novels (i.e., fiction). See Lawrence M. Wills, *Ancient Jewish Novels: An Anthology* (New York: Oxford University Press, 2002).

25. See, for example, Michael L. Satlow, *How the Bible Became Holy* (New Haven: Yale University Press, 2015).

26. Subtitled *Literary-Feminist Readings of Biblical Narratives*, published by Fortress Press, Minneapolis.

27. Although overstated, Clover's *Men, Women, and Chain Saws* makes this point quite clearly.

28. The story of Adam Smith's decipherment of the Utnapishtim episode is well-known. See, conveniently, Irving Finkel, *The Ark Before Noah: Decoding the Story of the Flood* (New York: Anchor Books, 2014).

29. For example, Amy Kalmanofsky, *Terror All Around: The Rhetoric of Horror in the Book of Jeremiah* (New York: T & T Clark, 2008).

30. I made this suggestion in *Holy Horror*.

31. Many editions and translations exist. Perhaps the most authoritative is that of Andrew George, *The Epic of Gilgamesh* (London: Penguin, 1999), based on his massive critical edition.

32. These scenes come from "the Baal Cycle," or KTU 1.1–6. A translation may be found in N. Wyatt, *Religious Texts from Ugarit* (London: Sheffield Academic Press, 2002). Details may be found in Neal H. Walls, *The Goddess Anat in Ugaritic Myth* (Atlanta: Scholars Press, 1992).

33. This is readily admitted by its fans. See Jason Zinoman, *Shock Value: How a Few Eccentric Outsiders Gave Us Nightmares, Conquered Hollywood, and Invented Modern Horror* (New York: Penguin, 2011) and Adam Rockoff, *The Horror of It All: One Moviegoer's Love Affair with Masked Maniacs, Frightened Virgins, and the Living Dead . . .* (New York: Scribner, 2015).

34. The literature on Revelation is massive. A good starting point for contemporary outlooks is John J. Collins, *The Oxford Handbook of Apocalyptic Literature* (New York: Oxford University Press, 2014). For a somewhat nontraditional view, see Elaine Pagels, *Revelations: Vision, Prophecy, and Politics in the Book of Revelation* (New York: Penguin, 2012).

35. See, for example, Gregory Mobley, *The Return of the Chaos Monsters: and Other Backstories of the Bible* (Grand Rapids, MI: Eerdmans, 2012).

36. Consider Andrew Tudor's early study, *Monsters and Mad Scientists: A Cultural History of the Horror Movie* (Oxford: Basil Blackwell, 1989) and Hutchings, *The Horror Film*.

37. See, for example, Amy J. Devitt, *Writing Genres* (Carbondale: Southern Illinois University Press, 2008). Even horror is divided into genres, as discussed by Chris Vander Kaay, and

Kathleen Fernandez-Vander Kaay, *Horror Films by Subgenre: A Viewer's Guide* (Jefferson, NC: McFarland, 2016); it is important not to let later categories interfere with the evidence contained in primary sources.

38. Jones, *Sleeping with the Lights On.*

39. Eva Mroczek, *The Literary Imagination in Jewish Antiquity* (New York: Oxford University Press, 2016) and Matthew Larsen, *Gospels before the Book* (New York: Oxford University Press, 2018), have demonstrated that reading ancient texts through the modern lens of "book" distorts them in ways that seldom find recognition.

40. Even seven-league boots may go back to ancient Near Eastern prototypes. See W. G. E. Watson, "Middle-Eastern Forerunners to a Folktale Motif," *Orientalia* 53 (1984): 533–36.

41. See conveniently David Brakke, *Demons and the Making of the Monk: Spiritual Combat in Early Christianity* (Cambridge, MA: Harvard University Press, 2006).

42. This is available in many translations and formats. A stripped-down version without commentary may be found in Athanasius, *Life of Anthony* (Pickerington, OH: Beloved Publishing, 2014). A little research suggests this was extracted from E. A. Wallis Budge's public domain translation from 1907.

43. This point is made by Darren Oldridge in *The Devil: A Very Short Introduction* (Oxford: Oxford University Press, 2012).

44. *The Exorcist* was a novel by William Peter Blatty published in 1971 (New York: Harper & Row).

45. For Mesopotamians, see Jeremy Black and Anthony Green, *Gods, Demons and Symbols of Ancient Mesopotamia: An Illustrated Dictionary* (Austin: University of Texas Press, 1992). A readable narrative account may be found in Jean Bottero, *Religion in Ancient Mesopotamia* (Chicago: University of Chicago Press, 2001).

46. This point also appears in Cowan's *America's Dark Theologian.*

47. A. Roger Ekirch, *At Day's End: Night in Times Past* (New York: W. W. Norton, 2005).

48. An obvious reason for this is that literary studies tend to focus on the mass dissemination of literature following the introduction of the printing press to Europe. The point here is that the groundwork was laid long before that particular invention led to fairly widespread literacy.

49. See, for example, Norman F. Cantor, *In the Wake of the Plague: The Black Death and the World It Made* (New York: The Free Press, 2001).

50. Seamus Heaney's *Beowulf* (New York: W. W. Norton, 2000) is an authoritative source here, as well as a noted translation.

51. A fine introduction to the late Middle Ages remains Barbara W. Tuchman, *A Distant Mirror: The Calamitous 14th Century* (New York: Ballentine Books, 1978).

52. For a recent treatment of Bosch, see Nils Büttner, *Hieronymus Bosch: Visions and Nightmares* (London: Reaktion Books, 2016).

53. On Holbein, see Oskar Bätschmann and Pascal Griener, *Hans Holbein* (London: Reaktion Books, 1997).

54. Consider Edward Grant, *The Foundations of Modern Science in the Middle Ages* (Cambridge: Cambridge University Press, 1996).

55. John N. King, *John Foxe's "Book of Martyrs" and Early Modern Print Culture* (Cambridge: Cambridge University Press, 2006).

56. These are readily acknowledged to have existed but are not traced back into their biblical origins.

57. Much has been written on both witches and the *Malleus Maleficarum.* See Christopher S. Mackay, *The Hammer of Witches: A Complete Translation of the Malleus Maleficarum* (Cambridge: Cambridge University Press, 2009).

58. As noted in Brakke, *Demons and the Making of the Monk.*

WORKS CITED

The Acts of Saint Agnes. New York: P. F. Cunningham, 1856.

Athanasius. *Life of Anthony.* Pickerington, OH: Beloved Publishing, 2014.

Bätschmann, Oskar, and Pascal Griener. *Hans Holbein.* London: Reaktion Books, 1997.

Black, Jeremy, and Anthony Green. *Gods, Demons and Symbols of Ancient Mesopotamia: An Illustrated Dictionary*. Austin: University of Texas Press, 1992.

Blatty, William Peter. *The Exorcist*. New York: Harper & Row, 1971.

Bottero, Jean. *Religion in Ancient Mesopotamia*. Chicago: University of Chicago Press, 2001.

Brakke, David. *Demons and the Making of the Monk: Spiritual Combat in Early Christianity*. Cambridge, MA: Harvard University Press, 2006.

Büttner, Nils. *Hieronymus Bosch: Visions and Nightmares*. London: Reaktion Books, 2016.

Byron, Glennis, and Dale Townshend, eds. *The Gothic World*. London: Routledge, 2014.

Cantor, Norman F. *In the Wake of the Plague: The Black Death and the World It Made*. New York: The Free Press, 2001.

Capote, Truman. *In Cold Blood*. New York: Random House, 1966.

Carroll, Noël. *The Philosophy of Horror, or Paradoxes of the Heart*. New York: Routledge, 1990.

Clasen, Mathias. *Why Horror Seduces*. New York: Oxford University Press, 2017.

Clover, Carol J. *Men, Women, and Chain Saws*. Princeton, NJ: Princeton University Press, 1992.

Cohen, Jeffrey Jerome. "Monster Culture (Seven Theses)." In *Monster Theory: Reading Culture*, edited by Jeffrey Jerome Cohen, 3–25. Minneapolis: University of Minnesota Press, 1996.

Collins, John J., ed. *The Oxford Handbook of Apocalyptic Literature*. New York: Oxford University Press, 2014.

Cowan, Douglas L. *America's Dark Theologian: The Religious Imagination of Stephen King*. New York: New York University Press, 2018.

———. *Sacred Terror: Religion and Horror on the Silver Screen*. Waco, TX: Baylor University Press, 2008.

Devitt, Amy J. *Writing Genres*. Carbondale: Southern Illinois University Press, 2008.

Dixon, Wheeler Winston. *A History of Horror*. New Brunswick, NJ: Rutgers University Press, 2010.

Ekirch, A. Roger. *At Day's End: Night in Times Past*. New York: W. W. Norton, 2005.

Finkel, Irving. *The Ark Before Noah: Decoding the Story of the Flood*. New York: Anchor Books, 2014.

Friedman, Lester D., and Allison B. Kavey. *Monstrous Progeny: A History of the Frankenstein Narratives*. New Brunswick, NJ: Rutgers University Press, 2016.

George, Andrew. *The Epic of Gilgamesh*. London: Penguin, 1999.

Grant, Edward. *The Foundations of Modern Science in the Middle Ages*. Cambridge: Cambridge University Press, 1996.

Harris, William V. *Ancient Literacy*. Cambridge, MA: Harvard University Press, 1991.

Heaney, Seamus. *Beowulf*. New York: Norton, 2000.

Hitchcock, Susan Tyler. *Frankenstein: A Cultural History*. New York: Norton, 2007.

Holmes, Richard. *The Age of Wonder: How the Romantic Generation Discovered the Beauty and Terror of Science*. New York: Vintage Books, 2008.

Hutchings, Peter. *The Horror Film*. Harlow: Pearson, 2004.

Ingebretsen, Edward J. S. J. *Maps of Heaven, Maps of Hell: Religious Terror as Memory from the Puritans to Stephen King*. Armonk, NY: M. E. Sharpe, 1996.

Jones, Darryl. *Sleeping with the Lights On*. Oxford: Oxford University Press, 2018.

Kalmanofsky, Amy. *Terror All Around: The Rhetoric of Horror in the Book of Jeremiah*. New York: T & T Clark, 2008.

King, John N. *John Foxe's "Book of Martyrs" and Early Modern Print Culture*. Cambridge: Cambridge University Press, 2006.

Larsen, Matthew D. C. *Gospels before the Book*. New York: Oxford University Press, 2018.

Mackay, Christopher S. *The Hammer of Witches: A Complete Translation of the* Malleus Maleficarum. Cambridge: Cambridge University Press, 2009.

Maier, Harry O. *New Testament Christianity in the Roman World*. New York: Oxford University Press, 2019.

Mariani, Mike. "Why Are Exorcisms on the Rise?" *The Atlantic* 322/5 (December 2018): 62–70.

Miller, Cynthia J., and A. Bowdoin Van Riper. *Divine Horror: Essays on the Cinematic Battle between the Sacred and the Diabolical.* Jefferson, NC: McFarland, 2017.

Mobley, Gregory. *The Return of the Chaos Monsters: and Other Backstories of the Bible.* Grand Rapids, MI: Eerdmans, 2012.

Montillo, Roseanne. *The Lady and Her Monsters: A Tale of Dissections, Real-Life Dr. Frankensteins, and the Creation of Mary Shelley's Masterpiece.* New York: William Morrow, 2013.

Moss, Candida. *The Myth of Persecution: How Early Christians Invented a Story of Martyrdom.* New York: HarperOne, 2013.

Mroczek, Eva. *The Literary Imagination in Jewish Antiquity.* New York: Oxford University Press, 2016.

Oldridge, Darren. *The Devil: A Very Short Introduction.* Oxford: Oxford University Press, 2012.

Osborne, Thomas M., Jr. "Virtue." In *The Cambridge Companion to Medieval Ethics, Cambridge Companions to Philosophy*, edited by Thomas Williams. Cambridge and New York: Cambridge University Press, 2019: 150–71.

Pagels, Elaine. *Revelations: Vision, Prophecy, and Politics in the Book of Revelation.* New York: Penguin, 2012.

Phillips, Kendell R. *Projected Fears: Horror Films and American Culture.* Westport, CT: Praeger, 2005.

Rockoff, Adam. *The Horror of It All: One Moviegoer's Love Affair with Masked Maniacs, Frightened Virgins, and the Living Dead.* New York: Scribner, 2015.

Roper, Lyndal. *Witch Craze: Terror and Fantasy in Baroque Germany.* New Haven, CT: Yale University Press, 2006.

Satlow, Michael L. *How the Bible Became Holy.* New Haven, CT: Yale University Press, 2015.

Seesengood, Robert Paul. "Seven Stations of Affect: Religion, Affect, and Mel Gibson's The Passion of the Christ." In *T&T Clark Companion to the Bible and Film*, edited by Richard Walsh, 174–86. London: T & T Clark, 2018.

Shelley, Mary. *Frankenstein: Annotated for Scientists, Engineers, and Creators of All Kinds.* David H. Guston, Ed Finn, and Jason Scott Robert, eds. Cambridge, MA: MIT Press, 2017.

Skal, David J. *The Monster Show: A Cultural History of Horror*, 2nd edition. New York: Faber and Faber, 1993.

Smith, Don G. *H. P. Lovecraft in Popular Culture: The Works and Their Adaptions in Film, Television, Comics, Music and Games.* Jefferson, NC: McFarland, 2006.

Temin, Peter. *The Roman Market Economy.* Princeton, NJ: Princeton University Press, 2013.

Trible, Phylis. *Texts of Terror: Literary-Feminist Readings of Biblical Narratives.* Minneapolis, MN: Fortress Press, 1984.

Tuchman, Barbara W. *A Distant Mirror: The Calamitous 14th Century.* New York: Ballentine Books, 1978.

Tudor, Andrew. *Monsters and Mad Scientists: A Cultural History of the Horror Movie.* Oxford: Basil Blackwell, 1989.

Vander Kaay, Chris, and Kathleen Fernandez-Vander Kaay. *Horror Films by Subgenre: A Viewer's Guide.* Jefferson, NC: McFarland, 2016.

Walls, Neal H. *The Goddess Anat in Ugaritic Myth.* Atlanta: Scholars Press, 1992.

Waterhouse, Ruth. "Beowulf as Palimpsest." In *Monster Theory: Reading Culture*, edited by Jeffrey Jerome Cohen, 26–39. Minneapolis: University of Minnesota Press, 1996.

Watson, W. G. E. "Middle-Eastern Forerunners to a Folktale Motif." *Orientalia* 53 (1984): 533–36.

Wiggins, Steve A. *Holy Horror: The Bible and Fear in Movies.* Jefferson, NC: McFarland Books, 2018.

Wills, Lawrence M. *Ancient Jewish Novels: An Anthology.* New York: Oxford University Press, 2002.

Wyatt, N. *Religious Texts from Ugarit.* London: Sheffield Academic Press, 2002.

Zinoman, Jason. *Shock Value: How a Few Eccentric Outsiders Gave Us Nightmares, Conquered Hollywood, and Invented Modern Horror.* New York: Penguin, 2011.

FILMOGRAPHY

The Conjuring. Directed by James Wan. Burbank, CA: Warner Brothers Pictures, 2013.

The Exorcist. Directed by William Friedkin. Burbank, CA: Warner Brothers Pictures, 1973.

King Kong. Directed by Merian C. Cooper and Ernest B. Schoedsack. New York: RKO Radio Pictures, 1933.

Nosferatu, eine Symphonie des Grauens. Directed by F. W. Murnau. Nederlandsche Bioscoop Trust, 1922.

The Passion of the Christ. Directed by Mel Gibson. Santa Monica, CA: Icon Productions, 2004.

Chapter Three

Mysterium Horrendum

*Exploring Otto's Concept of the Numinous
in Stoker, Machen, and Lovecraft*

Jack Hunter

This chapter[1] is about the essence of religious experience—the numinous—
and how it is conjured and expressed through the weird fiction of Bram
Stoker, Arthur Machen, and H. P. Lovecraft, and the many efforts at translating their work into film. The term "weird" is used here in the sense suggested
by Lovecraft himself, in his historical essay on the development of weird
fiction, "Supernatural Horror in Literature":

> The true weird tale has something more than secret murder, bloody bones, or a
> sheeted form clanking chains according to rule. A certain atmosphere of
> breathless and unexplainable dread of outer, unknown forces must be present;
> and there must be a hint, expressed with a seriousness and portentousness
> becoming its subject, of that most terrible conception of the human brain—a
> malign and particular suspension or defeat of those fixed laws of Nature which
> are our only safeguard against the assaults of chaos and the daemons of un-
> plumbed space.[2]

This chapter will argue that weird fiction in particular is effective precisely
because it induces in readers a sense of the "weird," and that the most
successful cinematic adaptations of the works of Lovecraft and Stoker are
those that most effectively inspire this sensation in the audience. Mark Fisher
highlighted the "sense of *wrongness*" associated with the weird:

> It is often a sign that we are in the presence of the new. The weird . . . is a
> signal that the concepts and frameworks which we have previously employed

are now obsolete. If the encounter with the strange . . . is not straightforwardly pleasurable . . . it is not simply unpleasant either.[3]

By highlighting the dual nature of the weird as simultaneously "pleasurable" and "unpleasant," Fisher is also locating the sensation of the weird as a relative of another dual natured "feeling response" identified by the theologian Rudolf Otto and labeled the "numinous." Before we proceed to consider how the "weird" and "numinous" are evoked in the writings of Stoker, Machen, and Lovecraft, let us take a moment to introduce Otto's work and ideas.

RUDOLF OTTO

The German theologian Rudolf Otto was born in a town called Peine, near Hannover in Prussia. Unfortunately, very little is known about his early life until he began his formal education, so this brief biographical sketch is little more than an overview of his academic accomplishments. It is known that he studied theology and philosophy at the University of Erlangen, writing his dissertation on Martin Luther's understanding of the nature of the Holy Spirit, before taking a post as a lecturer at the University of Göttingen in 1897. Here he taught courses on theology, the history of philosophy and the history of religion. Later, he was appointed professor of systematic theology at Göttingen, and in 1914 he became professor of theology at Breslau until 1917, when he was hired as professor of systematic theology (again) at the University of Marburg. He retired in 1929 after a long and distinguished career but continued to live in Marburg for the rest of his life. He died in 1937.

Unlike many of his late-nineteenth-century predecessors, Otto's area of study and experience was not solely limited to the Christian context—it reached much further afield. For a year, beginning in 1911, for example, Otto traveled widely through Northern Africa, Egypt, and into Palestine and the Middle East. His journeys took him through India, China, Japan, and the United States before finally returning to Germany.[4] These travels expanded his awareness of the fact that the category of religion is not necessarily synonymous with Christianity. His experiences in these disparate contexts influenced his thinking to include the many varieties of religious expression found throughout the world's cultures, paving the way for a phenomenological approach to the study of religion that looks beyond immediately obvious surface differences toward an altogether stranger foundational impulse and experience.[5]

Otto is best known for his groundbreaking book *Das Heilige*, translated to English as *The Idea of the Holy* (first published in 1917), in which he developed his concept of "the numinous" as the essential core of religious experience. This idea of the numinous, defined as an encounter with the "wholly other," is the main focus of this chapter, and it is a concept that is particularly well suited to exploring through the weird fiction writings (as well as some of the attempts at replicating them in film), of Bram Stoker, Arthur Machen, and H. P. Lovecraft, as other scholars have suggested.[6] Before we move into the realms of weird fiction and horror, however, let us first find out a little more precisely what Otto was referring to when talking about the numinous.

THE NUMINOUS

For Otto, the numinous referred to the "non-rational" component of religion—that is, the element of religion that cannot be explained in sociological, economic, political, or doctrinal terms. Religion is, after all, a particularly complex and nebulous phenomenon that can be analyzed in all of these fairly mundane and highly reductive terms but cannot be reduced to any of them in its totality.[7] We can quite easily approach and understand the sociological functions of religious belief, or look at the power relations within organized religions. We can create psychological profiles of religious believers or critically analyze the textual component of religious doctrine, for example, and yet, in spite of all of this, there remains an aspect of religion that is much more difficult to apprehend or understand in such terms. That aspect is *religious experience*, which Otto considered to be a *sui generis* phenomenon—meaning that it is irreducible to any other factor. Indeed, from Otto's perspective the doctrinal, ethical, political, social, and psychological dimensions of religion—which he termed "rational"—ultimately stem from religious experience—the "non-rational,"[8] rather than the other way around. Religious experience is, therefore, that element of religion sought out and described in mystical traditions or which leaks through unexpectedly into the mundane sphere in the event of ostensible miracles, visions, or other seemingly supernatural or paranormal occurrences. It is this transcendent, ineffable aspect of religion, grounded in direct feeling and emotion that Otto refers to as *numinous*.

Otto suggests that the sense of the numinous is conjured through our interactions with what he terms "the wholly other"—defined as "something which has no place in our scheme of reality but belongs to an absolutely different one."[9] Otto's understanding of the numinous experience arising from an interaction with the wholly other contrasts with the ideas of scholars such as Émile Durkheim, who argued that the "sacred" is socially constructed. For Otto the sacred is very real, existing independently of human consciousness and waiting to be interacted with.

Within the feeling-response that arises from interaction with the wholly other, Otto discerned two distinct, yet complimentary, characteristics of numinous experience, which he labeled the *mysterium tremendum* and the *mysterium fascinans*. Drawing on his extensive experience researching manifestations of the sacred in different contexts, Otto became acutely aware of the numinous's ability to be simultaneously terrifying (the *tremendum*) and fascinating (the *fascinans*)—the fear and awe of the supernatural that we, as a species—for whatever reason—cannot help but yearn for. This is what Otto called the "religious impulse." For Otto, this yearning for the sacred has its roots in the irreducible horror and beauty of the holy as a distinct kind of experience, and it is here that weird fiction, in its vivid explorations of supernatural and cosmic horrors and wonders, can begin to illuminate just what Otto was attempting to distill as the underlying basis of all religious expression. Timothy Beal draws out the relationship between the horror and religious experience through his seminal exploration of the religion and the monstrous:

> The *experience* of horror in relation to the monstrous is often described in terms reminiscent of religious experience. Both are often characterized as an encounter with mysterious otherness that elicits a vertigo-like combination of both fear and desire, repulsion and attraction. Both religious experience and horror are characterized as encounters with something simultaneously awesome and awful. [10]

Beal's understanding of religious experience embodies Otto's characterization of the numinous as dual natured—simultaneously beautiful and terrifying, tapping into a deep-rooted fear of the divine that has been largely eradicated from religion in the West. It is my contention, then, that horror and weird fiction (both in literature and film) might serve an important pedagogical function for students of religious experience by recreating within us something of the experiences they describe, giving us a hint of religious experience by invoking the numinous feeling-response itself—Otto would call this an "indirect means of expression of the numinous" through art, literature, and music. [11]

DRACULA

Let us turn first to perhaps the greatest (or at least most influential) vampire story ever written, Bram Stoker's classic *Dracula*, first published in 1897. As a whole, Stoker's masterpiece plays with a wide range of religious ideas but in a surprisingly subtle way for a book that deals with a supernatural struggle between the forces of good against evil. In an article on "Religion and Superstition in Dracula," for example, John Watters argues that the novel portrays a clash between traditional Catholic Christianity on the one hand—steeped in ritual and mystery—and a more rational, modern, and scientific form of Protestantism on the other. According to this interpretation, the Dutch doctor, metaphysician, and vampire hunter Abraham Van Helsing serves as the crucial link between these two competing worldviews, for he "understands the necessity of using 'tradition and superstition' to destroy 'tradition and superstition,'"[12] thus bringing forth a new, modern, scientific worldview.

But, just as Otto sought to uncover the non-rational, experiential core of the religious impulse, it is not these rational, doctrinal, or theological aspects of religion (i.e., issues relating to the clash of Catholic and Protestant theologies and science), that we are most concerned with in the context of this chapter (though it is undoubtedly an interesting subtext within the novel). Rather, it is Stoker's descriptions of uncanny, weird, and mystical horror that are of key importance in elucidating our understanding of Otto's concept of the numinous. We are most interested here in Stoker's attention to detail in describing the sensations, feelings, and emotions of horror—the phenomenology of the numinous—and how he conjures these in his readers, rather than with his particular doctrinal leanings. Turning toward the non-rational, then, Beth McDonald, in her book *The Vampire as Numinous Experience* writes of the functions of the vampire as a numinous encounter:

> The numinous value, or sacred functioning, of the vampire myth lies in the influence that an encounter with the numinous has on the individual. In vampire literature, an encounter with a vampire [induces] an effect or condition of perception which allows the reader, and perhaps the character, to experience a sense of powerlessness in the face of someone or some thing supernaturally powerful.[13]

It is this powerlessness in the face of the supernatural that runs at the core of Otto's conception of the numinous experience.[14] Take, for instance, a seminal scene from the novel, when Jonathan Harker first sees Dracula in a truly unnatural light—crawling headfirst down the cliff-like walls of his castle, resembling something akin to a monstrous bat scuttling tightly across the vertical surface like a lizard. Here Harker's suspicion that there is something deeply weird about Count Dracula is finally confirmed. Harker explains in his diary:

> I was at first interested and somewhat amused [. . .]. But my very feelings changed to repulsion and terror when I saw the whole man slowly emerge from the window, and begin to crawl down the castle wall over that dreadful abyss, face down, with his cloak spreading out around him like giant wings. At first I could not believe my eyes [. . .] but I kept looking, and it could be no delusion [. . .]. I feel the dread of this horrible place overpowering me; I am in fear—in awful fear—and there is no escape for me; I am encompassed about with terrors that I dare not think of.[15]

This horrific sight, and Harker's reaction to it, conjures perfectly the *mysterium tremendum* through an inversion of the normally assumed laws of nature (with which we are so familiar), and the blurring of distinctions between man and animal. In this dramatic scene gravity is defeated, and it is terrifying to behold—it is repulsive—and yet it is deeply fascinating and draws our gaze. We cannot help but look in terror and awe at the spectacle through Harker's eyes. We can imagine Harker asking himself, "What is this creature, and what does it mean that this is happening? Is it my imagination, or have I slipped through into some other world? Has a trace of some other world leaked through into our own?" We can vividly imagine and sense Harker's horror at seeing this monstrosity and his inability to stop himself from staring in disbelief as the feeling of encroaching terror builds within him. It is a perfect encapsulation of Mark Fisher's understanding of the weird:

> The weird is a particular kind of perturbation. It involves a sensation of *wrongness*; a weird entity or object is so strange that it makes us feel that it should not exist, or at least it should not exist here. Yet if the entity or object *is* here, then the categories which we have up until now used to make sense of the world cannot be valid. [16]

The essence of Dracula's weird numinous quality is also captured wonderfully in a seminal scene from Hammer Studios's 1970 movie *Scars of Dracula*, directed by Roy Ward Baker. [17] The scene shows Dracula, here powerfully portrayed by Christopher Lee, and his vampiric harem in their natural habitat, wandering somnambulistically through the dark, gloomy passages and chambers of the Count's moldering castle. It is almost as though we have slipped through into another world—the world of the vampire—a limbo world between the living and the dead (again a breakdown on the usually assumed laws of nature). Dracula and his maidens are haunting their lair, like zombified spiders awaiting their prey, who wander in unwittingly, entrapping themselves in the vampire's hypnotic web. The atmosphere is particularly eerie and otherworldly—Dracula's castle is a *truly haunted* house. Indeed, Otto comments specifically on the numinous quality of haunted spaces as a primeval form of religious experience:

> Even today the finer awe that may steal over us in the stillness and half-gloom of our present-day sanctuaries has ultimate kinship [. . .] with genuine "ghostly" emotions. The faint shiver that may accompany such states of mind is not unrelated to the feeling of "creeping flesh," whose numinous character we have already considered. [18]

From Otto's perspective, the vampire's lair—Dracula's castle—could be understood as a "sacred place"—a place that has an overwhelming and tangible effect on the consciousness of those who interact with it. Again, the spectacle is terrifying, but we cannot help but be fascinated by what we are seeing; we cannot look away—we are drawn in. Perhaps this is just another tool in the vampire's seductive repertoire, luring us in with their otherworldly fascination. In this scene we are given a glimpse beyond the veil, seeing what the "wholly other" is actually like in its own habitat, before it finally consumes us.

This same numinous intensity was also captured beautifully in Werner Herzog's 1979 remake[19] of F. W. Murnau's 1922 German Expressionist masterpiece *Nosferatu: A Symphony of Horrors*[20]—itself an unauthorized retelling of Stoker's Dracula story.[21] The *mysterium tremendum* is particularly tangible in the scenes where Jonathan Harker first meets Count Orlok (to avoid legal action) after his long journey through the Carpathian mountains and interactions with superstitious locals. Their encounter is infused with a slow-burning tension and dread, which gradually builds to a crescendo when the Count snatches his first taste of Harker's blood after he inadvertently cuts his thumb with a rusty bread knife. These moments capture the very essence of religious dread—an awe-inspiring fear arising from a confrontation with the wholly other.

The character of Dracula occupies an extreme polarity of the "sacred spectrum"—he is so profane, unclean, and diseased that he becomes spiritually powerful and highly dangerous.[22] Dracula is an embodiment of what Otto refers to as "daemonic dread," the "*mysterium horrendum*," or the "negative numinous," and his effect on the individual is to invoke what Otto called "creature-feeling"—"the emotion of a creature, abased and overwhelmed by its own nothingness in contrast to that which is supreme above all creatures."[23]

THE GREAT GOD PAN

Very often textbooks for students of religious studies use an extract from the chapter "The Piper at the Gates of Dawn" in Kenneth Grahame's *The Wind in the Willows* (1908) to express Otto's conceptualization of the numinous. In the chapter, Ratty and Mole unexpectedly come face-to-face with Pan—the ancient Greek god of the wild—while searching for their lost friend. Clearly expressed in their encounter are the mixed emotions of fascination, joy, and terror that Otto identifies as characteristic of the numinous:

> "Rat!" he found breath to whisper, shaking. "Are you afraid?"
> "Afraid?" murmured the Rat, his eyes shining with unutterable love. "Afraid! Of Him? O, never, never! And yet—and yet—O, Mole, I am afraid!"[24]

This famous encounter is an undeniably vivid illustration of Otto's conception of the numinous: Ratty and Mole, in the face of the figure of Pan, are entranced by the twin emotions of terror and awe. But there is another literary vision of Pan that is equally as evocative, and equally as illustrative of

Otto's concept, and it takes place in the Welsh author Arthur Machen's weird 1890 novella "The Great God Pan."

The story begins with Dr. Raymond—who is fascinated by what he calls "transcendental medicine"—and his colleague performing some experimental brain surgery. They explain that they are merely making "a slight lesion in the grey matter [. . .] a trifling rearrangement of certain cells, a microscopical alteration" to the brain of a young woman in the hope that it will (literally) open her mind to all the wonders of nature, behind the veil of illusion (echoing William Blake's cleansing of the doors of perception). Dr. Raymond explains to his colleague how the two worlds, the physical and the spiritual, are simultaneously separate and yet immanent, veiled only by the physiological structures of the human brain:[25]

> Look about you [. . .]. You see the mountain, and hill following after hill, as wave on wave, you see the woods and orchard, the fields of ripe corn, and the meadows reaching to the reed-beds by the river. You see me standing here beside you, and hear my voice; but I tell you that all these things—yes, from that star that has just shone out in the sky to the solid ground beneath our feet—I say that all these are but dreams and shadows; the shadows that hide the real world from our eyes. There is a real world, but it is beyond this glamour and this vision [. . .] beyond them all as beyond a veil. I do not know whether any human being has ever lifted that veil; but I do know [. . .] that you and I shall see it lifted this very night from before another's eyes. You may think this all strange nonsense; it may be strange, but it is true, and the ancients knew what lifting the veil means. They called it seeing the God Pan. [26]

Machen's portrayal of the numinous is one of a transcendent reality that interpenetrates our own, an idea also explored in his novel *The Three Impostors*,[27] where strange mysteries bubble away beneath the surface of everyday life in Victorian London. The numinous is ever-present. It lies waiting just beyond the illusory veil of reality that we are so comfortable inhabiting, requiring only a simple neurosurgical procedure to be revealed. But, when it does finally break through, the numinous can be extremely powerful, and extremely terrifying:

> Her eyes opened [. . .]. They shone with an awful light, looking far away, and a great wonder fell upon her face, and her hands stretched out as if to touch what was invisible; but in an instant the wonder faded and gave place to the most awful terror. The muscles of her face were hideously convulsed [. . .] the soul seemed struggling and shuddering within the house of flesh. [28]

Quite unlike Kenneth Grahame's fairytale depiction of Pan and his effects on Ratty and Mole, Machen's conjuration of the Great God is horrific. In the novella, Dr. Raymond's experimental patient is overwhelmed by the *mysterium tremendum*—at first staring in awe and wonder at the revelation unveiled before her eyes, and then screaming in terror at its frightful immensity. Three days later she goes completely insane and worse still becomes impregnated with the child of the Great God Pan. It is a jumble of existential terrors that suggest that the cosmos is vastly more chaotic, and even less empathetic toward human life, than we can possibly suppose. As Otto writes, "the transition from natural to daemonic amazement is not a mere matter of degree"[29]—it is something "wholly other." It is the feeling of cosmic immensities (or at least the possibility of them) conjured in Machen's writings that lends them their "numinous" quality. It is also what inspired the horror writer H. P. Lovecraft to write that "there is in Machen an ecstasy of *fear* that all other living men are too obtuse or timid to capture, and that even Poe failed to envisage in all its starkest abnormality."[30]

LOVECRAFT'S COSMIC HORROR

H. P. Lovecraft's definition of "cosmic horror" is actually a remarkably close approximation of Otto's notion of the *mysterium tremendum*. Lovecraft's fictional world is one of ineffable cosmic horrors and mysterious occult forces. As we have already seen, for Lovecraft true weird fiction, by its very nature, should *invoke in the reader* a sense of profound uneasiness and dread, it should hint at the inability of the human mind to comprehend the true nature of reality, which is far more terrible than we can imagine (as Machen's surgical revelation of Pan suggested), and it should cause us to question the stability of our faith in the established laws of nature (think again about Dracula's inversion of the laws of gravity). For Lovecraft, in fiction at least, true horror emerges at the point when we realize that we have not even come close to understanding the complexities of the cosmos in which we insignificantly live. In Lovecraft's multiverse the rational scientific models of Western civilization are conceived as a "safeguard" against chaos, but our fixed laws are just an illusion—a psychological defense mechanism to protect our sanity from the "daemons of unplumbed space." Jesse Norford summarizes the philosophy that arises from this perspective when he writes that Lovecraft's

> fictional universe creates a paranoid and misanthropic vision of human life as
> a disease and the reality beneath the veil of ordinary life as a creeping, crawl-
> ing chaos that would blight the mind if ever fully revealed.[31]

Lovecraft's horror is ineffable. The unintelligible guttural names of his pantheon of alien deities are an expression of this ineffability. Their names cannot even remotely be pronounced by human tongues—Cthulhu, Yog Sothoth, Shub-Niggurath—these are nothing more than human approximations of the sounds of their names. Lovecraft's daemons are completely ontologically alien—the "wholly other"—the very definition of the incomprehensible

numinous. Otto's notion of the *mysterium* also captures this sense of ineffable incomprehensibility:

> The truly "mysterious" object is beyond our apprehension and comprehension,
> not only because our knowledge has certain irremovable limits, but because in
> it we come upon something inherently "wholly other," whose kind and charac-
> ter are incommensurable with our own, and before which we therefore recoil
> in a wonder that strikes us chill and numb. [32]

The numinous-wholly-other-ness of Lovecraft's non-Euclidean interdimensional entities is expressed wonderfully in the 1970 film version of *The
Dunwich Horror*, directed by Daniel Haller and produced by Roger Cor-
man. [33] Instead of creating an elaborate B-movie monster costume to represent Wilbur Whately's twin, the filmmakers chose to signify his presence
using weird flashing lights, interspersed with cut-up footage of tentacles and
abstract writhing horrors, overlain with a soundtrack of terrified screaming.
Admittedly, this decision was probably greatly influenced by the film's limited budget, but the overall effect was to successfully conjure the unspeakable,
ineffable otherness of Lovecraft's pantheon of alien gods.

The physical characteristics (if we can even use that term to refer to the
"bodies" of interdimensional gods) of Lovecraft's pantheon also express this
"otherness." Yog-Sothoth is perhaps the most enigmatic expression of this
"otherness" in Lovecraft's fiction. While many of Lovecraft's creations are
described using features we are at least vaguely familiar with (such as tentacles, eyes, wings, etc.), albeit mangled into monstrous chimeric forms, Yog-
Sothoth is described as entirely other, as these extracts suggest:

> It was an All-in-One and One-in-All of limitless being and self—not merely a
> thing of one Space-Time continuum, but allied to the ultimate animating es-
> sence of existence's whole unbounded sweep—the last, utter sweep which has
> no confines and which outreaches fancy and mathematics alike. It was perhaps
> that which certain secret cults of earth have whispered of as YOG-SOTHOTH,
> and which has been a deity under other names; that which the crustaceans of
> Yuggoth worship as the Beyond-One, and which the vaporous brains of the
> spiral nebulae know by an untranslatable Sign. [34]

And in another tale featuring Yog-Sothoth, the interdimensional god is described as equally cosmic terms:

> great globes of light massing toward the opening, and not alone these, but the
> breaking apart of the nearest globes, and the protoplasmic flesh that flowed
> blackly outward to join together and form that eldritch, hideous horror from
> outer space, that spawn of the blankness of primal time, that tentacled amor-
> phous monster which was the lurker at the threshold, whose mask was as a

congeries of iridescent globes, the noxious Yog-Sothoth, who froths as primal slime in nuclear chaos beyond the nethermost outposts of space and time![35]

Such extracts read like mystical tracts attempting to convey the nature of reality as revealed during ecstatic visions and reveries, the likes of which might be found in any of the world's occult and mystical traditions. Take, for example, the following extract from the writings of the Christian Neoplatonist mystic Pseudo-Dionysius the Areopagite. Pseudo-Dionysius argued in favor of what has come to be known as the *via negativa*—or the *apophatic* way (from the Greek "to deny")—a means of talking about God that gets at its point not through describing what God is, but rather through describing what God is not:

> Beings are surpassed by the infinity beyond being, intelligences by that oneness which is beyond intelligence. Indeed the inscrutable One is out of reach of every rational process. Nor can any words come up to the inexpressible Good, this One, this Source of all unity, this supra-existent Being. Mind beyond mind, word beyond speech, it is gathered up by no discourse, by no intuition, by no name. It is and it is as no other being is.[36]

Later scholars were also influenced by Pseudo-Dionysius's perspective. St. Augustine, for example, referred to God as "*aliud, aliud valde,*" meaning "other, completely other." Pseudo-Dionysius's apophatic approach captures the essence of both Otto's idea of the "wholly other"—as an actually existing thing that exists in the cosmos that is beyond human conception—and Lovecraft's ineffable alien gods—which threaten to undo all rational thought.

CONCLUSION

Horror literature and the films that are inspired by them, especially those within the subgenre of weird fiction and cosmic horror, provide an ideal springboard for thinking more deeply about key themes in the study of religion—especially Otto's conception of the numinous. These stories play with religious ideas, and distort them, leading to new insightful metaphors and interpretations. In their revelation of the horrors and wonders that lie beyond the illusory veil of everyday sense experience, these stories challenge our understanding of our own place and role in the universe (multiverse?), encouraging us to ask questions about the nature of human life and its relation to a much wider cosmic context. In other words, horror stories, and weird fiction in particular, serve to relocate human life in a wider system of ecological connections and remove us from our position of "dominant species."[37]

For Lovecraft, who was a staunch, scientifically minded atheist,[38] the awe, fear, and horror of the cosmos was one of emptiness, meaninglessness, and futility. Human beings are of little significance in the grand scheme of the unforgiving multiverse, which is indifferent to our existence. Lovecraft explores the *mysterium tremendum* not so much as a transcendent or sacred reality, but rather as its antithesis—an excessively profane and cruel cosmos with no hope of salvation. His is a numinousness of the alien wholly other, incomprehensible and deeply, deeply weird. Similarly, Stoker created a time-less character, perpetually resurrected on the silver screen, who embodies the wholly other. Dracula's is a terrifying, soul destroying, numinous quality. He is the embodiment of the negative numinous, the darkness that counterpoints the holy as godliness. Dracula is a symbol of the primal fear and spiritual danger associated with the unclean, the profane, and the dead. For Machen, however, human beings are components and participants in a much broader worldview encompassing many overlapping worlds, with many different in-habitants. Machen was deeply religious, and his fiction could be understood as a reflection of his personal cosmology—informed by a mystical Celtic spirituality and involvement with magical and occult/esoteric groups such as the Order of the Golden Dawn.[39] His fiction, therefore, highlights the imma-nence and transcendence of the numinous, ever-present just beneath the illu-sory veil of reality, and exceedingly powerful when it slips through into our mundane sphere.

Each of these works expresses a different, admittedly frightening, aspect of the mysterium. The philosopher of religion John Hick proposes what he calls a pluralist approach to the study of the world religions, wherein idiosyn-cratic religious systems represent "different human responses to the same ultimate transcendent reality." Hick refers to this transcendent reality as the "Real," which is, in itself, "beyond the scope of human conceptual under-standing."[40] Dracula, The Great God Pan, and Yog-Sothoth might also, therefore, be understood as expressions of the same transcendent "Real," representative of each author's attempt at capturing something of the uncan-ny essence of its mysterious nature.

Above all, and perhaps most interestingly, these works of fiction and film put us in direct contact with the numinous itself.[41] Weird writing and film-making escape beyond the confines of the page or screen and touch the reader in strange ways, activating our species's deep-seated cosmic fear and wonder. In a sense, therefore, these works teach us about the numinous through firsthand experience, rather than through abstract scholarly theoriz-ing. By means of the written word, Stoker, Machen, and Lovecraft were able to invoke some of the same emotions and feelings of fascination and terror that Otto described in *The Idea of the Holy*, which is very powerful stuff for a genre that finds its expression in pulp paperbacks and B-movies.

NOTES

1. This chapter was first written as a presentation for *Weekend Otherworld* at The Cinema Museum, London. 25th October 2014.
2. Lovecraft, "The Supernatural in Fiction."
3. Fisher, *The Weird and the Eerie*, 13.
4. Almond, *Rudolf Otto*.
5. Almond, "Rudolf Otto."
6. Beal, *Religion and its Monsters*.
7. Bowker, *The Sense of God*.
8. Almond, "Rudolf Otto."
9. Otto, *The Idea of the Holy*, 29.
10. Beal, *Religion and its Monsters*, 7.
11. Otto, *The Idea of the Holy*, 61.
12. Watters, "Religion and Superstition in Dracula," 115.
13. McDonald, *The Vampire as Numinous Experience*, 37.
14. Linforth, "'Numinous' and 'Negatively Numinous.'"
15. Stoker, *Dracula*, 45–46.
16. Fisher, *The Weird and the Eerie*, 15.
17. *Scars of Dracula*.
18. Otto, *The Idea of the Holy*, 128.
19. *Nosferatu the Vampyre*.
20. *Nosferatu: A Symphony of Horrors*.
21. Saviour, "Absent Presences in Liminal Places."
22. Douglas, *Purity and Danger*, 123.
23. Otto, *The Idea of the Holy*, 10.
24. Grahame, *The Wind in the Willows*, 108.
25. This is an idea that was later explored by thinkers such as Henri Bergson and Aldous Huxley, with their "filter theory" of consciousness, whereby the brain is understood a "reducing valve" for conscious experience. The idea is also currently prevalent in the popular discourse around DMT, the pineal gland, and the apparent world revealed under the profound influence of the drug.
26. Machen, *The Great God Pan*, 4–5.
27. Machen, *The Three Impostors*.
28. Ibid., 12–13.
29. Otto, *The Idea of the Holy*, 27.
30. Letter from H. P. Lovecraft to Frank Belknap Long, 8 January 1924.
31. Norford, "Pagan Death," 172.
32. Otto, *The Idea of the Holy*, 28
33. *The Dunwich Horror*.
34. Lovecraft and Price, "Through the Gates of the Silver Key."
35. Lovecraft and Derleth, *The Lurker at the Threshold*.
36. Hick, *The Fifth Dimension*, 80.
37. Grieve-Carlson, "The Hidden Predator."
38. Houellebecq, *H. P. Lovecraft*.
39. Kandola, "Celtic Occultism and the Symbolist Mode."
40. Hick, *The Fifth Dimension*, 77.
41. Kripal, *Mutants and Mystics*.

WORKS CITED

Almond, Philip. "Rudolf Otto: The Context of His Thought." *Scottish Journal of Theology* 36, no. 3 (August 1983): 347–62.

Almond, Philip C. *Rudolf Otto: An Introduction to his Philosophical Theology.* Chapel Hill: University of North Carolina Press, 1984.

Beal, Timothy K. *Religion and its Monsters.* London: Routledge, 2002.

Bowker, John. *The Sense of God: Sociological, Anthropological and Psychological Approaches to the Origin of the Sense of God.* Oxford: Clarendon Press, 1973.

Douglas, Mary. *Purity and Danger: An Analysis of the Concept of Pollution and Taboo.* London: Routledge, 2005.

Fisher, Mark. *The Weird and the Eerie.* London: Repeater Books, 2016.

Grahame, Kenneth. *The Wind in the Willows.* London: Ariel Books, 1980.

Grieve-Carlson, Timothy. "The Hidden Predator." In *Greening the Paranormal: Exploring the Ecology of Extraordinary Experience*, edited by Jack Hunter. 225–38. Milton Keynes: August Night Press, 2019.

Hick, John. *The Fifth Dimension: An Exploration of the Spiritual Realm.* Oxford: Oneworld, 1999.

Houellebecq, Michel. *H. P. Lovecraft: Against the World, Against Life.* London: Gollancz, 2008.

Kandola, Sondeep. "Celtic Occultism and the Symbolist Mode in the Fin-de-Siècle Writings of Arthur Machen and W. B. Yeats." *English Literature in Transition, 1880–1920* 56, no. 4 (2013): 497–518.

Kripal, Jeffrey J. *Mutants and Mystics: Science Fiction, Superhero Comics and the Paranormal.* Chicago: University of Chicago Press, 2011.

Linforth, Lucy. "'Numinous' and 'Negatively Numinous' in Bram Stoker's *Dracula*." *Forum: University of Edinburgh Postgraduate Journal of Culture and the Arts* 14 (Spring 2012): 2–14.

Lovecraft, H. P. "The Supernatural in Fiction." In *At the Mountains of Madness: The Definitive Edition.* New York: Random House, 2005.

Lovecraft, H. P., and E. H. Price. "Through the Gates of the Silver Key." In *Omnibus 1: At the Mountains of Madness.* London: Voyager, 1999.

Lovecraft, H. P., and August Derleth. *The Lurker at the Threshold.* New York: Carroll & Graf Publishers Inc., 1998.

Machen, Arthur. *The Great God Pan.* Cardigan, UK: Parthian, 2010.

———. *The Three Impostors.* London: Everyman, 1995.

McDonald, Beth E. *The Vampire as Numinous Experience: Spiritual Journeys with the Undead in British and American Literature.* Jefferson, NC: McFarland & Company, Inc., 2004.

Norford, Jesse. "Pagan Death: Lovecraftian Horror and the Dream of Decadence," *The Gothic: Probing the Boundaries*, ed. Eoghain Hamilton. Oxford: Interdisciplinary Press, 2012.

Otto, Rudolf. *The Idea of the Holy.* Oxford: Oxford University Press, 1958.

Saviour, Catania. "Absent Presences in Liminal Places: Murnau's *Nosferatu* and the Otherworld of Stoker's *Dracula*." *Literature/Film Quarterly* 32, no. 3 (2004): 229–36.

Stoker, Bram. *Dracula.* London: Scholastic, Inc., 1999.

Watters, John. "Religion and Superstition in Dracula." In *Dracula: Mythe et metamorphoses*, edited by Claude Fierobe. Villeneuve d'Ascq: Presses Universitaires du Sepentrion, 2005.

FILMOGAPHY

The Dunwich Horror. Directed by Daniel Haller. Los Angeles: American International Pictures, 1970.

Nosferatu: A Symphony of Horrors. Directed by F. W. Murnau. Germany: Prana Film, 1922.

Nosferatu the Vampyre. Directed by Werner Herzog. Germany: Werner Herzog Filmproduktion, 1979.

Scars of Dracula. Directed by Roy Ward Baker. United Kingdom: Hammer Studios, 1970.

Part II

Christianizing the Monster

Chapter Four

Priests, Secrets, and Holy Water

All I Ever Learned about Catholicism I Learned from Horror Films

Karrà Shimabukuro

When I was little, much too little to understand the references, I have clear memories of my mother sharing her personal experiences with *The Exorcist*. My mother saw *The Exorcist* when it first came out, the same time that "Local newscasts reported viewers fainting, vomiting, and fleeing the theater" which were initially credited to the horrific content and disturbing images involving Regan MacNeil. However, it is more likely that these reactions were due to the subliminal images that were included in opening versions of the film and later removed.[1] My mother's experience with the subliminal images was heightened by the fact that she saw the film while tripping and was never able to watch the film again. After seeing the movie, she quit her job because it required her to walk past the M Street stairs that Father Karras falls to his death at the end of the movie. She said she was too disturbed to walk past them every day, twice a day. I also remember my mom telling me that *The Exorcist* was based on a true story, and according to her it was based on Shirley MacLaine's experiences, which is why MacLaine became so interested in the spiritual later in life, and which explained Ellen Burstyn's look in the movie.[2] When I was a little older we went out to Long Island to visit my godfather and were out running errands when he pointed out the Amityville-in-so-many-miles sign on the side of the road and said "that's where the house is." Like my mother's stories, I had no idea what he was referencing, but the idea that something bad had happened there was clear, and as I got older and actually saw these films, I viewed them through this lens, that they were true stories and reflected personal experiences.

Most people growing up have a story to tell about their hometown. Maybe it's a haunted house in the neighborhood, or a regional tale about witches, or a wronged woman who steals and drowns children, a murdered man who haunts the road he dies on. The details may be vague and different people may tell it with different details, but many of these stories are presented as true, actual history of the area. The different versions can be seen as the childhood game of telephone, where the story told today rarely resembles the original. Whether or not an outsider believes the stories, they are presented as historical truth, authentic, and are accepted as popular knowledge and belief. These narratives are often specific to a region or area; although, some may be restricted to a cultural or racial group, in general. These stories are widely known. Horror movies often present their narratives as based on a true story or inspired by a true story, and the stories they tell feel similar to the local stories people grew up with. Many horror movies include a scene early in the film that tells the lore of the villain that is vital to the film's narrative and the authenticity of the tale. The emphasis on the realness of the threat is important for these stories to have weight. The beliefs of the characters in these stories, and their acceptance that this threat is real, is vital to the action of the film. The threat must be real for the movie to work. The evil must be able to affect the characters physically, in the real world, to emphasize what is at stake. Likewise, the characters must believe they can ultimately defeat this evil or else there is no satisfaction to the movie. In some movies this battle is framed in a generic good vs. evil framework, but in many cases the enemy is a specific demon or the devil himself, casting the main character(s) on the side of holiness, God, and the church.

THE POWER OF POPULAR BELIEF IN HORROR FILMS

Horror movies have a complicated relationship and history with the Christian church. Individual churches and faiths have often condemned films for glorifying Satanism and the demonic as well as for featuring witchcraft and other supernatural elements they characterized as evil or inviting evil influences. *Rosemary's Baby* (1968) and *The Omen* (1976) both focus on the idea of intentionally bringing the Antichrist into the world in order to rule. *Carrie* (1976) frames her fundamentalist mother as the catalyst for the death and destruction Carrie's abilities cause. *Halloween* (1978) is the beginning of the popularity of slasher and horror films which feature nudity, premarital sex, alcohol and drug use, and graphic depictions of sex and murder, all behaviors categorized as sins or sinful.

The Exorcist (1973), *The Rite* (2011), and *The Conjuring* (2013), are different from the movies, material, and criticisms mentioned above. These movies center the Catholic Church to varying degrees, but each recognizes the authority of the Church. They present priests as powerful, knowledgeable men who are providing an important and necessary pastoral duty. These films accurately show the Rite of Exorcism and treat the other symbols of Catholic ritual with respect. They are also clear representations of the importance of faith and accepting the power of God. Each movie presents the Rite of Exorcism as the ultimate performance and test of faith.

The Catholic Church teaches that evil and the devil and his minions are real threats to people's souls. They train priests to perform exorcisms, and how to recognize the signs, differentiating from mental or physical illness. Their stance is that there is a need for exorcism. I argue that these films feature true, authentic representations that support Church doctrine, and as such display for the public lessons on the dangers of evil and the necessity of faith. But how can we reconcile beliefs in literal evil, in demons, and the fantastical, often over the top, genre of horror? The problem is not that horror films do not treat Christianity, or faith, or God, as necessary or accurately. Rather the issue is that the majority of audiences no longer accept evil or the devil as a literal threat, so in characterizing the threat as fantasy, they also characterize the answer to the threat in the same way. This can be seen in movies such as *Stigmata* (1999), *End of Days* (1999), *Constantine* (2005), *The Exorcism of Emily Rose* (2005), *The Last Exorcism* (2010), and *The Possession* (2012). I argue that while the initial reaction may be to dismiss the portrayal of Catholicism in these films as another aspect of fantasy, as generic elements of horror films, the movies themselves are expressions and performances of faith as much as the rite they focus on. These acts of faith are constructed for a general populace by a priestly figure imbued with the authority of the Church, through the performance of rituals and prayers, often in Latin, which demonstrates their knowledge and skill.

The Exorcist, The Rite, and *The Conjuring* all claim to be based on real events, to be authentic, trustworthy narratives of exorcisms. William Peter Blatty, author of the 1971 novel *The Exorcist,* as well as the 1973 screenplay for the film, says he based the book on the 1949 Prince George's County case of Roland Doe, a fourteen-year-old boy who was allegedly possessed and had an exorcism performed. *The Rite* opens with Pope John Paul II's quote from May 1987: "The battle against the devil, which is the principal task of Saint Michael the Archangel, is still being fought today because the devil is still alive and active in the world."[3] The movie claims its first authority by invoking the head of the Catholic Church. The text that appears after is, "What follows is inspired by true events." Out of all the movies, *The Rite* makes the most changes to the original story. *The Rite* is based on Matt Baglio's 2009 book, *The Rite: The Making of a Modern Exorcist.* Baglio is an American journalist, not a priest, who while living in Rome spent time shadowing and interviewing Father Gary Thomas when he was apprenticed to an exorcist. Baglio also spent time at the exorcism school at Regina Apostolorum. In the movie, the character of Michael Kovak (played by Colin O'Donoghue) is an amalgam of both Baglio and Father Thomas, while the character of Angeline (played by Alice Braga), a journalist, is also meant to represent Baglio, with Father Trevant (played by Sir Anthony Hopkins) as an amalgam of priests Baglio interviewed and observed during his time in Rome.

The Conjuring establishes its authenticity from the opening scenes. Ed and Lorraine Warren (played by Patrick Wilson and Vera Farmiga) are interviewing three young adults about the doll Annabelle that has been tormenting them and won't leave them alone. The scene then shifts to the Warrens showing the footage of this interview to a group in a lecture hall. As they introduce themselves as demonologists the frame freezes and yellow text scrawls across the screen. It establishes their credentials by saying that Lorraine is "a gifted clairvoyant" and Ed "is the only nonordained Demonologist recognized by the Catholic church." It goes on to frame the Perron story as, "Out of the thousands of cases throughout their controversial careers, there is one case so malevolent, they've kept it locked away until now." There is a space, then the text says, "Based on the true story." Then the title scrolls and the movie begins in earnest. Text appears that says "1971 Harrisville, Rhode Island," with a shot from inside a house, framed through a window of a family in a station wagon pulling up, a shot that recalls the opening scenes of *The Amityville Horror* (1979) when the Lutz family moves in. This opening establishes the truth and authenticity of the movie in several ways. It is presented as truth, a real-life interview meant to reinforce the idea that the Warrens, and the movie itself, are based on fact and authentic. It also recalls the look and use of found footage in horror films. Next the text establishes the credentials of the Warrens, privileging Ed's experience by stating his authorization by the Church. Finally, the opening, similar to the *Amityville* opening, claims authenticity by association, despite the Perron story occurring first. In reality, the Perron family of a father, mother, and five daughters moved into a large farmhouse in January 1971 and almost immediately began to experience odd things. Ed and Lorraine Warren did come out to investigate and did perform a seance where Carolyn Perron appeared possessed, but they never performed an exorcism. The family continued to live in the house until 1980.

In addition to claims or presentations of these movies as real, or at the very least, inspired by real events, the events and characters of these movies must also be understood in the context of the beliefs of the Catholic Church. The Church recognizes only men as capable of being priests, who are responsible for the daily, pastoral care of the physical, mental, and spiritual well-being of their parish. This care is performed through the Sacraments of the Church: Baptism, Reconciliation, the Eucharist, Confirmation, Marriage, Holy Orders, and the Anointing of the Sick. These visible rites make up the daily, regular lives of Catholic laypeople and the ministry of Catholic priests. The Rite of Exorcism is part of the "category of sacramentals" connecting it to the Sacrament of Reconciliation as it allows people's sins to be forgiven, allowing for the pursuit of grace, which in turn enables them to fight evil. The Rite of Exorcism is a detailed way to contain evil within the ministry. In part this is a remnant from the early modern period where the Catholic Church had to condemn magic[4] and distinguish exorcism from necromancy.[5] Necromancers used demons for their own end while exorcists called demons out to defeat them.[6] The United States Conference of Catholic Bishops (USCCB)[7] recognizes exorcism as a necessary Sacrament that is rarely performed, requires a detailed, lengthy process before being performed, and is conducted by experienced, knowledgeable professionals. The USCCB warns that people become possessed through association with specific people such as "healers, mediums, psychics"; through certain practices such as "cleansings, New Age religion, Reiki"; and through direct contact with things that are "the dominion of the devil" such as "magic, witchcraft, Satanic worship."[8] Exorcism is not a rite unique to Catholicism, or even Christianity, although certainly Catholic exorcisms are the most commonly referenced.[9] What some would take as the biblical foundation for exorcism is seen in just a handful of passages, such as the two demon-possessed men and the herd of pigs in Matthew 8:30, the mention of a man possessed by a demon who claims "we are legion" in Luke 8:30, what appears to be demonically caused epilepsy in Luke 9:39, as well as demonically caused muteness in Luke 11:14 and a bent back Luke 13:10–13.[10] In each case the remedy for possession is the utterance of words, or the performance of a rite, by a figure authorized or blessed by the Church.

A BRIEF HISTORY OF EXORCISM

In the Medieval Period, exorcism was associated mainly with saints, further proof of the miracles they performed. Cathar heresy in the thirteenth century forced the Church to reconsider their approach.[11] Later it became an instrument of conversion and "part of the campaign against magicians."[12] Liturgical exorcism was revived in the fourteenth century, and a variety of approaches was shown in "the widespread appearance of exorcism manuals in the fourteenth century."[13] By the fifteenth century, exorcism texts covered a wide range of topics, addressed witchcraft, and reflected the fluid nature of what defined evil.[14] The Catholic Rite of Exorcism was codified in 1614.[15] The codification encouraged the exorcist to use critical thinking before claiming someone was possessed and identified the common signs of possession like speaking an unknown language, strength beyond what they should have, and the demons being able to mimic people and illnesses.[16] "The 1614 rite remained the Catholic Church's official liturgy until January 1999, making it the longest lived of all Tridentine liturgies."[17] This history, the appearance of inflexibility, is also what provides structure, stability, and comfort, all elements that are reflected in popular culture as positives.

The Catholic Church itself claims possession is real and the Rite of Exorcism and exorcists are necessary. After the Second Vatican Council the Church walked a fine line between supporting a rite that was often seen as "medieval superstition" and presenting the image that the Catholic Church was part of the modern world. They urged "priests and bishops to seek professional medical assistance in cases where the true nature of what seems to be diabolical possession is in doubt."[18] In 2000, Pope John Paul's chief exorcist Father Gabrielle Amorth performed an exorcism on a nineteen-year-old Italian woman.[19] The Catholic Church has 404 fully trained exorcists and 124 assistants worldwide. Since 2005, the Vatican's Pontifical Athenaeum Regina Apostolorum has hosted an annual "Course on Exorcism and Prayers of Liberation."[20] A 2018 article reported that the "demand for exorcisms is up threefold in Italy."[21] In July 2019, a Colombian priest, Rubén Darío Jaramillo Montoya, sprinkled holy water from a helicopter over the city of Buenaventura, performing an exorcism to "purge the area of demonic infestation."[22] It's worth noting that each of these stories was reported as news in reputable publications. This conveys an acceptance of the Church's story and the exorcisms themselves. Because these stories are reported in the mainstream news, they are both seen as true and enter the public imagination. While the audience was probably not aware of the exorcism case that inspired Blatty, the novel of *The Exorcist* was out for two years before the movie, and was a best seller, making it likely that an audience member of the movie had at least heard some of what the movie was about. This reception context of passing familiarity is the same for *The Rite* and *The Conjuring* released in the years after the Vatican's 1999 revision of the Rite of Exorcism as well as the numerous news articles and stories that reported on the renewed theological interest, training, and conferences. In addition to these events the Catholic Church is often in the news for their consultations on exorcism films. While the Church did not consult on *The Exorcist*, Blatty wrote both the book and screenplay with knowledge of the area and Church, and even Catholic film critics have said it accurately portrays the Rite. Both Matt Baglio, the author of the book *The Rite* is based on, and Father Gary Thomas, who Baglio shadowed to write the book, consulted on the film.[23]

THE POWER OF PRIESTLY FIGURES
AND CHURCH AUTHORITIES

Regardless of how the Catholic Church may feel about these films and their often sensationalized content they must still contend with the (mis)representation they provide to the general populace. This is particularly true of horror films that claim to be based on a true story like *The Exorcist, The Rite,* and *The Conjuring,* which all implicitly or explicitly claim authority through authenticity.[24] The Showtime made-for-television movie *Possessed* (2000) is a more accurate rendition of the Doe story than *The Exorcist*; however, because it was limited to Showtime subscribers and was not widely released or known, it is not included here. Each film builds to an ending where performing an exorcism is the only way to save an innocent, and only a priestly figure has the necessary knowledge, faith, and experience to perform it. Priestly figures such as Father Merrin in *The Exorcist* (played by Max von Sydow) and Father Trevant in *The Rite* are older figures whose expertise is grounded in their years of experience. They are paired with younger, more inexperienced priests, Father Karras from *The Exorcist* (played by Jason Miller) and Michael Kovak from *The Rite*. In addition to being inexperienced, these men also suffer from crises of faith and confidence.

The presence of these priestly figures as saviors signifies a need for a clear authority, a simple solution to a seemingly insurmountable issue. Ed Warren fits this description as well, although he is a revision of the priestly figure because he is not a priest, but he is granted similar experience, knowledge as the others. Father Gordan is the only priest featured in the film, and when the Warrens meet with him, it is clear he seeks out their help and respects their perspective and knowledge. This works to convey the authority of the Church onto them, in particular onto Ed. In each case these clear, uncomplicated answers are provided in the context and backdrop of incredibly complicated times. The anxieties reflected in *The Exorcist* focus on concerns that "the Catholic Church had become an archaic, ineffective, and altogether irrelevant institution in the context of the seemingly more enlightened twentieth century."[25] The movie also wrestles with "other sociocultural anxieties of the period, including those regarding urban decay, the emergence of the gay rights movement, the decline of religious morality and perceived ethical corruption of society, and the dissolution of the traditional family."[26] The slasher films of the 1980s and 1990s reflected different concerns over sexuality, "the emergence of the neoconservative movement," and the push to "return to the traditional 'family values' and conservative religious beliefs of the 1950s."[27] Both *The Rite* and *The Conjuring* can be read through the lens of the culture wars that were revived in the wake of America electing, then reelecting its first Black president and the backlash of white rage, exposing the lie of post-racial America. However, they must also be read through the lens of life after the terror attacks of 9/11, which "inspired a whole new set of sociocultural anxieties; people around the world feared sudden, unexpected violence, and they became increasingly anxious about religion."[28] *The Rite* offers the safety of nostalgia, setting its events in an indeterminate time that nonetheless feels safely ensconced in the 1950s or 1960s, before the Church changed with the Second Vatican Council (1962–1965). *The Conjuring* is set in 1971 but does not focus on the anxieties seen in *The Amityville Horror* about the dangers of divorce, blended families, and the loss of the traditional family. Instead, *The Conjuring* does not focus on deficits but models that emphasize the importance of the mother figure to the family, the power of faith, and a need for Church authority. The dangers are real and have horrific consequences, but there are still simple, clear answers to dealing with these threats.

Popular films that feature demonic possession and exorcism have made the Catholic Rite of Exorcism, and the priests who perform it, part of the popular imagination. "The isolated case of 'The Exorcist' has become the archetype of a genre that currently enjoys great success even in more secularized and protestant countries,"[29] showing that the Catholic ideology and iconography has moved beyond its strictly religious boundaries into popular culture. These films use the readily recognizable signifiers of the priestly vestments, prayer, and ritual on the commentary for their particular historical and cultural moment.

For many Americans these films may be their only source of knowledge about the Catholic Church. Regardless of race, religion, or culture, most people would recognize the black-clothed figure of a priest with his white collar and purple stole. Westerners most likely recognize him through popular culture as the benevolent figure setting the background scene of a wedding or baptism or funeral, playing an important but inconsequential role in the action. Other than the figure and appearance of the Catholic priest, Catholicism in popular culture and imagination is constructed through the performance of rituals and prayers, often in Latin. For example, the phrase "*In nomine Patris et Filii et Spiritus Sancti*" is recognizable to many non-Catholics, as well as the symbolism of objects like the rosary. Unlike comedies or dramas, in horror films when the priest performs a ritual, their presences and actions are essential to the plot. In addition, in horror films priests present arcane knowledge that enables them to perform rituals that no one else can. They are visually recognizable, as are the trappings required for these rituals. Because the above movies claim to be true stories, the presentation of the priests and the Rites of Exorcism they perform become part of popular belief and understanding of the Rite but also of Catholicism at large. These movies provide an insight into how the general public is informed and educated about Catholicism and how these films are a rupture of particular tensions and concerns. These American-made films that claim to tell the true story and center exorcism and the priests that perform them inform people's knowledge and perspective of the Catholic Church, represent specific concerns of the time, and become part of popular belief that the Church itself must then contend with. In addition to claiming their stories were true, *The Exorcist*, *The Rite,* and *The Conjuring* present evil, the Devil, and possession, as real and literal threats, not metaphorical symbols of internal struggles.

It is important to note that the families shown in these films present a white concept of normality and family. This vision of an "all-American" family is white, generally middle class, and follows gender stereotypes that a family is a father, mother, and children. Movies that counter this nuclear family narrative do so at their own peril, as evidenced in *The Exorcist* when Regan's possession is at one point blamed on the divorce of her parents. These movies represent a white, Western world where priests are commonly understood as a benevolent figure who is there to help and not a symbol of child abuse, or conquest, or colonization. An analysis of the Black experience of *The Exorcist*, would be very different.[30] I know of only one film that features a Black character who is possessed, 1974's *Abby.* Dr. Williams, an academic on an archaeological dig in Nigeria finds a puzzle box, which he opens, seemingly releasing a spirit who travels to Kentucky, possessing his son's wife, Abby. Dr. William returns home and is able to free Abby from the spirit. The film does not refer to the Catholic Rite of Exorcism, and references a trickster god, Eshu, and not the Christian devil, as the source of the problem.[31]

In Western culture as reflected in the horror genre the priest is a person of knowledge, a savior figure, and a trusted source who lends assistance. Father Merrin (played by Max von Sydow) from *The Exorcist* and Father Lucas Trevant (played by Anthony Hopkins) in *The Rite* both fit this description. Ed and Lorrain Warren (played by Patrick Wilson and Vera Farmiga) in *The Conjuring* are also presented in this manner. These figures are depicted as experts in these unnatural matters who have the knowledge and firsthand experience to help the people in need. Both *The Exorcist* and *The Rite* center a pair of priests in their plots. One older priest, Father Merrin and Father Lucas Trevant, is depicted as having years of practical experience with exorcisms. A reluctant, younger priest is sent to support or learn from the older. Despite the fact that these priestly figures are presented as gifted and unique for the knowledge they possess they are also innately human, sometimes tragically so. Fathers Merrin and Trevant are older men, and with both the physical toll of their experiences affects their ability to perform, it weighs on them. Father Merrin has a heart condition that the demon Pazuzu[32] takes advantage of. The younger men who are framed as apprentices to the older men are shown as weak and falling short because of their lack of faith and confidence. These relationships are set up for the older generation to teach, help, and inspire, to pass on their knowledge of the Rite but to also serve as spiritual advisors.

While Fathers Merrin and Trevant are similarly presented, their impacts on their protégés differ radically. While both Father Karras and Michael Kovak struggle with their faith only one of them learns from their exorcism experience. Father Karras, while ultimately saving the innocent and possessed Regan, is only able to do so by committing the mortal sin of suicide. He is too weak to complete the ritual and save Regan the "right" way. In this he is very much a reflection of the time. Where did a priestly figure fit in post Second Vatican Council? How did a priest educated in a scientific and clinical field reconcile the two worlds he traversed? While the Second Vatican Council was meant to allow the Church to change and adapt to best serve their parishioners many older American Catholics saw the changes, the modernizations, as a betrayal. The sweeping changes to the Latin Mass, the allowance of laity participation in Mass, the changes in the appearance of nuns, and the fear that honored traditions like the rosary would be removed left many feeling unmoored.[33] The 1960s and 1970s also saw changes in science, gender roles, politics, and the economy, which also could be seen as threats to the traditional Catholic family. These concerns ruptured in different ways with some leaving the Church and others questioning their faith. Father Karras wrestles with his sense of guilt and obligation as a son to a distant mother, his conflicting beliefs in his roles as psychiatrist and priest, and his confusion over what he should be doing. When Father Karras is at the bar at the beginning of the movie, he says he wants out of the job, says he "can't cut it anymore" and "I need out, I'm unfit," which reads differently now in light of the revelations of decades of sexual abuse of children by Catholic priests. Karras says "I think I've lost my faith, Tom." In the end Karras fails as both a psychiatrist and a priest. He cannot save Regan in either role, he lacks the knowledge she needs, and he lacks the faith necessary to act on that knowledge. His suicide does result in the defeat of the demon but only as proof of his ultimate failure as a priest. Karras is an object lesson in what is at stake if the men and women of the 1970s cannot reclaim their moral center.

The opening of *The Rite* does not privilege or focus on the Church, instead focusing on Michael Kovak, an unremarkable man working in the family business. In the beginning Michael Kovak is neither a believer nor a priest. He joins the priesthood to get a free college education, and the movie opens with his calculated plan to quit the priesthood once he graduates so he doesn't have to take his vows. Even his motivation of a college education isn't pure as he pursues it to avoid taking over his father's mortuary business, not because he has any great interest. In the opening of the movie there is nothing to distinguish Michael from anyone else, yet after seeing him perform Last Rites on an accident victim, Father Matthew sees something in him and offers him a delay in making a decision, sending him to Rome to learn from Father Xavier, saying the Church sees a need for exorcists to deal with the "half a million reports of demonic encounters." Michael goes because it buys him time and because Father Matthew tells him if he quits he has to pay back the $100,000 the Church paid for his education, not because he suddenly finds his faith. Throughout the movie he says "I don't know what I believe in." Part way through Trevant's exorcism, he tells Angeline "I can do it. It's more than just saying the words." She responds, "You've seen him, what's not to believe in?" and Michael says, "Me." While both Father Karras and Michael suffer from crises of faith, Michael succeeds where Karras fails, both as a man and a priest. He believes in himself as a priest, which allows him to perform the exorcism and save Trevant. Yet the lesson of Michael Kovak is more hopeful than that of Father Karras. While the dangers are shown as more numerous in this more modern world, the response needed as more elaborate and ongoing, Michael is ultimately able to find his faith and his calling, which enables him to fulfill his purpose.

The lesson of the 2011 film is that just mouthing the words, "playing" at faith is not enough. In order to face the daily, regular threats that evil presents, one must find their inner strength and confidence through faith. This then provides the guidance and knowledge to do what has to be done. It is a more hopeful lesson than Karras because Michael succeeds where Karras failed, but it is also a more complicated picture. Karras's failure revolved around a single event which represented his failure at a single thing, being a man of faith in the 1970s. Michael shows that in the modern world it is not a single battle that needs to be fought and won but a daily decision to choose good, choose faith, choose God. That the demons, dangers, and threats come for anyone from everywhere and that they must be defeated again and again. There is hope to be found but only if you are willing to fight and sacrifice for it.

The 1971 setting of *The Conjuring* presented through the lens of 2013 shows a need for faith, structure, rituals that matter, but also places the need for the patriarchal authority of priests and Church in a muted and secondary role. Neither Ed nor Lorraine Warren are priests, and yet each has separate but complementary gifts that allow them to act as priestly figures. While they have no official standing within the Church, their interactions with Father Gordan indicate they are trusted to investigate for the Church, lending them authority. They possess the same arcane, occult knowledge as the other priestly figures; this is supplemented by their own practical experience, not just with possession but with other unnatural and demonic events. This allows them to act as experts, even if it is beyond their normal purview of just investigation for the Church. If he was unable to perform a successful exorcism, he would not be a priestly figure. The proof that Ed is able to act as a priestly figure is in that he succeeds.

Beginning with their opening interview, lecture, and their appearance at
the Perron house, Ed and Lorraine Warren are presented as a complementary
partnership that throughout most of the film privileges the power and authority of Lorraine's gifts. When Father Gordon meets with them, he treats them
as equals, certainly conveying that the Church sees them this way. Yet at the
end of the movie Lorraine abdicates her agency as evidenced by her handing
Ed the materials necessary to perform the exorcism. Ed becomes the pre-
sumptive priestly figure. While this may seem like a betrayal of the characters, the film sets up Lorraine as the weaker figure from the beginning. Ed
says he worries about her last experience, what it took out of her. Like
Merrin and Trevant, the physical weight and toll of these experiences, the
cumulative effect, is shown in Lorraine's tiredness, her need to rest. This is
further seen by the physical effects she suffers as a result of her psychic gifts
once she is in the Perron house. The shift from partnership to Ed as the
priestly figure occurs toward the end when he makes the decision that they're
leaving because he's concerned about the toll it's taking on Lorraine. What
seems like a jarring power shift is really just the logical conclusion to how
the movie has set up the power dynamic. Viewed through the 1971 setting
and the 2013 production this is a step back. The movie reasserts the idea that
no matter how talented or gifted the woman, she cannot take on the role of
priest; she will always be inherently weaker and therefore lacking, not up to
the task.

THE POWER OF PRAYER AND RITUAL

In *The Exorcist, The Rite,* and *The Conjuring,* the priestly figure is the con-
duit for the knowledge, but the actual Rite of Exorcism is the demonstration
and symbol of the Church's power. Before the Church can assert this control
and prove its dominance the illusion of omniscience that the modern world
offers must first be disproved. In *The Exorcist,* Chris MacNeil only accepts
the necessity for the Rite after she has tried everything else, only turning to
the "superstition" of the Catholic Church once she is desperate. The technology of tests, X-rays, MRIs, and shock therapy all fail to cure Regan. Father
Karras tries to use taped evidence as proof against possession but is unable
to. *The Rite* shows the Rite as daily ministry, part of the priest's pastoral duty
toward his parishioners. We never see Father Trevant perform Mass or act as
a parish priest, but his actions are shown as similar to this type of ministry.
The presentation of a nostalgic time, and in Rome, frames the action as set in
the past, not the modern world, which reads as a way of distancing itself from
claims of authority and realism regarding the Church and exorcism. The
Italians that Trevant encounters all have faith in him, in the Church, in
demons. The modern scientific world does not intrude on the narrative. *The*

Conjuring blends science and faith. The Warrens use technology to make their case to the Church. They take photographs, use infrared, take video and temperatures. While these technologies are used to prove that something exists in the Perron house it also has limitations. Technology can only offer proof; it is incapable of acting on this knowledge.

In addition to showing the failure or limits of technology, another rejection of the modern world in the films is the domestic settings. All of the exorcisms occur in homes, defenses of the family, and these spaces. In *The Exorcist* Father Merrin travels to Chris's home to minister to Regan. In *The Rite* Father Trevant performs exorcisms in his home and travels to the home of others. In *The Conjuring* Ed and Lorraine begin in their home, the repository for evil and possessed objects, their way of protecting the outside world from these forces, and then travel to the Perron home. The exorcisms then are not just the Rite of removing the possessed but of defending these domestic spaces and connecting these domestic spaces to regular ministry, daily acts of faith. In these spaces across time periods and geography what is necessary for the family to thrive is the presence of a strong priestly figure and the recognition of their authority and the authority of the Catholic Church as necessary.

These priestly figures are trained and trusted by the Catholic Church. While some of the authority of the individual exorcist rests on the teaching from the Church of the Rite of Exorcism, Fathers Merrin and Trevant and Ed Warren have authority because of their experiences outside of Church teachings. The opening scenes of *The Exorcist* place Father Merrin at an archaeological dig in northern Iraq. We never learn why he is there, in civilian clothes, with no visible connection to the Church, but these scenes serve as evidence of his wide range of knowledge and present the knowledge he does have through an exotic lens. He appears at home navigating this world, the language, the geography of the ruins and the streets. While these opening scenes have little dialogue the visual arguments present Merrin as an authority.

Father Karras's knowledge and authority is grounded in the authority of Georgetown University, the oldest Catholic and Jesuit university in the United States. Yet it is the university, and not the Jesuit, that Karras privileges. He frequently appears in civilian clothes, removing his collar, a visual representation of his rejection of the Church's authority and knowledge, at the earliest opportunity, and often with frustration. He mentions again and again his belief in science, clinical evidence, and psychiatry. He refuses to acknowledge other types of evidence, even the evidence of his own eyes. When he first encounters Regan and witnesses the furniture moving, her physical distortion, he is unmoved. Throughout the movie, he insists on framing all the information he gets through a psychiatrist's perspective instead of a priest's. When Chris asks Karras, "How do you go about getting an exorcism?" he responds that, "It just doesn't happen anymore." His role as psychiatrist means he cannot accept a world where an exorcism is necessary. He offers to see Regan only as a psychiatrist and later, when the Church approves Father Merrin performing the exorcism, Karras agrees to attend because "there should be a psychiatrist present anyway," not to support the actual Rite.

Both Father Karras and Chris MacNeil demonstrate the myriad of ways that modern science, medicine, psychiatry, fails to address the spiritual challenges and threats people face.[34] Father Karras tries to get Chris MacNeil to accept his help only as a psychiatrist, and she is emphatic that is not what she needs. Chris MacNeil tries to get help from the scientific and medical community, but no one is able to treat Regan or provide answers. The scientific and medical characters and scenes emphasize that they do not know what they are encountering. The majority of the film covers Chris and Regan's struggles, their journey from one doctor to another, each one performing test after test with equipment that is both modern and inexplicable. Some of these tests seem to cause Regan pain, and none yield any results. The doctors hide their inability to help through medical jargon and by refusing to answer Chris's questions. The only answers they have are to order more scans, more tests, to see "what we missed" without acknowledging their ignorance. Among themselves though they wonder "what we missed" while also refusing to admit their knowledge has limits, just ordering more scans and more tests. These experiences are shown through Chris's eyes, with Regan the object of the tests but because of her condition shown as less than human. These experiments demonstrate the failure of science and medicine but also seek to frame Chris as a failure and therefore a cause of Regan's condition. The doctors suggest her movie-star lifestyle, exposure to drugs, and being divorced, could all have made Regan sick. Even when a doctor finally suggests exorcism it is not because he believes it will work, but because he believes it will have a placebo effect. Regan "believes" she's possessed so she might "believe" she's cured if an exorcism is performed. Chris's rejection of modern science is an act of desperation, not faith, but because she is a woman and therefore cannot be a priestly figure, her faith is not important, only that she prove the necessity for the knowledge of the Church.

The Rite acknowledges the knowledge and power of the Catholic Church, its priests, and the Rite of Exorcism. In the beginning of the film Father Matthew states as fact that the Vatican has ordered an exorcist in every diocese, emphasizing the necessity of this ministry, this sacramental. His words carry weight because he holds a position of authority at the university Michael attends. Father Xavier has authority because Father Matthew recommends him, and then his authority is demonstrated by his placement in a lecture hall, teaching others about exorcism, listing the identifiable signs of possession, using film and photos as proof as the opening of *The Conjuring* later does. Father Xavier's authority is then transferred to Father Trevant when he recommends Michael go see him, telling him Trevant will "be happy to provide you with the type of proof you seem to need." With Trevant the concept of knowledge, authority, and power is demonstrated by what he does. The authority of Fathers Matthew and Xavier is largely conveyed through their position in the Church. Trevant is the first person whose power and knowledge doesn't have to be taken on faith. Like Father Merrin, the source of his knowledge and experience is never explained, and it does not need to be, as the enacting of this knowledge proves his right to be an authority.

In each film the knowledge and performance of the Rite of Exorcism represents something different. In *The Exorcist* the performance of the Rite of Exorcism is shown as the answer. If Father Merrin or even Father Karras had been able to complete the Rite then Regan could have been saved and Karras could have embraced his role as priest over psychiatrist. Because the Rite is not completed, the narrative's conclusion is unsatisfying despite Regan being saved. We see this in the denouement as Chris and Regan leave their house to return to Los Angeles and encounter Father Dyer. The knowledge necessary to keep people safe is lost because of Merrin's death and Karras's suicide. Father Dyer has been left out of the loop, and his confusion on what actually occurred is seen in his hesitant interactions with Chris at the end. *The Rite* presents faith as the necessary component of exorcism. Michael's knowledge is partially from books, his participation in the classes at the Vatican, but for the most part it comes from his observance of Trevant, the exorcist apprenticeship. Yet it is not this knowledge that enables him to save Trevant; it is the fact that he finds his confidence, his faith, and embraces his role as a priest. *The Conjuring* is similar in that it shows the Rite as what enables people like Carolyn Perron to make the right choice. Ed and Lorraine's exorcism is successful because it is powered by their faith which in turn enables them to save the Perrons.

"THE POWER OF CHRIST COMPELS YOU": PERFORMING FAITH

The Rite of Exorcism is relatively simple given the enormity of the wished-for goal and possible consequences. The priest, who is designated by the bishop, goes to confession or offers an act of contrition or performs Mass and asks for God's help. He puts on his vestments, the surplice (white linen vestment) and purple stole which indicates the priest is performing/celebrating a Sacrament (despite the Rite of Exorcism not being a Sacrament). He makes the sign of the cross on himself, bystanders, and the possessed, sprinkling everyone with holy water, then he kneels and says the Litany of Saints. He then commands the demon to obey, and lays hands on the possessed, praying for them. Next, he reads selections from the Gospels, and casts the demon out. There is another round of prayers, then the Rite is repeated. The Rite does not require a lot of material trappings or people. The simplicity of the concept and ceremony may help explain why it has become part of the public imagination. The Rite itself is shown pretty accurately. Movie critic Pauline Kael contended "the film was 'the biggest recruiting poster the Catholic Church had had since the sunnier days of *Going My Way*[35] and *The Bells of St. Mary's*."[36] Friedkin, a non-Catholic, called it "wrong-headed" at the time. Later however, he allowed that he knew "many people who went into the priesthood because of that."[37] In *The Exorcist,* Fathers Merrin and Karras don the surplice and stole, absolve each other of sin, sprinkle holy water, and follow the order of prayer. Father Trevant's performance of the ritual is conducted in Italian, as are all his conversations with the possessed, but he wears the stole, invokes prayer, emphasizes the need for contrition before performing the Rite, and uses holy water. While Father Merrin cycles through the Rite, the movie does present it as something that only has to be performed once, as does *The Conjuring,* while *The Rite* shows it as a sacramental that must be performed again and again. The presentation of the ritual from the priestly vestments to the prayers and performance of the ritual, emphasizes the permanence and stability of the Catholic Church. Whether accepted or derided by popular, modern culture, the Church continues; the Church and its knowledge and authority lives on. The presentation of the Rite in these films is relatively unchanged from 1973–2013, representing an enduring understanding.

CONCLUSION

In each of these movies the actual Rite of Exorcism does not occur until the end, indicating that it is not the Rite itself that is important but the commentary that there is a need for it even in the modern world. In this way these movies can be understood as making the case for the importance of the Church itself, its priests, its institutional knowledge, its purpose. In *The Exorcist* Father Merrin begins the Rite an hour and thirty-seven minutes into the two-hour movie, and it gets only sixteen minutes of screen time. In *The Rite* the exorcism only takes up thirteen minutes of screen time out of a one hour and fifty-four minute movie, and in *The Conjuring,* only a little over six minutes out of a one hour and fifty-two minute movie. Despite their brief appearances the outcomes of these movies hinge on the performance of the Rite of Exorcism. Regan's, Trevant's, and Carolyn's souls and lives are on the line as well as all the parishioners who could be potentially saved by the priests in each film. In each film the Rite is used as a deus ex machina that offers simple, clear solutions to complicated issues. Chris MacNeil becomes a better mother, prioritizing her daughter over her career. Michael Kovak becomes a priest. Carolyn Perron chooses her children and her family, thus embracing the traditional role and norm expected of her. The brevity of the screen time supports the reading of the power of exorcism as mystical, magical, and unknown. It works because of faith and God. If you believe, the ritual gives you power and you disbelieve at your own peril.

In *The Exorcist, The Rite,* and *The Conjuring,* the only true performances of faith are the ones that enable the Rite of Exorcism. Father Merrin is pure of faith, Michael Kovak finds his faith, and Ed Warren's faith frees Carolyn. These representations of faith, these lessons on the importance of God, and the recognition of literal evil, do not assume a perfect world, or occur in a vacuum. *The Exorcist* reflects concerns of the state of the home and family in the 1970s, the danger divorce and single parenting can have, the threat presented by women acting outside of accepted gender norms. Chris and Regan MacNeil are examples of what happens when a mother ignores and neglects her home, accepting a role outside of her domestic space. *The Rite* and *The Conjuring* emphasize the need for daily ministry and faith. They also demonstrate the necessity of the institutional knowledge and authority of the Church in defeating the demonic threats that exist. The Church is the answer to loss of faith and skepticism. Regardless of time period, politics, or claims of modernity, the Catholic Church fills a need, even for non-Catholics who are given access to these things through the role of priestly figures, their knowledge, and the rituals they enact through popular culture. When so much seems uncertain and science and facts are doubted it is not hard to see why audiences would find comfort in the simple answers and solutions that these rituals present. The Catholic Church cannot erase these presentations from the minds and imaginations of the general populace or reframe the narrative. They must operate in a world where these preconceptions exist. Perhaps the lesson is that regardless of the framing or historical moment, faith and guidance is always wanted and needed.

NOTES

1. Jake Rossen, "The Terrifying Subliminal Image Hidden in *The Exorcist,*" *Mental Floss,* October 10, 2016. http://mentalfloss.com/article/87245/terrifying-subliminal-image-hidden-exorcist.

2. Burstyn's look actually comes from the fact that Beatty was neighbors and friends with MacLaine and wanted her in the film. So I guess my mother wasn't completely wrong, https://www.washingtonpost.com/wp-srv/style/longterm/movies/features/dcmovies/exorcist.htm.

3. Father Gabriele Amorth, *An Exorcist Tells His Story* (San Francisco: Ignatius Press, 1999): 26.

4. Brian Levack, *The Devil Within: Possession and Exorcism in the Christian West* (New York: Yale University Press, 2013): 64.

5. Ibid, 71.

6. Ibid, 64.

7. "Exorcism," *United States Conference of Catholic Bishops,* Accessed 24 August 2019, http://www.usccb.org/prayer-and-worship/sacraments-and-sacramentals/sacramentals-blessin

gs/exorcism.cfm.

8. Ibid.

9. Brian Levack, *The Devil Within: Possession and Exorcism in the Christian West* (New York: Yale University Press, 2013): 82.

10. King James Bible.

11. Francis Young, *A History of Exorcism in Catholic Christianity* (Cambridge: Palgrave Macmillan, 2016): 62.

12. Ibid, 63.

13. Ibid, 67.

14. Ibid, 77.

15. Ibid, 101.

16. Ibid, 117.

17. Ibid, 119.

18. Ibid.

19. "Interview with the Exorcist," *Newsweek,* September 20, 2000, 1.

20. Barbie Latza Nadeau, "Vatican Assembles Avengers of Religion to Beat the Devil," *The Daily Beast,* May 8, 2019, https://www.thedailybeast.com/vatican-exorcist-convention-tries-innovative-ways-to-beat-the-devil.

21. Doug Stanglin, "Demand for Exorcisms Is Up Threefold in Italy, so Vatican Is Holding Conference, *USA Today,* February 23, 2018. https://www.usatoday.com/story/news/world/2018/02/23/vatican-host-international-exorcism-conference-meet-growing-demand/367735002/.

22. Harriet Sherwood, "Bishop Will Take to the Skies to Exorcise Entire Columbian City," *The Guardian,* July 10, 2019, https://www.theguardian.com/world/2019/jul/10/bishop-take-skies-exorcise-colombian-city-helicopter-buenaventura.

23. "The Rite: The Story Behind the Film," *Franciscan Media,* Accessed 20 August 2019, https://www.franciscanmedia.org/the-rite-the-story-behind-the-film/.

24. Paul Vitello, "William Peter Blatty, Author of 'The Exorcist,' Dies at 89, *The New York Times,* January 13, 2017, https://www.nytimes.com/2017/01/13/books/william-peter-blatty-author-of-the-exorcist-dies-at-89.html.

25. Christopher J. Olson and Carrielynn D. Reinhard, *Possessed Women, Haunted States: Cultural Tensions in Exorcism Cinema* (New York: Lexington Books, 2017): 21.

26. Ibid, 23.

27. Ibid, 88.

28. Ibid, 103.

29. Marco Innamorati, Ruggero Taradel, and Renato Foschi, "Between Sacred and Profane: Possession, Psychopathology, and the Catholic Church," *History of Psychology,* 22 no. 1 (2019):12.

30. James Baldwin, *The Devil Finds Work* (New York: Vintage International, 1976): 125.

31. "Abby," 1974, *IMDB,* Accessed 24 August 2019, https://www.imdb.com/title/tt0071095/?ref_=fn_al_tt_1.

32. He is never specifically named in the movie, but it is a statue of him that Merrin sees in Iraq at the beginning of the movie.

33. Sylvia Poggioli, "Vatican II: A Half-Century Later, A Mixed Legacy," *NPR* October 11, 2012, https://www.npr.org/2012/10/11/162594956/vatican-ii-a-half-century-later-a-mixed-legacy.

34. Octavia J. Cade's "Sifting Science: Stratification and *The Exorcist*" offers a clear analysis of the complexity of science in the film.

35. 1944 movie musical with Bing Crosby.

36. 1945 movie with Bing Crosby and Ingrid Bergman.

37. Peter E. Dans, *A Century of Saints and Sinners: Christians in the Movies* (Lanham, MD: Rowman and Littlefield, 2009): 206.

WORKS CITED

"Abby," 1974, *IMDB*, Accessed 24 August 2019, https://www.imdb.com/title/tt0071095/?ref_=fn_al_tt_1.

Amorth, Father Gabriele. *An Exorcist Tells His Story.* San Francisco, CA: Ignatius Press, 1999.

Baldwin, James. *The Devil Finds Work.* New York: Vintage International, 1976.

Cade, Octavia J. "Sifting Science: Stratification and *The Exorcist*," *Horror Studies* 7, no. 1 (April 2016): 61–72.

Dans, Peter E. *A Century of Saints and Sinners: Christians in the Movies.* Lanham, MD: Rowman and Littlefield, 2009.

"Exorcism." *United States Conference of Catholic Bishops,* Accessed 24 August, 2019. http://www.usccb.org/prayer-and-worship/sacraments-and-sacramentals/sacramentals-blessings/exorcism.cfm.

Hesse, Josiah. "Why Are So Many Horror Films Christian Propaganda?" *Vice,* 2018. https://www.vice.com/en_us/article/gqkj84/why-are-so-many-horror-films-christian-propaganda.

Innamorati, Marco, Ruggero Taradel, and Renato Foschi, "Between Sacred and Profane: Possession, Psychopathology, and the Catholic Church," *History of Psychology* 22, no. 1 (2019): 1–16.

"Interview with the Exorcist." *Newsweek,* September 20, 2000.

Levack, Brian. *The Devil Within: Possession and Exorcism in the Christian West.* New York: Yale University Press, 2013.

Nadeau, Barbie Latza. "Vatican Assembles Avengers of Religion to Beat the Devil." *The Daily Beast,* May 8, 2019. https://www.thedailybeast.com/vatican-exorcist-convention-tries-innovative-ways-to-beat-the-devil.

Olson, Christopher J., and Carrielynn D. Reinhard. *Possessed Women, Haunted States: Cultural Tensions in Exorcism Cinema.* Lanham, MD: Lexington Books, 2017.

Poggioli, Sylvia. "Vatican II: A Half-Century Later, A Mixed Legacy." *NPR* October 11, 2012. https://www.npr.org/2012/10/11/162594956/vatican-ii-a-half-century-later-a-mixed-legacy.

"The Rite: The Story Behind the Film." *Franciscan Media,* Accessed 20 August 2019. https://www.franciscanmedia.org/the-rite-the-story-behind-the-film/.

Rossen, Jake. "The Terrifying Subliminal Image Hidden in *The Exorcist*." *Mental Floss,* October 10, 2016. http://mentalfloss.com/article/87245/terrifying-subliminal-image-hidden-exorcist.

Sherwood, Harriet. "Bishop Will Take to the Skies to Exorcise Entire Columbian City." *The Guardian,* July 10, 2019. https://www.theguardian.com/world/2019/jul/10/bishop-take-skies-exorcise-colombian-city-helicopter-buenaventura.

Slovick, Matt. "The Exorcist." *The Washington Post,* 1996. https://www.washingtonpost.com/wp-srv/style/longterm/movies/features/dcmovies/exorcist.htm.

Stanglin, Doug. "Demand for Exorcisms Is Up Threefold in Italy, so Vatican Is Holding Conference." *USA Today,* February 23, 2018. https://www.usatoday.com/story/news/world/2018/02/23/vatican-host-international-exorcism-conference-meet-growing-demand/367735002/.

Tagliabue, John. "The Pope's Visit: The Doctrine; Vatican's Revised Exorcism Rite Affirms Existence of Devil." *The New York Times,* January 27, 1999. https://www.nytimes.com/1999/01/27/us/pope-s-visit-doctrine-vatican-s-revised-exorcism-rite-affirms-existence-devil.html.

Vitello, Paul. "William Peter Blatty, Author of 'The Exorcist,' Dies at 89." *The New York Times,* January 13, 2017. https://www.nytimes.com/2017/01/13/books/william-peter-blatty-author-of-the-exorcist-dies-at-89.html.

Young, Francis. *A History of Exorcism in Catholic Christianity.* Cambridge: Palgrave Macmillan, 2016.

FILMOGRAPHY

Carrie. Directed by Brian De Palma. Beverly Hills, CA: Red Bank Films, United Artists, 1976.

Constantine. Directed by Francis Lawrence. Los Angeles: Village Roadshow Pictures, Warner Brothers, 2005.

End of Days. Directed by Peter Hyams. Santa Monica, CA: Beacon Pictures, 1999.

Going My Way. Directed by Leo McCarey. Hollywood: Paramount Pictures, 1944.

Halloween. Directed by John Carpenter. Los Angeles: Compass International Pictures: 1978.

Possessed. Directed by Steven E. de Souza. New York: Showtime Networks, 2005.

Rosemary's Baby. Directed by Roman Polanski. Hollywood: Paramount Pictures, 1968.

Stigmata. Directed by Rupert Wainwright. Culver City, CA: Metro-Goldwyn-Mayer, 1999.

The Amityville Horror. Directed by Stuart Rosenberg. Los Angeles: American International Pictures, 1979.

The Bells of St. Mary's. Directed by Leo McCarey. Culver City, CA: RKO Pictures, 1945.

The Conjuring. Directed by James Wan. Los Angeles: New Line Cinema, 2013.

The Exorcism of Emily Rose. Directed by Scott Derrickson. Culver City, CA: Screen Gems, 2005.

The Exorcist. Directed by William Friedkin. Burbank, CA: Warner Bros., 1973.

The Last Exorcism. Directed by Daniel Stamm. Paris: Studio Canal, 2010.

The Omen. Directed by Richard Donner. Los Angeles: Twentieth Century Fox, 1976.

The Possession. Directed by Ole Bornedal. Beverly Hills, CA: Ghost House Pictures, 2012.

The Rite. Directed by Mikael Håfström. Los Angeles: New Line Cinema, 2011.

Chapter Five

"We Have to Stop the Apocalypse!"

Pre-Millennial (Mis)Representations of Revelation and Eschaton in Horror Cinema

Kevin J. Wetmore, Jr.

Beginning in the late eighties, horror cinema embraced the concept of the end of the world as posited in the biblical Book of Revelation. As with much of pop culture, these films conflated the eschaton (the end of the age/the end of time) with apocalypse (hidden things revealed).[1] Revelation offers vivid depictions of the end and supernatural consequences of worldly actions that can be readily used by horror filmmakers to create terror outside of the original Christian contexts and theologies. The Christian theology(s) of last things are appropriated, their material, imagistic, and character elements reappropriated in secular contexts in which individuals must fight to stop the end of the world, which is presented as evil and wrong. Films such as *The Omen* (1976), *Prince of Darkness* (1987), *The Seventh Sign* (1988), *The Prophecy* (1995), *Stigmata* (1999), *End of Days* (1999), *Bless the Child* (2000), and *Lost Souls* (2000), to name but the best-known examples, construct the eschaton using the language and imagery of Revelation, presenting it as a horrific experience akin to the terrors of other horror cinema and, oddly, something to be stopped, rather than embraced.

Ironically, Revelation, a book meant to give hope and comfort to a community that was facing persecution (or imagined itself as being persecuted), is adapted with a focus on its horrific imagery, constructed to terrify the viewer. Yet, Revelation, and the horror cinema that gets it so wrong, both actually imagine the same result—after a horrific battle of some kind, evil is defeated and cast away. The key difference is, in the latter, the evil is working in opposition to God, who also seems to be intent on destroying the world, but at the last minute allows the eschaton to be stopped. The Christian theology of Revelation is one that requires the eschaton to go forward, resulting in a happy ending, whereas the theology of horror cinema's happy ending is an eschaton postponed or cancelled altogether. Yet both end in evil being banished.

This chapter will examine the adaptation of Revelation's images in premillennial horror cinema (meaning films made before the year 2000); consider how such adaptation reinforces the idea of the end of the age as a battle with evil that must be stopped in order to preserve the status quo, rather than changing it, as Revelation postulates; and explore how such depictions actually are influenced by and reinforce pop Christian narratives such as the *Left Behind* series and *The Late Great Planet Earth*, while simultaneously shaping how the apocalypse (in all senses of the word) is understood in mainstream culture. What is fascinating about these premillennial horror films is that without exception they all posit scenarios in which a select few must "stop the apocalypse," rather than see it as the fulfillment of scripture.

A PRIMER IN HIDDEN THINGS REVEALED

The word "apocalypse" means "lifting the veil," or "hidden things revealed," hence the biblical Apocalypse of John is also called The Revelation to/of John. There are many other apocalyptic works, both canonical (such as in Daniel 7–12), and noncanonical (such as Enoch, The Shepherd of Hermas, and the Apocalypse of Peter). There are Jewish apocalypses, Christian apocalypses, and apocalypses from non-Abrahamic religions.[2] Apocalypses often feature an otherworldly journey or a vision of a new age, following a period of judgment. Under Christianity, apocalypses included messianic as well as adversarial figures. 2 Thessalonians chapter two, for example, entirely concerns "the Man of Lawlessness," whom Jesus will destroy, but not before the people are led astray and deceived. The last book of the New Testament is the Apocalypse of John, a Christian living in exile on the island of Patmos, who sends information of his vision of the end to come to seven churches: Ephesus, Smyrna, Pergamum, Thyatira, Sardis, Philadelphia, and Laodicea.

There is disagreement over the dating of the book and the extent to which it may or may not reflect persecution from Domitian, Galba, Nero, or other emperors. David E. Aune's authoritative and comprehensive summary of the internal and external evidence for the date of composition of Revelation toward the end of the reign of the emperor Domitian, around 95 CE, although as Aune notes, "there are some dissenting voices suggesting earlier and later dates."[3] Regardless of the date, the book presents a vision of the end of history and a radical transformation of reality.

Revelation is presented as a vision received by John of what is to come. Revelation 1:1–3 opens:

> The revelation of Jesus Christ, which God gave him to show his servants what must soon take place; he made it known by sending his angel to his servant John, who testified to the word of God and to the testimony of Jesus Christ, even to all that he saw. Blessed is the one who reads aloud the words of the prophecy, and blessed are those who hear and who keep what is written in it; for the time is near. [4]

Note from the very opening of the book, John states Jesus and his angel showed him "what must soon take place" and that "the time is near." When that time is depends upon one's interpretive lens, as will be discussed below.

Revelation is written in poetic, metaphoric language to a community in crisis or perceived crisis, as noted above. As Christians are persecuted (or think themselves about to be persecuted) by the Roman Empire, John tells of his vision. Christ appears to him, showing a scroll with seven seals, each one broken by Christ in turn, bringing about disaster and destruction. After the seven seals, seven angels blow seven trumpets, each blow also bringing about global disaster and destruction. A satanic being, often called the Antichrist in pop apocalypses (though the word does not appear in Revelation, which instead denotes "the Beast" as the adversary of God), and his false prophet rise and wage a campaign against Christians, culminating in chapter nineteen in a climactic battle that sees the defeat of the Beast, the kings of the earth, and their armies, and the reign of Christ in a New Heaven and New Earth without suffering or fear, while those who opposed Christ are thrown into a lake of fire for eternity.

John is instructed by Christ in Revelation 1:19, "Now write what you have seen, what is, and what is to take place after this." There is no suggestion that there are alternatives. This unavoidable future is presented as a good thing. Evil does not have the final word; the eschaton brings about the triumph of God and of good. Nowhere in John does it say to stop it. Nowhere in John is there the option for a different outcome. The irony is that a literal reading of Revelation (particularly through the futurist mode, described below) indicates it states exactly what will happen, that it is God's will, there is no other possible path, and that it is good. Evil will be defeated and a New Heaven and New Earth will be made and everyone will live in peace and harmony forever. Tangentially, we should note that within apocalyptic theology and scholarship there are numerous schools of interpretation, traditionally broken into four types: futurist (everything after chapter four in Revelation will take place in the future), historicist (everything in Revelation has been progressively fulfilled through Church history), preterist (the events described in Revelation have happened already), and idealist (Revelation describes a symbolic fight between good and evil). Apocalyptic horror offers only a futurist reading of Revelation.

Revelation is meant as a book of comfort in times of crisis. It promises justice, and an end to suffering. Those who persecute us now will suffer in the future, the book argues, and we who suffer now will be triumphant. Indeed, as Eugen Weber reminds us, "Ninety-eight verses (of over four hundred) in the Apocalypse of John speak of catastrophe, and 150 refer to joy, consolation, brightness and hope."[5] In Revelation, death is not the end, although twentieth-century apocalyptic cinema often presents death as the ultimate bad ending, simply because in horror cinema, death is when the bad guys get you. In Revelation, the physical body is resurrected at the end of the age, and one is rewarded or punished for eternity in one's physical body. The end cannot be changed, God brings it about, and it is a good thing for all believers.

CINEMA GETS HOLD OF REVELATION

Based on the films of the end of the twentieth century, one would assume Revelation was Satan's plan to ruin everything and take over God's kingdom, and that God was completely against the eschaton and the apocalypse. Alternately, one would assume that the word "apocalypse" means "the end of the world," and that Christians got it from a whole series of secular end-of-the-world narratives that take the form of everything from natural disasters, including the Earth being struck by an object from space, climate change, and floods, through nuclear war, disease, the emergence and domination of zombies, or the rise of artificial intelligence.

Apocalypse, since it presents a community in crisis and can be read as predicating the eschaton (end of time/end of things), has been interpreted to mean "the end." "The Apocalypse" now has been thoroughly secularized and means the end of the world as we know it, to the point where scripture and theology have nothing to do with it. In *Apocalypse Movies: End of the World Cinema*, Kim Newman's subtitle summarizes his approach to apocalypse. Further, he argues that the biblical account of end times is a creative fabrication, not a sincerely held belief: "Before the cultivation of fiction as an art form, images of mass devastation usually had to be dressed up as religion."[6] His example is "Revelations" [sic] in which the actual end of the world is "a sub-plot in the last battle between our Redeemer and the Anti-Christ."[7] Newman's book covers various end-of-the-world scenarios: nuclear war, "big bug," aliens, global disasters, but leaves little room for religious apocalyptic films, meaning *The Omega Man* is discussed, while *The Omen* is glaringly absent. Similarly, Wheeler Winston Dixon's volume *Visions of the Apocalypse: Spectacles of Destruction in American Cinema* does not mention a single film that engages the Christian eschaton; all the apocalypses here are films that deal with the violent destruction of humanity and annihilation through nuclear war or natural disasters.[8] Diane Sippl writes, "I would like to define apocalypse as simply this: the end of the world as we know it."[9] Except, it's not. Words mean things. In this essay, I use the term apocalypse to refer to films that are premillennial (meaning made before the year 2000), show the potential end of the world (averted through the efforts of the heroes), and use the Christian sense of the word meaning "uncovering of hidden things" in that these films also show the Christian eschaton happening and what the heroes can do to stop it.

ENTER HAL LINDSEY: MAKING SACRED SECULAR APOCALYPTIC FILMS

In the seventies, however, Christian apocalyptic cinema began to emerge. It took two forms. The first is a specifically Christian cinema, made by, for, and about Christians. Most notably is the 1972 film *A Thief in the Night*, which went on to spawn three sequels set in the same world with the same characters. In that original, brief (69-minute) movie, Patty, a young woman, marries a Christian man and wakes up one day to find that he has been raptured along with millions of other believers and she now lives in a world in which the United Nations has set up a one-world government that requires all to receive "The Mark of the Beast" in order to engage in commerce. She wakes up again to realize it was all a dream, but that her husband has again been raptured. The film warns that the end of the world could begin at any moment and cautions Christians to be prepared for what will follow. This film marks the beginning of Christian pop apocalyptic cinema.

The second is the subject of this essay: the mainstream film that uses the Bible and the culture of rapture, Antichrist, and eschaton to tell a tale of the coming end of the world. The key difference between the two forms (and there are many differences), is that the believer-based film posits the events as a *fait accompli* from God, and the secular films posit the events as being manipulated by Satan or a cabal (usually within the Catholic Church) and can thus be stopped.

The Late, Great Planet Earth, first published in 1970, followed by a paperback release in 1973, was the best-selling nonfiction book of the decade. Hal Lindsey (with often uncredited coauthor C. C. Carlson) offers a quasi-literalist reading of Revelation, a premillennial dispensationalist eschatology connected to John Nelson Darby's theology, which found its most extensive expression in the *Scofield Reference Bible* (1909). According to this theology, the end of the current age (or "dispensation") is imminent. True Christian believers will be raptured into Heaven and everyone else on

Earth must undergo a seven-year "tribulation" in which the Antichrist rises
and reaches a climactic fight at the battle of Armageddon. Jesus will come in
the clouds with a sword in his mouth and defeat Antichrist and all who
followed him, sending them all to a lake of fire, establishing a New Heaven
and a New Earth. Lindsey charts the rise of Antichrist, his seven-year rule,
the Rapture, and the final conflict between God and the enemies of God but
locates them in contemporary politics. Lindsey wrote another twenty books
on the subject, which collectively construct a contemporary Christian futurist
and quasi-literalist approach to Revelation which understood the book as
"coming true" by the end of the twentieth century.

Lindsey's follow-up volume, *Satan is Alive and Well on Planet Earth*
(1972) argues not only that Satan is real, but functions in the world, controlling all politics. "This book is an attempt to define a personal enemy who
rules our world system," Lindsey writes, "Whether we know it or not, he also
influences every life to some degree."[10] It is Lindsey's concept of Satan that
appears in dispensationalist apocalyptic films: Satan has control over much
of the world, but also exerts an influence on any individual alive. From the
young man hit by a bus to Gabriel Byrne whispering across the street in *End
of Days* to the homeless surrounding the church in *Prince of Darkness* to the
corridors of power in Washington in the *Omen* series, cinema does not depict
a scriptural Satan so much as the malevolent, medieval politician/personal
demon of Lindsey. As the very title of the book suggests, Satan is a physical
presence currently on the planet, echoed in the films explored here.

Interestingly, throughout his multiple books on the coming eschaton,
Lindsey claims to read the Bible literally, although his "literal" reading of the
Bible is malleable and arbitrary, insisting that one passage be read literally
and claiming that in the next passage the language of Revelation is metaphoric or poetic. For example, Revelation 9:7–9 reads:

> In appearance the locusts were like horses equipped for battle. On their heads
> were what looked like crowns of gold; their faces were like human faces, their
> hair like women's hair, and their teeth like lions' teeth; they had scales like
> iron breastplates, and the noise of their wings was like the noise of many
> chariots with horses rushing into battle.

Lindsey interprets this through a modern lens and admits that approach is
"deductive" (i.e., speculative):

> I personally tend to think that God might utilize in his judgments some modern
> devices of man which the Apostle John was at a loss for words to describe
> nineteen centuries ago! In the case just mentioned, the locusts might symbolize
> an advanced kind of helicopter. This is just one example of the fast-moving,
> contemporary, and often deductive manner in which I have chosen to approach
> the Book of Revelation.[11]

Although claiming a literal reading, Lindsey argues the locusts are helicopters as viewed by a first century Christian. Similarly, the bow wielded by the Antichrist in Revelation 6:1–2, is how John describes ICBMs, according to Lindsey.[12] Lindsey allowed for the literal reality of the Revelation of John while also allowing for poetic license in making the apocalypse (in the secular sense) contemporary. The supernatural aspects of this interpretation of end-time events included (in fact, needed), modern technology. This was Lindsey's gift to horror cinema—a means to interpret scripture in a contemporary context to make the horrors of Revelation possible and relevant in the last decades of the twentieth century.

Even films not directly presenting the eschaton still manage to invoke Antichrist. *The First Power*, for example, a film ostensibly about a serial killer resurrected by Satan to continue his work, begins with a nun reading from Revelation to a bishop and priest: "And when they shall have finished their testimony, the beast that ascendeth out of the bottomless pit shall make war against them, and shall overcome them, and kill them" (Rev 11:7–8).[13] The priest responds:

> Sister, we're all aware of the Book of Revelation. You can twist those words to mean almost anything. . . . Sister, this is the twentieth century—one mustn't mention Satan in polite company.

The bishop then jokes that if they discuss devil worship in public, "we might all end up on *Geraldo*." He suggests the nun mediate less on Satan and more on the love of Christ.

The film demonstrates the error in the clergy's thinking; the devil is an active presence in Los Angeles, giving the serial killer the eponymous "First Power," the ability to come back from the dead. Ironically, however, the response of the clergymen is actually very close to the actual Catholic position: literalist readings of Revelation are in error, and one should focus less on Satan and more on the love of Christ.[14]

The most obvious example of a Lindsey-esque apocalypse is *The Omen* (1976), obviously indebted to *The Exorcist* (1973) (and called "*The Exorcist* for Protestants" by some) and rooted in the world of international politics. Robert Thorn (Gregory Peck) is the American ambassador to the Court of St. James and is active in European as well as American politics. His wife Katherine (Lee Remick) gives birth to a stillborn in a hospital in Rome, and a priest convinces Robert to take the baby he claims was born of a mother who died in childbirth. Robert does so, not telling Katherine, and Damien is raised as their own child. Damien, however, was actually born of a jackal and is the Antichrist. He is raised as the child of an ambassador, although his nanny commits suicide on his birthday in front of the party, exclaiming "It's all for you, Damien." Anyone who uncovers the truth or tries to harm Damien is killed horribly in seemingly random accidents.

Once Robert realizes that his son is indeed the Antichrist, the film shifts. Flying to Israel he meets archeologist/exorcist Carl Bugenhagen (Leo McKern in an uncredited appearance) who gives him "the seven Daggers of Megiddo," explaining if he can stab all seven into his son the Antichrist will die forever. This moment becomes the model for all mainstream films that show the end-times. A weapon, or a person, or an event can be used or killed in order to stop Satan and prevent "the apocalypse." Thorn drags Damien into a church but is shot by police before he can use the daggers. Damien is then sent to live with the American president in the White House at the end of the film. In *Damien: Omen II* (1978), Bugenhagen uncovers a painting of the Antichrist at Megiddo (where the last battle will be fought, according to Revelation 16:16), which resembles Damien, who is now twelve years old. Bugenhagen writes a letter explaining Damien is the Antichrist and the daggers can kill him. Although buried alive in a supernaturally caused cave-in, Bugenhagen asserts with his dying breath that God will win. The daggers are then sent to the Thorn museum where once again an attempt is made to kill Damien with the daggers, but instead, all around him are killed. In the final film of the original trilogy, *The Final Conflict* (1981), a now adult Damien (Sam Neill) is the ambassador to Great Britain and knows the Christ child has been reborn in the United Kingdom. He plans to kill the boy and dominate the world but is conflicted by his love for a reporter (Lisa Harrow). At the climax, the journalist stabs Damien with one of the Megiddo daggers as he confronts the boy Christ, killing him. The film then ends quoting Revelation 21:4: "he will wipe every tear from their eyes. Death will be no more; mourning and crying and pain will be no more, for the first things have passed away," implying when the Christ boy matures he will begin his reign of peace.

This plot bears no resemblance to scripture. There are no sacred daggers with which to kill the Antichrist in Revelation. According to popular futurist interpretations of Revelation, the text says that Christ will return in the clouds. Other interpretive approaches see the cloud motif as one of judgment coming upon Israel, echoing similar Hebrew Bible passages, and one fulfilled in the past rather than the future. Not one of popular interpretations of Revelation see Christ born again as a child. Most of all, the Antichrist cannot be stopped by stabbing him, and we skip the tribulation and all the other things mentioned in the book. That a mainstream film uses the Bible, Christian theology, and religion to present their own narrative spin that doesn't fit well with popular Christian interpretations is no surprise. What is important to be aware of is that *The Omen* sets the model for all films that follow. As noted above, a means of stopping the end-times is introduced. This motif is one that will repeat throughout twentieth-century apocalyptic horror. The danger of the Catholic Church, or at least a secret cabal working within it to bring about the end, is presented. Often, another cabal that will violate a number of laws in order to stop the Antichrist is also posited. Whereas a renegade group of priests and nuns at a hospital in Rome kill the Thorn child and give them the Antichrist baby, in *The Final Conflict* a cabal of seven monks led by Father De Carlo (Rossano Brazzi) are willing to endanger others and use children as bait in order to kill Damien.

A larger pattern within both Evangelical Christianity and mainstream religious apocalypse movies is this construction of the Catholic Church as a problematic element of the apocalypse. Often, the Church is either entirely corrupt, home to a small but influential corrupt element, ineffective or overzealous in its response, or there is a radical element within the Church that either seeks to bring about the end or is overzealous in its efforts to prevent it.

Satanic Catholics are found in *The Omen*, whereas overzealous clergy willing to kill innocents to stop the Antichrist can be found in *End of Days*, *Stigmata*, *The Seventh Sign*, and *The Final Conflict*. Ineffective priests and nuns can be found in *Prince of Darkness*, *Lost Souls*, *The Prophesy*, and *Bless the Child*. Given the shaping influence of Lindsey's theology on these films, it is not to be unexpected that the Catholic Church is ineffective at best and dangerous at worst. This view of the Catholic Church is not a modern phenomenon. Martin Luther believed the pope was the Antichrist. Jack Chick, the creator of many anti-Catholic tracts, understood the Roman Catholic Church as the "great whore of Babylon" referred to in Revelation 17.[15] Even Hal Lindsey looks askance at the Catholic Church as a faith that misunderstands Jesus Christ and might just be a player for Antichrist during the end-times.

In *Contemporary Apocalyptic Rhetoric*, Barry Brummett defines apocalyptic by function rather than its elements:

> a mode of thought and discourse that empowers its audience to live in a time of disorientation and disorder by revealing to them a fundamental plan within the cosmos. Apocalyptic is that discourse that restores order through structures of time or history by revealing the present to be a pivotal moment in time, a moment in which history is reaching a state that will both reveal and fulfil the underlying order and purpose in history.[16]

The buildup to the millennium was certainly one such "time of disorientation and disorder."

Hal Lindsey and those who share his theology reveal a premillennial dispensationalist hermeneutic for understanding the "fundamental plan within the cosmos." Dispensationalist pop Christian apocalypse films, while certainly echoing Lindsey-esque thinking on the surface, actually filter scripture through secular apocalyptic films.

Secular apocalypses are all about stopping the end of the world. In films such as *Fail-Safe* (1964), *Terminator 2: Judgement Day* (1991), *Twelve Monkeys* (1995), *Deep Impact* (1998), and *Armageddon* (1998), characters aware of a potential world-ending event—nuclear war, the future rise of a genocidal AI program, the spread of a virus, or an asteroid crashing into Earth, respectively, all work to stop the catastrophic event. Indeed, the narrative pattern in such films involves the discovery of the threat, the race to prevent the event from happening, and the subsequent fallout from positive and negative results of that race. Dispensationalist premillennial apocalyptic films also follow this model. In other words, films that employ Christian elements to narrate a coming apocalypse rely as much if not more on secular apocalyptic movies as they do the Bible.

These films almost all feature the same parallel plot: the birth, rise, or awakening of the person who will bring about the apocalypse and the investigation or discovery of the approaching apocalypse by a person who might be able to stop it. Many of these films begin with the events that will start the end-time commencing. The protagonist is made aware of a prophecy or the coming apocalypse. Often, the film requires someone to identify the Antichrist. In *The Omen*, for example, Bugenhagen tells Thorn to look for a hidden "666" birthmark on the body of his son, which, of course, he finds. Identifying that the end is now upon us and identifying the players in that end scenario are vital to these films, which is ironic, although also Lindsey-esque because both Lindsey and apocalyptic cinema claim you can predict the end.

STOPPING THE APOCALYPSE

What Steve A. Wiggins says of *The Seventh Seal* could apply to virtually all of these films: "The entire universe of *The Seventh Seal* is biblical. This is 'the apocalypse' predicted by scripture."[17] In these films the Bible is taken both literally and symbolically (much in the manner Lindsey does). Characters consult the Bible, quote it (often incorrectly) to each other, and offer the Bible as proof that the end-times are here. But as noted above in the analysis of *The Omen* trilogy, all of the Christian theology, clerical characters, biblical imagery, and scripture quoting is employed in the service of an apocalypse that must be stopped, the exact opposite of what Revelation states.

The forerunner of these films is *Rosemary's Baby* (1968). Rosemary is duped by her husband and neighbors, raped by the devil, and gives birth to Satan's son, who will usher in a new Satanic age. Unlike in subsequent films, when she realizes her baby is the child of Satan, perhaps born to bring about the end of the world, she becomes a comforting and willing mother. There is no fight, no attempt to stop the child, no defeat of evil. Satan wins, at least this first round, in Polanski's film.

John Carpenter's *Prince of Darkness* (1987) involves a group of scientists teaming up with the local Catholic Church in Los Angeles when the death of a priest uncovers a mysterious artifact at an urban Church. A linguist translates a book that contains the true history of reality: Jesus was an alien sent to Earth to warn us about the "Anti-God" attempting to enter this reality. The Anti-God's son was reduced to a green liquid and sealed in a glass chamber under the Church of St. Goddard in Los Angeles.[18] The characters are all plagued by a dream showing a monstrous being exiting the front of the church while hearing a voice say, "This is not a dream. . . . We are using your brain's electrical system as a receiver. We are unable to transmit through conscious neural interference. You are receiving this broadcast as a dream. We are transmitting from the year one, nine, nine, nine. You are receiving this broadcast in order to alter the events you are seeing." One character explains they are seeing a message from the future, sent on tachyon particles (which theoretically travel so fast they move backwards in time), in which Satan is incarnating and entering this reality to bring about the end. Note the message is being sent "in order to alter the events."

The characters attempt to survive the night in the church, surrounded by possessed homeless people who kill them if they attempt to leave. The characters are slowly each possessed, until the woman originally possessed by Satan attempt to use a mirror to bring the Anti-God into this world. Catherine (Lisa Blount) tackles the Satan-possessed woman, throwing both of them through the mirror, which then is shattered by a priest (Donald Pleasance), ending the threat of apocalypse. Interestingly, one of the messages sent by Satan to the group appears on a computer screen: "You will not be saved by the holy ghost. You will not be saved by the god Plutonium. In fact, YOU WILL NOT BE SAVED!" This message denies the possibility of salvation, whether by faith or science. In the end, as in most Carpenter films, it is the power of self-sacrifice and camaraderie that provide salvation (of a sort). In other words, the film shows a group of people realizing the end-times are upon them and working to stop this apocalypse, both in the present moment and in the future ("the year 1999"). *Prince of Darkness* is the silly eighties version of *The Omen*, following the same path and prescribing the same solution (kill the son of Satan and the apocalypse is over).

The following year *The Seventh Sign* (1988) relied upon Jewish mysticism to present an apocalypse to be stopped. The Guf is the "treasury of souls" which exists under the throne of God. Once it is empty, the Son of David (i.e., the messiah) will appear and the world will end.[19] The film combines this Jewish element with Revelation, showing "David Bannon" (Jürgen Prochnow), who is really Christ returned, literally breaking open seals on envelopes (not scrolls), to bring about the disasters listed in Revelation. The Guf is almost empty. Abby Quinn (Demi Moore), who has seen several pregnancies end in miscarriage, is pregnant with what is revealed will be the first baby born without a soul (in other words, dead) and will signal the end of the world.

The secret Satanic Catholic element is present in the form of Father Lucci (Peter Friedman), who investigates mysteries for the Church and informs the Vatican "these are not signs of the apocalypse," even though he knows they are. He is revealed to be the Roman soldier who flogged Christ, cursed to wander the Earth until it is no more, so he has a vested interest in the world ending. John Heard plays an ineffective priest, one to whom Abby goes for comfort and who dismisses her thoughts about the end of the world: "And you're forgetting the most important aspect of eschatology: that when the end comes, with it comes eternal life for those who are saved." "What if no one is saved?" asks Abby, despite the fact that the nameless priest is essentially correct. The film raises the truth of Revelation and then refutes it—the end of the world is a bad thing if it means children die, therefore it must be stopped. And stopped it is. Abby first tries to prevent the execution of "the last martyr"; according to the film that is one of the things that must happen before the end. When Father Lucci kills the last martyr, Abby gives birth to a dying child and tells David/Jesus that she is willing to die for the child; he tells her not only will her baby live, "The Guf has been filled." In other words, in response to her agreeing to die in childbirth, God just made billions of more souls to populate the Earth in order to preserve the status quo.

A variant apocalypse is offered in *The Prophecy* (1995), in which a failed priest-turned-homicide-cop discovers angels are having a war in Heaven when he finds a Bible containing an extra chapter for Revelation, chapter twenty-three. His new chapter tells of a second war in Heaven (the first is when Lucifer and a third of the angels fell). The angel Gabriel (Christopher Walken) comes to Earth to find the soul of a war criminal who can help him end the war in Heaven. Gabriel objects to "talking monkeys" (humans) being elevated above angels by God, and other angels are fighting against his faction. The soul has been placed in a young girl, Mary, by another angel, seeking to hide it from Gabriel. Thus, we have an adaptation of the Gospel of Luke in which the angel Gabriel seeks a young woman named Mary who has a supernatural spirit within her. It falls to Detective Thomas Dagget (Elias Koteas) to protect the girl, using guns, a Native American exorcism ritual, and the help of Lucifer (who does not want to see the status quo change) to defeat and kill Gabriel, sending him to hell and averting the apocalypse. This film is notable in that it is Lucifer who works to stop the apocalypse, as he is interested in maintaining the balance between Heaven and hell. Rather than the enemy of God found in Revelation, this satanic figure is a manager keeping the current business model in place.

In what is perhaps the greatest blending of secular apocalypse with mainstream end-of-the-world cinema, *End of Days* (1999) wears the shaping influence of *Terminator* (1982) and the aptly named *Terminator 2: Judgement*

Day (1991, featuring Arnold Schwarzenegger as both herald of and force against the robotic end-times). A comet called "The Eye of God" appears in the heavens in 1979, signaling the birth of a young woman who will either lead humanity into a period of peace and goodness or will give birth to the Antichrist. The Catholic Church is aware of this; some favor assassinating her rather than taking a chance. The pope says faith is called for; but a cardinal counters, "If she lives to bring about the End of Days, there will be no redemption. All our souls will perish," a line seemingly disconnected to the book of Revelation or Catholic belief.[20]

Protecting the girl in the dying days of 1999 is Jericho Cain (Arnold Schwarzenegger), whose name is profoundly biblical (the city that fell before Joshua, combined with the name of the first murderer). He is deeply conflicted and suicidal, but when he learns that the devil, in the form of Gabriel Byrne, plans to impregnate Christine (Robin Tunney), whose name seems intentionally suggestive of Christ and Christians, on New Year's Eve, he decides the best way to save her is through gunfights, chase scenes, jumping off of buildings, and otherwise recreating scenes from the *Terminator* films, except instead of saving John Connor (JC?) he is now saving a girl who could be good or evil.[21]

Cain must also save Christine from a rogue group of priests who attempt to kill her with daggers, echoing *The Omen*. Rescuing her from a Satanic temple in the New York subway system before Satan can impregnate her and running to a church, Schwarzenegger throws himself upon the sword of a statue of St. Michael the archangel so that he will not be possessed by Satan either. Midnight passes and according to the film's prophecy, she can no longer be impregnated by Satan on January 1. Given that the book of Revelation posits no specific dates, the film creates arbitrary magical rules for ending the end-times and preserving the status quo, which according to *End of Days* is apparently what God wants. "It is in our darkest hour that we must have faith," the Pope tells the conclave of Cardinals who know about the girl. The faith we should have, however, is that Jericho Cain, the human terminator, will stop Satan through gunplay and heroic sacrifice. No need for Jesus in this film; Arnold's got it.

Lost Souls (2000) opens with a fictitious quote from scripture: "A man born of incest will become Satan / And the world as we know it will be no more. . . . Deuteronomy Book 17." The film then depicts an exorcism in a mental hospital. Maya Larkin (Winona Ryder), who was exorcized of a demon when she was a teenager, works with priests as a lay assistant during exorcisms. She becomes convinced that self-help author Peter Kelson (Ben Chaplin), Damien-like, has been bred to be the Antichrist. During their investigations, they learn he was indeed born of incest, between his mother and a priest who is also his uncle. Since the Deuteronomy prophecy says this man will become Satan, she accompanies him to see if at the designated time he is indeed possessed by Satan. The two of them sit in a car as the seconds tick down. At the designated time he is initially relieved, but then becomes obviously possessed. Maya shoots him in the head, killing him instantly, thus ending the apocalypse in record speed, and much more efficiently than Arnold Schwarzenegger did.

Lastly, *Bless the Child* (2000) follows many of the same plotlines. A junkie gives birth to Cody, a girl who may be the second coming of Jesus. She brings dead birds back to life and knows things no child should. She is being raised by her psychiatric nurse aunt Maggie (Kim Basinger). All of the children born at the same time as Cody are slowly being killed as Eric Stark, a child actor who as an adult becomes the Antichrist, seeks to destroy Christ. Stark marries Jenna, Maggie's sister and Cody's mom, so that he might adopt the child and stop her. FBI agent Travis (Jimmy Smits) specializes in religious crimes. Working with Maggie, he tracks down Stark and Cody to a church, where angels come to the rescue, destroying Stark and all his followers and allowing Cody to go back to school. Oddly, this second coming is a repeat, not an apocalyptic one. Cody will heal and teach and encourage people to be good to one another and love God, not bring about a New Heaven or New Earth—just make this one a little better.

INVERSION: CHRISTIAN CINEMA DOES THE SAME

If mainstream (read: secular) apocalypse movies that draw upon Christian themes, symbols, and texts transform Revelation into an action horror movie, then Christian cinematic approaches to apocalypse (films made by Christian filmmakers with an explicitly evangelical intent) also transform Revelation into a horror movie. The *Left Behind* films are the most prominent movies in an entire subgenre of biblically based apocalypse horror. *A Thief in the Night* (1972) and its sequels paved the way for such fare as *The Omega Code* (1999), *The Moment After* (1999, its own title echoing the secular end-of-the-world television movie *The Day After*), *Tribulation* (2000), *Meggido: The Omega Code 2* (2001), *Jerusalem Countdown* (2011), and *Revelation Road: The Beginning of the End* (2013), to name but a handful of dozens. The secular and Christian apocalypse movies began to echo each other during the postmillennial period. In *World Gone Wild: A Survivor's Guide to Post-Apocalyptic Movies*, David J. Moore asserts an influence on postmillennial secular apocalyptic films by Christian apocalyptic pop culture. The 2009 film *Knowing*, concerning the coming destruction of the world from solar flares, is, according to Moore, a secular rapture film: "instead of Christ returning to earth to take Christians, aliens (or angels, depending on how you look at it) rapture up children who have heard the calling to go with them," who are then literally deposited on a new Earth (another planet) while the original earth is burned to a cinder (in a lake of fire?).[22] The Christian concept of the Rapture is secularized into aliens taking the chosen children into the heavens, sparing them the tribulation of the destruction of the home planet.

Similarly, Jason C. Bivins traces a profound influence of secular horror cinema on Christian depictions of the end-times. In *Religion of Fear: The Politics of Horror in Conservative Evangelism*, Bivins notes the *Left Behind* series uses "narrative strategies appropriated from conventional page-turners," and inscribes its characters and scenarios with horror tropes.[23] Unlike the secular horror films which concern stopping (or at least postponing) the end, the *Left Behind* films conversely seek to prepare audiences for what the artists perceive as the inevitable end predicted in Revelation. What is interesting, however, is that despite having the exact opposite narrative goal (bringing about as opposed to stopping), they employ the same exact dramatic and narrative techniques as secular horror. "[Nicolae] Carpathia himself is depicted as a horror figure," Bivins argues, seeing elements of vampires, the Frankenstein monster, and cinematic demons in him.[24] The novels and the films based upon them employ "splattery images of bodily destruction and sci-fi inspired violence," both supernatural and conventional, such as "the oft-used guillotine (an iconic horror reference given new life in this series)."[25] Bivins goes on to compare Tim LaHaye and Jerry Jenkins (the authors of the series) with Stephen King, noting that King uses horror and gore "in the name of effective writing, [but] LaHaye and Jenkins are distinct insofar as their devices are combined with religious sensibilities and political concern."[26] There is more violence, gore and body destruction, disease, decay and wartime degradations in the *Left Behind* series than in any series of slasher films, all in the name of Christ. Bivins quotes a fifteen-year-old *Left Behind* fan: "The best thing about the *Left Behind* books is the way the non-Christians get their guts pulled out by God."[27] He could just as easily have been a horror fan speaking of Freddy Krueger or Jason Voorhees.

The result of the blending of these approaches to the eschaton is that the apocalypse (in the secular sense) is now entirely coded as horror, for both secular film fan and Christian alike. The key difference is the secular film apocalypse must be stopped or untold horrors will be unleashed on the world and the status quo will end. For the believer, the apocalypse will unleash untold horrors on the world and the status quo will end, and that is a good thing. If the secular filmmakers misread Revelation in crafting narratives that see the Church and a handful of characters who know "the truth" trying to stop the end of the world, Evangelical filmmakers also misread Revelation, crafting narratives in which pleasure is to be found in the torture and death of nonbelievers before God finally sends them all to hell.

POSTMILLENNIAL HORROR—MORE OF THE SAME

Interestingly, with the passing of the year 2000, apocalypse cinema continued, shaped further by the experiences of 9/11 and by reshaping apocalyptic horror often as a local phenomena (*The Reaping*, 2007). The influence of 9/11 experience, but also the survival of the year 2000 and all the fears of Y2K (and then again the year 2001, when the new millennium actually began) made the films less about the end of days than needing to fight against and stop local apocalypses or religious terrorists.

Legion (2010) is a perfect example of dispensationalist horror bleeding into post-9/11 apocalyptic cinema. God loses faith in humanity and sends His angels to start the apocalypse. The archangel Michael arrives with a bag full of guns to fight the possessed people and angels coming to attack the diner that is the film's setting. Michael explains that Charlie, the pregnant waitress at the diner, will give birth to a child that will lead humanity "out of the darkness." The film thus combines the backstories of *The Terminator* and the gospel of Matthew: a child will be born that will save humanity in the future but first must be protected from adversaries both natural and supernatural. This is, however, not the biblical apocalypse. This event is simply God, as in Genesis, deciding to wipe out humanity as if Jesus had never come in the first place:

> Michael: The last time God lost faith in man, He sent a flood. This time, He sent what you see outside.
> Percy: Are you saying this is the apocalypse?
> Michael: I'm saying this is an extermination.

It is interesting to note not that we have lost faith in God but that He has lost faith in us and will simply let the angels kill us all. In *The Prophesy*, God chooses not to intervene in the war in Heaven, letting the angels duke it out. In fact, God is mostly absent from apocalyptic films altogether. He is, at best, an absent father. This is, as Michael notes, a nonapocalypse apocalypse.

The overall effect of these secular religious horror films is to remove God almost altogether from the equation. Angels fight in Heaven and on Earth; the Antichrist attempts to end creation, and through it all God is absent, spoken of only in the third person. These films offer a Godless apocalypse, one in which we are free to fight and prevent change to the status quo, just as in secular apocalyptic films.

CONCLUSION

Throughout the late twentieth century, Hollywood offered a conflation of Christian eschatology with secular apocalypse films, and a belief that God is not behind the end-times but rather would prefer we somehow stop them. These films evince a shaping influence of dispensationalist theology of Hal Lindsey and other fundamentalist Christians, who, in turn, craft their own horrific versions of end-times narratives shaped by secular horror cinema. All of this is possible, because as Stephen Prothero indicated in his book *Religious Literacy*, "One of the most religious countries on earth is also a nation of religious illiterates."[28] We know Revelation is a book about the end of the world. We know the end of the world is a bad thing. Therefore, it must be a book about God trying to stop the end of the world. Enter filmmakers.

We should not be surprised (and indeed I suspect most of us are not surprised) that Hollywood gets Revelation "wrong." More important for our purposes seems to be the mutual fascination of secular Hollywood and what I shall term Religious Hollywood (makers of the films such as the *Left Behind, Omega Code,* and *A Thief in the Night* series). Religious cinema employs the tropes of horror cinema to present the eschaton and the events that build to it, just as secular films employ the language, scriptural references, and narrative tropes of Revelation. Each group employs elements associated with the other to achieve their desired cinematic effect and affect, which is fear. In the case of religious filmmakers, it is fear that will reinforce the belief of the viewer or convert the unbelievers. In the case of secular filmmakers, they find in Revelation the elements of horror that lend themselves to creating a scary film. We do not necessarily learn anything about the book of Revelation from these films, but we do begin to see how religion functions within a society to create fear, especially for those outside that religious tradition.

Pop apocalypse horror films construct the eschaton using the language and imagery of Revelation, presenting it as a horrific experience akin to the terrors of other horror cinema and, oddly, something to be stopped, rather than embraced. *The Omen* provided the model for films about individuals who had learned about the reality of the coming end (hidden things revealed), and were given weapons, knowledge, and scenarios by which that end might be prevented. This genre was profoundly shaped by the fundamentalist, dispensationalist seventies theology of Hal Lindsey, and in turn the genre then provided a model for evangelical apocalyptic horror (*Left Behind* being the best-known example) to craft its own version of Revelation using the tropes of horror cinema.

NOTES

1. See John Collins's *The Apocalyptic Imagination* for a background on apocalyptic. I follow Tina Pippen in this essay in that there is a great deal of scholarly work on apocalyptic literature, and these terms bear very specific meanings within theological and religious contexts, but I shall use the terms "apocalypse" and "apocalyptic" rather expansively, as understood in popular culture, to refer to any scenario that imagines the end of society.

2. For simplicity of reference, canon refers to a number of different books of text. The Hebrew Bible, commonly called the Old Testament by Christians, has 46 books according to Catholics but only 39 in Protestant Bibles. Both Catholic and Protestant Bibles have 27 books in the New Testament, which is the canonical writings of the early Christian church. A number of noncanonical apocalyptic texts can be found in both the Hebrew and Christian traditions. For more information on early apocalyptic canonical and noncanonical texts, see Murphy and Schedtler, eds. *Apocalypses in Context.*

3. Aune, *Revelation 1–5*, lvii–lxx. For additional information on the dating of the book and possible persecutions (or imagined persecutions) it was written in response to, please see Collins, *Crisis and Catharsis*; Blount, *Revelation*, as well as Steven Cook's work on the sociology of apocalypse *Prophecy and Apocalypticism.*

4. All scriptural citations are taken from the New Revised Standard Version (NRSV) as found in the *Harper Collins Study Bible.*

5. Weber, *Apocalypses*, 230.

6. Newman, *Apocalypse Movies*, 18.

7. Ibid.

8. Dixon, *Visions of the Apocalypse.*

9. Sippl, "Tomorrow is My Birthday," 5.

10. Lindsey and Carlson, *Satan is Alive and Well*, 1.

11. Lindsey and Carlson, *The Late, Great Planet Earth*, 1.

12. Lindsey, *The Apocalypse Code*, 72.

13. Oddly, the nun quotes the King James Version, which Catholics neither accept nor use.

14. See chapter two, article seven of the *Catechism of the Catholic Church.*

15. Bivins, *Religion of Fear*, 57.

16. Brummett, *Contemporary Apocalyptic Rhetoric*, 9–10.

17. Wiggins, *Holy Horror*, 60. We should note that when Wiggins says the universe is "biblical," he means "biblical" as interpreted through the lens of culture.

18. Note that there is no "St. Goddard." This is Carpenter mixing science and religion as he does throughout the film, as Robert H. Goddard (1882–1945) was an engineer, scientist, and physicist (as are the majority of the characters in the film) who developed the first liquid-fueled rocket, thus heralding not only space travel but also the potential for the end of the world in the form of missiles.

19. Dennis, *The Encyclopedia of Jewish Myth, Magic and Mysticism*, 184.

20. See chapter two, article seven of the *Catechism of the Catholic Church.*

21. See Michelle Fletcher, "'Behold, I'll Be Back' in Copier and Vander Stichele, *Close Encounters between Bible and Film.*

22. Moore, *World Gone Wild*, 15.

23. Bivins, *Religion of Fear*, 20, 205.

24. Ibid., 205.

25. Ibid., 206.

26. Ibid., 208.

27. Ibid., 208.

28. Prothero, *Religious Literacy*, 2.

WORKS CITED

Aune, David E. *Revelation 1–5*, Word Biblical Commentary 52A. Dallas, TX: Word, 1997.

Bivins, Jason C. *Religion of Fear: The Politics of Horror in Conservative Evangelicalism.* Oxford: Oxford University Press, 2008.

Blount, Brian. *Revelation: A Commentary.* Louisville, KY: Westminster John Knox Press, 2013.

Brummett, Barry. *Contemporary Apocalyptic Rhetoric.* New York: Praeger, 1991.

Catechism of the Catholic Church. New York: William H. Sadler, 1994.

Collins, Adela Yarbro. *Crisis and Catharsis: The Power of the Apocalypse.* Philadelphia: The Westminster Press, 1984.

Collins, John. *The Apocalyptic Imagination: An Introduction to Jewish Apocalyptic Literature.* 3rd ed. Grand Rapids, MI: Eerdmans, 2016.

Cook, Steven. *Prophecy and Apocalypticism: The Postexilic Social Setting.* Minneapolis, MN: Augsburg Fortress Publishers, 1995.

Dennis, Geoffrey W. *The Encyclopedia of Jewish Myth, Magic and Mysticism*, 2nd ed. Woodbury, MN: Llewellyn Publications, 2016.

Dixon, Wheeler Winston. *Visions of the Apocalypse: Spectacles of Destruction in American Cinema.* London: Wallflower, 2003.

Ehrman, Bart D. *The New Testament: A Historical Introduction to the Early Christian Writings.* 9th ed. Oxford: Oxford University Press, 2008.

Fletcher, Michelle. "'Behold, I'll Be Back': *Terminator*, the Book of Revelation, and the Power of the Past," in *Close Encounters between Bible and Film*, eds. Laura Copier and Caroline Vander Stichele. Atlanta: SBL Press, 2016.

Harper Collins Study Bible. London: Harper Collins, 1993.

Lindsey, Hal. *The Apocalypse Code.* Palos Verdes, CA: Western Front, 1997.

———. *There's A New World Coming, A Prophetic Odyssey.* Santa Ana, CA: Vision House, 1973.

Lindsey, Hal, and C. C. Carlson. *The Late, Great Planet Earth.* New York: Bantam Books, 1973.

———. *Satan is Alive and Well on Planet Earth.* Grand Rapids, MI: Zondervan, 1972.

Moore, David J. *World Gone Wild: A Survivor's Guide to Post-Apocalyptic Movies.* Atglen PA: Schiffer, 2014.

Murphy, Kelly J., and Justin Jeffcoat Schedtler, eds. *Apocalypses in Context: Apocalyptic Currents Through History.* Minneapolis, MN: Fortress Press, 2016.

Newman, Kim. *Apocalypse Movies: End of the World Cinema.* New York: St. Martin's Griffin, 2000.

Pippin, Tina. *Apocalyptic Bodies: The Biblical End of the World in Text and Image.* London: Routledge, 1999.

Prothero, Stephen. *Religious Literacy: What Every American Needs to Know—And Doesn't.* San Francisco, CA: Harper Collins, 2007.

Sippl, Diane. "Tomorrow is My Birthday: Placing Apocalypse in Millennial Cinema." *CineAction* 53 (2000): 2–21.

Weber, Eugen. *Apocalypses: Prophesies, Cults, and Millennial Beliefs through the Ages.* Cambridge, MA: Harvard University Press, 1999.

Wiggins, Steve A. *Holy Horror: The Bible and Fear in Movies.* Jefferson, NC: McFarland & Company, 2018.

FILMOGRAPHY

Armageddon. Directed by Michael Bay. Burbank, CA: Buena Vista Home Entertainment/ Touchstone, 1998.

Bless the Child. Directed by Chuck Russell. Los Angeles: Paramount, 2000.

Damien: Omen II. Directed by Don Taylor. Los Angeles: 20th Century Fox Home Entertainment, 1978.

Deep Impact. Directed by Mimi Leder. Los Angeles: Paramount Home Video, 1998.

El Dia de la Bestia. Directed by Alex de la Iglesia. Madrid: Twentieth Century Fox Home Entertainment España, 1995.

End of Days. Directed by Peter Hyams. Los Angeles: Universal Pictures Home Entertainment, 1999.

Fail-Safe. Directed by Sidney Lumet. Culver City, CA: Columbia TriStar Home Video, 1964.

The Final Conflict. Directed by Graham Baker. Los Angeles: 20th Century Fox Home Entertainment, 1981.

The First Power. Directed by Robert Resnikoff. Beverly Hills, CA: MGM Home Entertainment, 1990.

Good Against Evil. Directed by Paul Wendkos. Golden Valley, MN: Mill Creek Entertainment, 1977.

Jerusalem Countdown. Directed by Harold Cronk. Los Angeles: Universal Pictures Home Entertainment, 2011.

Knowing. Directed by Alex Proyas. Los Angeles: Universal Pictures Home Entertainment, 2009.

Left Behind. Directed by Vic Armstrong. Toronto: Entertainment One, 2014.

Left Behind: The Movie. Directed by Vic Sarin. Toronto: Entertainment One, 2000.

Left Behind II: Tribulation Force. Directed by Bill Corcoran. Culver City, CA: Sony Pictures Home Entertainment, 2002.

Legion. Directed by Scott Stewart. Culver City, CA: Sony Pictures Home Entertainment, 2010.

Lost Souls. Directed by Janusz Kaminski. Los Angeles: New Line Home Video, 2000.

Meggido: The Omega Code 2. Directed by Brian Trenchard-Smith. New York: GoodTimes Home Video, 2001.

The Moment After. Directed by Wes Llewellyn. Los Angeles: Universal Studios Home Entertainment, 1999.

The Omega Code. Directed by Robert Marcarelli. New York: GoodTimes Home Video, 2000.

The Omega Man. Directed by Boris Sagal. Burbank, CA: Warner Home Video, 1971.

The Omen. Directed by Richard Donner. Los Angeles: 20th Century Fox Home Entertainment, 1976.

Prince of Darkness. Directed by John Carpenter. Los Angeles: Shout! Factory, 1987.

The Prophesy. Directed by Gregory Widen. New York: Dimension Home Video, 1995.

The Reaping. Directed by Stephen Hopkins. Burbank, CA: Warner Home Video, 2007.

Revelation Road: The Beginning of the End. Directed by Gabriel Sabloff. Los Angeles: Universal Pictures Home Entertainment, 2013.

Rosemary's Baby. Directed by Roman Polanski. Los Angeles: Paramount Home Video, 1968.

The Seventh Sign. Directed by Carl Schultz. Culver City, CA: Columbia TriStar Home Video, 1988.

Stigmata. Directed by Rupert Wainwright. Beverly Hills, CA: MGM Home Entertainment, 1999.

The Terminator. Directed by James Cameron. Los Angeles: 20th Century Fox Home Entertainment, 1984.

Terminator 2: Judgment Day. Directed by James Cameron. Santa Monica, CA: Lionsgate Home Entertainment, 1991.

A Thief in the Night. Directed by Donald W. Thompson. Des Moines, IA: Mark IV Pictures, 1972.

Tribulation. Directed by André van Heerden. Culver City, CA: Sony Pictures Home Entertainment, 2000.

Twelve Monkeys. Directed by Terry Gilliam. Los Angeles: Universal Pictures Home Entertainment, 1995.

Chapter Six

Gnostic Terror

Subverting the Narrative of Horror

Alyssa J. Beall

Within a given culture, there are particular characters or ideas that a segment of the population will find terrifying. Within one generation, one area, or one interest group, those things we find the most horrific might not be shared with our closest friends; fears are both culturally conditioned and individually specific, influenced by a range of factors.[1] I begin this chapter by discussing how fears in a society are transmitted and how they change between places and times; my primary interest, however, is not the specifics of *what* we're afraid of but whether there is a unifying theme to our current fears. As our perspectives on authority and knowledge change, so does the way our fears are expressed.

I am positing an orthodox/heterodox dichotomy as a way to examine horror in our current media. In what I will be calling the "orthodox" or "traditional" narrative in horror, the problem is centered around a lack of knowledge; horror is caused by the unexplained or the unseen, and the fear is that something is really lurking under the bed or in the closet.

However, in a society where knowledge can be accessed far more quickly and easily than in previous decades, "the unknown" is no longer always our primary concern. Rather, we live in a state of fear where knowledge is no longer enough to chase away the demons. Drawing on the theological concept of gnosticism or "secret knowledge,"[2] I argue that when the framing narratives of particular shows and films are placed in direct opposition to, or directly challenge, the orthodox worldview, we can see this confrontation of ideas in both the visuals and the narratives of recent film and television. There are multiple discussions around the term "gnostic," including whether it should be used as a catchall term at all, and if so, for what? Here, I am using the term as it is influenced by discussions of early Christian texts: a knowledge (*gnosis*) that is supposed to be salvific and was—at least in certain settings—limited to the members of each group. There is therefore a level of separation, secrecy, or mysteriousness also wrapped up in the term. My question revolves around the nature of what gnosis points to: Can it be more terrifying to have knowledge than to *not* have it? What if the knowledge that was supposed to be salvific is, instead, horrifying?

We can see this confrontation of the orthodox/gnostic dichotomy in both the visuals and the narratives of recent film and television. As such, these filmic texts can be read as reclaiming both the theological power—and terror—of knowledge itself. As heretical—or heterodox—popular culture, they change the rules of the horror genre and speak to a changing perspective in society today.

This change in perspective can be linked to the religious affiliations and interests of Generation X and the Millennial generation. Drawing on data from the Pew Religious Landscape Studies, I argue that recent perspectives on authority and knowledge—not simply perspectives on religion—are impacting the genre of horror in popular culture.

TRANSMITTING FEAR: WHAT SCARES US?

Much has been written on the idea that our fears are culturally determined and culturally transmitted. In *Sacred Terror* Douglas Cowan discusses sociophobic themes in horror films: "fear of change in the sacred order; fear of sacred places; fear of death, of dying badly, and of not remaining dead; fear of evil that is both externalized and internalized; fear of fanaticism and the power of religion; and finally, fear of the flesh and the powerlessness of religion. Exploiting these fears, filmmakers make us shiver, scream, and seek comfort beneath the bedclothes."[3] Giving examples for each of these categories, he outlines why films need not be directly religious in order to reflect these core fears.

Rather than the direct, specific religious context and symbolism that is found in some horror films, Cowan argues, there can still be a religious orientation that "remains a significant material disclosure of deeply embedded cultural fears of the supernatural and an equally entrenched ambivalence about the place and power of religion in society as the principal means of negotiating those fears."[4] Writers and directors still draw on a society's overarching ideas *about* religion to tap into the fears of their viewers. This also explains why horror films vary from culture to culture—"religion" itself is not a stable concept.

In *Monsters in America*, W. Scott Poole argues that monsters "emerge out of the central anxieties and obsessions that have been a part of the United States from colonial times to the present and from the structures and processes where those obsessions found historical expression."[5] Examining topics like science, slavery, war, and disease, Poole adds another layer to the idea of the social construction of our fears. As old anxieties are resolved, new ones arise; the landscape of terror is constantly evolving in response to our society.

I take as an established point, then, that horror film and TV express our cultural fears, that they vary in times and places, and that what scares one person may have little or no impact on another. This chapter attempts to look at a different facet of the social nature of our fears: the relationship of horror to how we know, and understand, the world around us.

SEA MONSTERS AND SEX DEMONS: TERROR AND EPISTEMOLOGICAL CONCERNS

In *Demon Lovers: Witchcraft, Sex, and the Crisis of Belief,* Walter Stephens discusses how over the centuries of the Inquisition period, the fears of witch hunters, the educated elites, and the common people all changed and adapted to different types of theologically based fears.

> Witchcraft narratives became necessary because theories of sacramental effi-
> cacy were increasingly difficult to believe when stated in the scientific terms
> of Scholastic theology. Witchcraft theorists intuited that Christian dogma was
> more convincing when presented as literature. The translation from theory to
> narrative makes readers' "willing suspension of disbelief" easier by engaging
> their emotions as well as their intellect.[6]

Of note here is both the theological transformation *and* the use of popular culture: Witchcraft stories act as replacements for sermons and lectures to the general public.

Stephens is not just discussing *what* scared people during the period of the Inquisition but also how they came to be *made terrified*. He argues that the inquisitors—whom he calls "witchcraft theorists"—are in large part writing in response to the dilemma of epistemological skepticism: What if there is no way to know what we absolutely should know? In the case of the inquisitors, he argues, this fear was about the reality of God. Proving that people had sex with or were possessed by demons proved the reality of those beings and defended against the unraveling of belief in the supernatural.

There was a major change in the worldview of the Inquisition period with the rise of a fear about *lack* of knowledge or, more specifically, about the fear that certain things could not be known. Coming up with proof for the supernatural—in this period, proving that demons were both possessing and having sex with witches (though usually not doing both simultaneously) addressed the very real concern that the supernatural, both good and evil, was not provably real. If inquisitors could prove the existence of demons, they were also proving by extension the existence of God.

I focus on this particular period because of the direct connections to *what people feared* during—and because of—this theological shift. Looking at trial transcripts, woodcuttings, and folktales rather than horror movies and TV shows, we can still see how an overarching theological concern about the status of knowledge itself manifested in terrifying images of the period. These ideas, according to Stephens, eventually trickled down through society: from theologians, to other learned elites, to the common people; eventually, scary stories about demons became popular, and the fear was spread throughout the more general culture.[7]

Looking back further historically, Timothy Beal examines another facet of the theological horror-knowledge relationship. His examination of the book of Job reveals the sheer terror addressed within:

> Nowhere else in the Hebrew Bible, indeed nowhere else in the known literature of the ancient Near East, is the particularity of the face of pain, and the theological horror written across it, so carefully attended to than in the book of Job. Nowhere else is the voice of utter disorientation, and the theological horror shrieking through it, so carefully sustained than in the book of Job. The book of Job is a giant breach in the biblical corpus, sending cracks through the rest of Scripture, interrogating the systems and strategies of Torah and wisdom for making theological sense of pain.[8]

Here, then, we have what we can characterize as the popular horror of generations past. Beal explores what this "breach" in the Bible means in terms of knowledge about God, particularly for generations of rabbis who attempted to interact with and respond to the book of Job.

Though the book of Job would be used in multiple ways, Beal argues that the perspective taken toward specific monsters in the text functioned in a particular way as shown in rabbinic discussions: the monsters, and the perspective of God *toward* the monsters, "canonized their ambiguity."[9] Yes, the book of Job was terrifying, but it was terrifying because it presented a perspective on knowledge itself that conflicted with the accepted order of the universe.

"In Job's story, the moral universe affirmed elsewhere in biblical tradition, according to which righteousness equal blessed well-being and disobedience equals curse suffering, is turned inside out and upside down."[10] This reversal, then, becomes an epistemological keystone for the reading of the *rest* of the biblical text: questions about how we can know the things we know seep out from Job into the rest of the Bible, and the inclusion of the story of Job into the canon demands that this perspective on knowledge be addressed in every piece of the whole.

In different time periods, different epistemological stances influenced the culture of the day. We can look at beliefs about the production and reliability of knowledge in the same way that we examine any other facet of culture: high culture can trickle down and influence popular culture, or it can be bracketed off, rejected, or reframed for a different audience. For the purpose of examining cultural fears and their popular expressions, how *sub*cultures respond to mainstream culture is particularly interesting. "Subcultural consumption is consumption at its most discriminating. Through a process of 'bricolage,' subcultures appropriate for their own purposes and meanings the commodities commercially provided. Products are combined or transformed in ways not intended by their producers; commodities are rearticulated to produce oppositional meanings."[11] How knowledge is produced and used, then, can be appropriated for a subculture's own purposes and meanings as well; the dominant ideas about knowledge in any mainstream culture can be transformed and rearticulated.

To move into our present day, I turn from witch-hunting manuals and Talmud to popular TV and film. There is a new cultural transition at hand; horror in TV and film reflects this transition, and I will compare the role of knowledge in horror in the 1980s–2000s to what scares us today. I make this comparison by examining three specific examples from the last decade: *Cabin in the Woods*, *The Walking Dead*, and *The Haunting of Hill House*. Each is a slightly different form of popular culture: wide release film, (extended) cable series, and streaming (Netflix) series.

THE ROLE OF KNOWLEDGE IN TERROR

In the classic or mainstream U.S. terror/horror scenario, the problem is often centered around a lack of knowledge; the main characters (and we, as viewers) are terrified by the unexplained or the unseen. From *Alien* (Scott, 1979) to *Bird Box* (Bier, 2018), the main characters and the viewer need to solve the puzzle of the situation in order to rescue others, be rescued, or find safety. If that solution is discovered, the horror is generally contained—though usually after one last, climatic scene. Once the problem is solved, the escape is complete, or the monster is vanquished, the characters can go on with their lives, and the viewer can walk out of the theater (or living room) with a sense of resolution.[12]

One example of this U.S. narrative in the 1990s and early 2000s (along with the follow-up short series in 2016) is *The X Files* (Carter et al., 1993–2001; 2016–2018). The show is predicated on the idea that "the truth is out there," and is supposedly accessible if the characters follow the correct leads, avoid all kinds of red herrings and interference, and stay true to their primary goal. In this type of fiction, some kind of metanarrative—be that aliens in *the X-Files* or gods in the long-running series of *Stargate* shows—functions to prove that there is order in the universe . . . if only they/we can find it. The attainment of that knowledge, generally through some version of Protestant work ethic along with a bit of luck—has the hope of fixing whatever problems the characters face.

A subsection of this type of narrative proves the usefulness of knowledge even further: If the problem remains unsolved or if knowledge is *not* attained, the characters are trapped, and the terror continues. One excellent example of this lack of resolution, both narratively and cinematically, is the original *Blair Witch Project* (Sánchez and Myrick, 1999): In the final scene we get only a brief, shaky glance at Mike standing in a corner before the primary (visual) narrator Heather is apparently attacked and drops her camera to the ground. We see—from her perspective—that *nothing* is resolved, and we participate in her lack of answers as the screen goes black.

One of the most significant examples of a film genre during this period is the group of narratives exemplified by *The Sixth Sense* (Shyamalan, 1999) and *The Others* (Amenábar, 2001). Both films prove the existence of, and our interaction with, the supernatural by sharing knowledge at the end of the film. That knowledge, when put into place, reveals the "true" storyline of each film: Malcolm Crowe and Grace are revealed to be part of the supernatural, despite the fact that even *they* are not aware of their status. As characters they are as surprised by this revelation of knowledge as we, the viewers, are.

For both character and viewer the result is resolution: Malcolm and Grace can "move on," though in very different ways, having finally understood the events of their death. Both Malcolm and Grace go through periods of near-frantic behavior as the pieces of the puzzle come together, but once the mystery is resolved, the characters are calm and at some sort of peace. As well, we as viewers can now view the film again and enjoy understanding the intricate clues left by the filmmakers throughout.[13]

KNOWLEDGE AS TERRIFYING: *CABIN IN THE WOODS*

In the last decade, we have seen the rise of a popular subgenre or subculture in which the situation has been reversed. The main characters (and by extension, we as viewers) know what's happening, may even know *why* it's happening, and yet that knowledge does nothing to fix the problem or make the terror go away. These filmic texts can be read as reclaiming the horror of gnosis: knowledge in these films is already a given, at least for some characters. In the end, however, their knowledge solves nothing and, in many cases, is actually dangerous or deadly for the characters who know the most.

In my three examples, the orthodox horror narrative remains stable for either a part of the show's timeline *or* from one group's perspective. In season one of *The Walking Dead* (Darabont et al., 2010), there is a search for knowledge as the hoped-for resolution to the zombie problem; in *The Cabin in the Woods* (Goddard, 2012), one set of characters is quite literally trapped in a classic horror film; in *The Haunting of Hill House* (Flanagan, 2018), one of two timelines (the past) follows the classic haunted house story. However, in each of these three texts, there is a secondary narrative that blatantly breaks with the traditional storylines. This secondary narrative—what I'm calling the "gnostic narrative"—acts as a frame for the orthodox narrative, and questions the very essence of what we, as viewers, fear. These competing narratives are conveyed to the viewer both in the storyline and in the visual techniques employed throughout; in each case, they are brought together in the climax of the episode, series, or film.

In *Cabin*, we open with two groups: the college students and the Technicians (also known as the "puppeteers"). The college students, in the traditional horror narrative, are out for a weekend trip to an isolated cabin. The puppeteers, in the framing narrative, are responsible for controlling most of the actual events of that weekend, unbeknownst to the students. The college students are, for the majority of the film, unaware of the puppeteers, while the puppeteers have almost complete knowledge of the actions of the college students via complicated surveillance technology.

Over the course of the film, we find out that groups of puppeteers throughout the world are responsible for setting up a situation of various traditional sacrifices to appease The Ancient Ones, lest the Ancient Ones fully wake and destroy the world. The rest of the film is quite literally framed by this narrative; our U.S.-based puppeteers are the opening sequence of the movie, and the (now-enlightened) remaining students are the last scene of the film.

Our college-student group of stereotypes, consisting of the virgin, whore, jock, brain, and fool, unknowingly choose their method of eventual torture and death by selecting various objects in a creepy basement of the cabin. The puppeteers, meanwhile, are apparently so blasé about the yearly project that they place bets on which deadly enemy will be selected—Giant Snake, Mutants, Angry Molesting Tree, and Sexy Witches, among others.[14] In the midpoint of the film when the winning creatures—Zombie Redneck Torture Family—are chosen, a new member of the tech crew is nonplussed:

Truman: They're like something from a nightmare.
Lin: No. They're something nightmares are from. Everything in our stable is remnant of the old world, courtesy of (pointing down) you-know-who.
Truman: Monsters? Magic? Gods?
Lin: You get used to it.

Truman: Should you?

We, as the viewers, know exactly what's happening, the puppeteers know what's happening, and the college students are completely in the dark. As Michael J. Blouin discusses in "'A Growing Global Darkness': Cultural Borders in Goddard's *The Cabin in the Woods*," the very people who possess knowledge are quite obviously bored by it:

> Armed with cameras, chemicals with which to lower the intelligence and increase the libido of the characters, and a whole cast of dreadful (if canny) supernatural beings to release, these two working stiffs nonetheless seem bored with their task. An apathetic Hadley (Bradley Whitford) laments that he is never permitted to unleash his beloved mermen on unsuspecting teens. The two men orchestrate bets on which monster will be chosen, largely indifferent to the the fate of the characters on-screen.[15]

At the same time, the knowledge of the puppeteers does absolutely nothing to ease the danger that they are in: If the sacrifice does not work, they are in as much trouble as everybody else.

We see the framing of the traditional horror narrative, as well as the idea of culturally determined fears, even more clearly in one very short scene nearing the end of the film. A Japanese group of puppeteers are the only others who are close to succeeding with their sacrifice to the Ancient Ones. Their sacrifice—a classroom of 8-year-old girls—defeat "Japanese Floaty Girl" (a reference to female revenge-seeking spirits or *yōkai* common in Japanese horror films[16]) by gathering in a circle, singing, and transforming the spirit into a lucky frog or *kaeru*. This type of sacrifice, and this resolution, is not something that would be available to the puppeteers in the context of the United States; our "nightmares" are culturally ours as are the stereotypical sacrifices that must be given to the Ancient Ones.[17]

The resolution to *Cabin* drives home the fact that knowledge is absolutely *not* salvific. Dana ("the virgin") and Marty ("the fool") are the only two survivors of the college-student group. Because they are not yet dead, the sacrifice is not completed, and all other groups of puppeteers have failed to complete their sacrifices as well. As Dana and Marty break into the domain of the puppeteers all the monsters are released, and the puppeteers meet various horrific ends. Dana and Marty transition from the traditional narrative to the framing story by descending through various levels of monsters, and finally meet The Director. The Director explains to them the mechanics of what has been happening, and that they are part of "something bigger, something older than anything known." They also discover that the world of the framing narrative is now completely out of hand, and Dana is given the option to kill Marty in order to complete the sacrifice, save the world, and possibly live. Deciding, quite quickly, that the state of humanity is not worth saving, Dana and Marty instead choose to smoke a joint and wait for sunrise.

> Marty: Giant Evil Gods.
> Dana: I wish I could have seen them.
> Marty: I know! That would have been a fun weekend.
> The building collapses around them; the gigantic hand of an Ancient One comes out of the earth, destroying the cabin and reaching toward the sky. The credits roll.

In the end, though there is knowledge for Dana and Marty, their choice is chaos: to release, so to speak, the uncontrolled Leviathan. Knowledge, in this scenario, is neither positive nor redemptive: it is terrifying and deadly.

KNOWLEDGE AS USELESS: *THE WALKING DEAD*

We see a variation on the theme of gnostic terror in *The Walking Dead*. As in other zombie films and shows, the first season of *The Walking Dead* seeks to answer the question of *why*: What happened, why are people suddenly resurrecting from the dead as zombies, and—most importantly—how can we fix it? Not only is the search for answers key to the plot in other postapocalyptic films, a major part of the resolution is usually the attainment of knowledge. [18] However, this storyline in *The Walking Dead* is short-lived because the answers accomplish absolutely nothing.

In the episodes "Wildfire" and "TS-19," Rick and the other survivors journey to the Centers for Disease Control and Prevention (CDC) outside Atlanta in hopes of getting both a cure and an explanation for recent events.

> Rick: What if we can get him help? I heard the CDC was working on a cure.
> Shane: I heard that too. Heard a lot of things before the world went to hell.
> Rick: What if the CDC is still up and running?
> Shane: Man, that is a stretch right there.
> Rick: Why? If there's any government left, any structure at all, they'd protect the CDC at all costs, wouldn't they? I think it's our best shot. Shelter, protection . . .

The CDC—literally the center of medical knowledge—represents salvation for the group; little do they know while on their way there that the single remaining employee at the facility has lost any hope of understanding the problem. After they join the surviving CDC employee, Jenner, he shows them the recording of a recently deceased and reanimated person (Test Subject 19), explaining the stages of death after being bitten. However, when asked about the "resurrection" event, Jenner can provide facts but no real explanation:

Andrea: You have no idea what it is, do you?
Jenner: It could be microbial, viral, parasitic,—fungal.
Jacqui: Or the wrath of God?
Jenner: There is that.
Andrea: Somebody must know something. Somebody somewhere.
Carol: There are others, right? Other facilities?
Jenner: There may be some. People like me.
Rick: But you don't know? How can you not know?
Jenner: Everything went down. Communications, directives . . . all of it. I've
been in the dark for almost a month.
Andrea: So it's not just here. There's nothing left anywhere? Nothing? That's
what you're really saying, right?

Despite the best scientific equipment and direct experimentation on various subjects, any knowledge gained at the CDC is completely useless. The group is left with *less* hope, not more, after gaining (some) of the answers they sought.

KNOWLEDGE AS DEADLY: *THE HAUNTING OF HILL HOUSE*

Netflix's 2018 hit series *The Haunting of Hill House* is another example of the orthodox/gnostic horror narrative, with a different twist. In *Hill House*, the competing narratives are happening to all the same characters but at different stages of their lives; in the flashback timeline we see the orthodox horror narrative of the classic haunted house, while in the present timeline we are presented with the heterodox narrative. These two narratives meet at various points in the series, but knowledge and resolutions are constantly shown to be anything *but* positive.

In the orthodox narrative of *Hill House*, a young family has moved into an abandoned mansion and, while the mother (Olivia) and father (Hugh) attempt to renovate the building, they all experience a variety of different hauntings. Olivia and one of her daughters, Teddy, have particularly close relationships with the supernatural figures of the house; Olivia can see many of the ghosts, and Teddy can sense things by touching objects or humans. By the end of the first episode we, as viewers, know that the family has fled the house, and that the mother is dead.

In the later storyline, all of the children have grown up, their relationship with each other and their father is fraught with difficulty, and each sibling has different problems to face. Drug abuse, infidelity, financial problems, child abuse, and depression are only some of the very real human issues that *Hill House* addresses. As these storylines develop, we constantly flash back to the traditional narrative, and parts of that earlier story are revealed little by little. Throughout the adult storyline, the power and horror of knowledge are constantly being revealed and discussed, a theme that is most clear in the storyline of Nellie/Nell.

Throughout the first five episodes, the youngest girl, Nellie, is visited and terrified at various times by an apparition she calls "the Bent Neck Lady." These visions vary: for young Nellie, they seem to come almost randomly— as she is asleep or as she is trying to fall asleep. In her later life, the Bent Neck Lady seems to appear during pivotal moments in Nell's life: the death of her husband, the night she is checking her twin brother into a rehab center. For Nellie/Nell (and for the viewer) the figure is always terrifying.

In the later, gnostic storyline, the issue of the Bent Neck Lady is resolved. However, for the character of Nell, understanding this ghost is directly linked to Nell's own death; the reveal in episode five is that the Bent Neck Lady *is* Nell and that she has been visiting her younger self after her own death by hanging. It is, essentially, her fully knowledgeable older self who visits young Nellie over and over, eventually driving her to her own death. The scream of older Nell as she hangs in an abandoned Hill House becomes the terrifying figure that haunts Nellie throughout her entire life.

Olivia and Teddy are two other characters who are harmed, rather than helped, by their own knowledge of the situation in the house. Their direct forms of knowledge—visual and tactile, respectively—seemingly make the horror of the house both more personal and more dangerous. Olivia's constant contact with the ghosts of the house eventually leads her to commit murder, while Teddy is forced to contain her own means of special knowledge by physically blocking it with gloves. While neither of these characterizations is particularly original in the terror/horror genre, both elements do underscore the fact that, in *Hill House*, knowledge is the exact opposite of salvation or liberation.

The ghosts themselves are another aspect to the production of *Hill House*; when the show first debuted, it became quickly apparent that quick shots of various figures were hidden throughout the setting of the house.[19] Throughout the series, these often unseen characters set the tone of the show, an intentional move on the part of the showrunners: "We don't call any attention to them, but they're there. If you look in a door frame, or under the piano, or behind a curtain in a lot of otherwise ordinary scenes, you'll see someone there."[20] As the show drew to a conclusion, many of these ghosts became more and more obvious and, as with other aspects of the show, awareness does not equal resolution. In the penultimate episode "Screaming Meemies," one of the ghosts appears for several very obvious seconds in the kitchen. Rather than being *less* scary by being so directly visible, the direct revelation of the ghosts makes the terror all the more real.

The last episode of *Hill House* attempts to resolve the overarching narrative in a much more positive light; the other siblings move on, and the hauntings are essentially shown to be nothing to fear. As several reviewers of the show noted, this final episode seemingly has very little to do with the overall tone of the previous nine episodes and leaves us with "a forcibly sentimental ending that winds up coated in ectoplasmic sap."[21] Disappointment in a weak ending aside, the final episode also demonstrates a need to reject the less-than-comforting buildup of the rest of the season as I have discussed it here; the desire for knowledge to redeem the characters may have outweighed the overarching theme of the show. The director, Mike Flanagan, noted that he changed the ending of the series on the last day of filming: "The night before it came time to shoot it, I sat up in bed, and I felt guilty about it. I felt like it was cruel. That surprised me. I'd come to love the characters so much that I wanted them to be happy."[22] Interestingly, "happy" apparently means that each character understands the house and its inhabitants—again, the classic horror resolution—whereas previous episodes sought to convey the danger of such knowledge.

THE RISE OF THE NONES: QUESTIONING KNOWLEDGE

The final question at hand is *why* this particular subgenre of horror has begun to appear on our screens. Here I necessarily resort to some unresolved questions, but combining the age group many of these shows and films are popular with, along with the age groups that are most likely to watch (or binge) them, looking at the religious affiliations—and more generally the sources of authority for—particular age groups may be enlightening.

Since the Pew Religious Landscape Studies of 2007 and 2014, much has been made of the "Rise of the Nones,"[23] defined as "A growing share of Americans are religiously unaffiliated, including some who self-identify as atheists or agnostics as well as many who describe their religion as 'nothing in particular.' Altogether, the religiously unaffiliated (also called the 'Nones') now account for 23% of the adult population, up from 16% in 2007."[24] It is not surprising that film and TV shows, dependent on these age groups for much of their popularity, would reflect the changing interests of those groups. The two largest groups are ages 18–29 (35 percent unaffiliated) and ages 30–49 (37 percent unaffiliated).[25] Seventy-two percent of the unaffiliated fall into the category of Millennial or Gen X.[26] While it is difficult to make age-related comparisons to viewership of particular shows due to lack of specific data, the success of a show like *Haunting* is fairly obviously based on the age groups using Netflix: 77 percent of ages 19–29 are Netflix members, while 66 percent of ages 30–44 are members. This figure drops by 20 percent for the next age category of 45–54 years, with only 46 percent membership.[27]

"Religion" as a category is no longer the compelling authority it once was. Again drawing on the Pew figures for the unaffiliated, only 7 percent cite religion as their source of guidance for right and wrong, while 57 percent state they look to "common sense."[28] This movement of popular culture away from depicting religious knowledge as authoritative, or depicting knowledge itself as salvific, makes perfect sense when these figures are taken into account.

Certainly there may be other explanations for the popularity of this type of horror, and the explanation behind the "rise of the Nones" is itself a question that many researchers are currently exploring.[29] As further research continues into the question of the Nones, the connections between religious preferences and popular culture trends may become clearer. I am not arguing that we are moving away from religious or supernatural *themes* in our popular culture horror choices. I agree with Cowan:

> The issue is not one of *secularization*—that cinema horror discloses to us the abandonment or minimization of religious belief in late modern society—but an overwhelming *ambivalence* toward the religious traditions, beliefs, practices, and mythistories by which we are confronted, in which we are often still deeply invested, which we are distinctly unwilling to relinquish, and which we just as often only minimally understand.[30]

Each example I have used above for the issue of knowledge incorporates some type of fear that can be, and has been, expressed through religions. In *Cabin*, we can actually see the monsters and the gods; the ghosts in *Hill House* and the zombies in *Walking Dead* both draw on ideas from a variety of religious traditions—some local, some global. However, they are not dependent on a *particular* traditional religion, and religion itself is not put forth as the solution in any of these three cases.

The ambivalence seen in these examples is toward the idea that knowledge—religious knowledge, in particular—accomplishes anything. Rather, what we are left with in this subgenre of gnostic terror is that knowledge is simply *not enough*. When something goes bump in the night, turning on the light doesn't scare away the monsters; it just makes them more clearly terrifying.

NOTES

1. For discussion, see, for example, Cowan, *Sacred Terror* and Byron, ed., *Globalgothic*.
2. For an overview of the category of "gnosticism," see King, *What Is Gnosticism*. For discussion and debate about the topic, see Williams, *Rethinking Gnosticism*.
3. Cowan, *Sacred Terror*, 59.
4. Ibid., 9.
5. Poole, *Monsters in America*, 4.
6. Stephens, *Demon Lovers: Witchcraft, Sex, and the Crisis of Belief*, 237.
7. Both Protestants and Catholics participated in the persecution of so-called witches during this period. As Margaret Miles points out in her review of *Demon Lovers*, Stephens's claim that the Catholic tradition of demonology is longer-standing than that of Protestant Christianity is a given, since Catholicism is the (far) older tradition. See Miles, review of *Demon Lovers*.
8. Beal, *Monsters*, 37.

9. Ibid., 57.
10. Ibid., 40.
11. Storey, *Cultural Studies*, 120.
12. See Carroll, *Philosophy of Horror*, 97ff. Carroll discusses characteristic horror plots, including what he calls "the complex discovery plot" as well as variations.
13. See Davis, "Skeptical Ghost" for a detailed discussion of both *The Others* and *The Sixth Sense* through the lens of skepticism.
14. See "Monsters: The Cabin in the Woods," *Fandom*, https://thecabininthewoods. fandom.com/wiki/Monsters for a full listing of possible monsters.
15. Blouin, "Global Darkness."
16. See Wee, *Japanese Horror Films*.
17. See Blouin, "Global Darkness" for an extended discussion of *Cabin* and the regional limits of horror vs. the possibility of global fears.
18. Examples of the idea of knowledge as salvific can be found across the terror/horror post-apocalyptic and virus film spectrum. From *Outbreak* (1995) to *Bird Box* (2018), the characters depend on knowledge for continued survival and/or complete resolution.
19. Tallerico, "Haunting of Hill House,"
20. Abrams, "*Haunting of Hill House* Director."
21. Stuever, "Final Episode."
22. Bloom, "Creator Addresses."
23. For further discussion of the Pew data, see Hout, "Religious Ambivalence."
24. Pew Research Center, "U.S. Public Becoming."
25. Pew Research Center, "Religious Landscape Study."
26. Ibid.
27. Statista, "Netflix members."
28. Pew Research Center, "Religious Landscape Study."
29. There are multiple recent articles and texts looking at the "Nones" and new trends or explanations. See, for example, Scheitle, et al., "Rise of the Nones;" Strawn, "'Nones-Sense.'"
30. Cowan, *Sacred Terror*, 51.

WORKS CITED

Abrams, Simon. "*The Haunting of Hill House* Director on the Biggest Changes From Shirley Jackson's Novel." *Vulture*, October 12, 2018. https://www.vulture.com/2018/10/haunting-of-hill-house-netflix-mike-flanagan-interview.html.

Beal, Timothy K. *Religion and Its Monsters*. New York: Routledge, 2002.

Bloom, Mike. "'The Haunting of Hill House' Creator Addresses the Show's Biggest Terrors and Twists." *The Hollywood Reporter*, October 15, 2018. https://www.hollywood reporter.com/live-feed/haunting-hill-house-finale-mike-flanagan-interview-1151590?utm_source=twitter.

Blouin, Michael J. "'A Growing Global Darkness': Cultural Borders in Goddard's *The Cabin in the Woods*." *Horror Studies* 6, no. 1 (2015): 83–99.

Byron, Glennis, ed. *Globalgothic*. Manchester and New York: Manchester University Press, 2013.

Carroll, Noel. *The Philosophy of Horror: Or, Paradoxes of the Heart*. New York: Routledge, 1990.

Cowan, Douglas. *Sacred Terror: Religion and Horror on the Silver Screen*. Waco, TX: Baylor University Press, 2008.

Davis, Colin. "The Skeptical Ghost: Alejandro Amenábar's *The Others* and the Return of the Dead." In *Popular Ghosts: The Haunted Spaces of Everyday Culture,* ed. María del Pilar Blanco and Esther Peeren, 64–75. New York: Continuum, 2010.

Fandom. "Monsters: The Cabin in the Woods." https://thecabininthewoods.fandom.com/wiki/Monsters.

Hout, Michael. "Religious Ambivalence, Liminality, and Increase of No Religious Preference in the United States, 2006–2014." *Journal for the Scientific Study of Religion* 56, no. 1 (March 2017): 52–63.

King, Karen L. *What is Gnosticism?* Cambridge, MA: Belknap Press, 2003.

Miles, Margaret M. Review of *Demon Lovers: Witchcraft, Sex, and the Crisis of Belief* by Walter Stephens. *Journal of the American Academy of Religion* 71, no. 3 (September 2003): 720–23.

Pew Research Center. "U.S. Public Becoming Less Religious," November 3, 2015. https://www.pewforum.org/2015/11/03/u-s-public-becoming-less-religious/.

———. "Religious Landscape Study: The Unaffiliated." Accessed June 12, 2019. https://www.pewforum.org/religious-landscape-study/religious-tradition/unaffiliated-religious-nones/.

Poole, W. Scott. *Monsters in America: Our Historical Obsession with the Hideous and the Haunting.* Waco, TX: Baylor University Press, 2011.

Scheitle, Christopher P., Katie E. Corcoran, and Caitlin Haligan. "The Rise of the Nones and the Changing Relationships between Identity, Belief, and Behavior." *Journal of Contemporary Religion* 33, no. 3 (2018): 567–79.

Statista. "Netflix Members in the U.S. 2017, by Age Group." Accessed August 23, 2019. https://www.statista.com/statistics/720723/netflix-members-usa-by-age-group/.

Stephens, Walter. *Demon Lovers: Witchcraft, Sex, and the Crisis of Belief.* Chicago: University of Chicago Press, 2002.

Storey, John. *Cultural Studies and the Study of Popular Culture.* Athens: University of Georgia Press, 1996.

Strawn, Kelley D. "Whats Behind the Nones-sense? Change Over Time in Factors Predicting Likelihood of Religious Nonaffiliation the United States." *Journal for the Scientific Study of Religion* 58, no. 3 (September 2019): 707–24.

Stuever, Hank. "Until the Final Episode, 'The Haunting of Hill House' Is the Perfect Horror Show." *The Washington Post*, October 12, 2018. https://www.washingtonpost.com/entertainment/tv/until-the-final-episode-the-haunting-of-hill-house-is-the-perfect-horror-show/2018/10/12/fad39d62-cccf-11e8-a3e6-44daa3d35ede_story.html.

Tallerico, Brian. "The Haunting of Hill House: All the Hidden Ghosts You Missed." *Vulture*, October 2, 2018. https://www.vulture.com/2018/10/the-haunting-of-hill-house-hidden-ghosts.html.

Wee, Valerie. *Japanese Horror Films and Their American Remakes: Translating Fear, Adapting Culture.* New York: Routledge, 2014.

Williams, Michael Allen. *Rethinking "Gnosticism": An Argument for Dismantling a Dubious Category.* Princeton, NJ: Princeton University Press, 1996.

FILMOGRAPHY

Alien. Directed by Ridley Scott. Burbank, CA: 20th Century Fox, 1979.

Bird Box. Directed by Susanne Bier. Los Gatos, CA: Netflix, 2018.

The Blair Witch Project. Directed by Eduardo Sánchez and Daniel Myrick. Orlando, FL: Haxan Films, 1999.

The Cabin in the Woods. Directed by Drew Goddard. Santa Monica, CA: Lionsgate, 2012.

The Haunting of Hill House. Directed by Mike Flanagan and Ciarán Foy. Los Gatos, CA: Netflix, 2019.

The Others. Directed by Alejandro Amenábar. New York: Dimension Films, 2001.

The Sixth Sense. Directed by M. Night Shyamalan. Los Angeles, CA: Hollywood Pictures, 1999.

The Walking Dead. Directed by Frank Darabont et al. Beverly Hills, CA: Anchor Bay Entertainment, 2010.

The X-Files. Created by Chris Carter. Los Angeles: 20th Century Fox Television, 1993–2001; 2016–2018.

Part III

Paranormal World, Monstrous History

Chapter Seven

A Longing for Reconciliation

The Ghost Story as Demand for Corporeal and Terrestrial Justice

Joshua Wise

This chapter will explore how the traditional ghost story, involving the themes of unresolved injustice, strong personal moral evil, haunting memory, and the haunted location, challenges the assumptions of a nonmaterial spirit anthropology[1] and reflects a position more in line with a biblical concern for enfleshed justice. I will draw from numerous sources and types of ghost stories including short stories, novels, movies, and video games. However, due to space limitations, not even all of the most commercially or culturally popular examples will be considered here. As well, I will not be considering ghost stories in non-Western cultures except in passing. My focus here is the Victorian and post-Victorian Anglophonic ghost story (hereafter, ghost stories) that has come to form the standard fare for short stories, novels, ghost tours, and often smaller, slower-paced movies and audio dramas.

TWO JUDGMENTS

Two images of divine judgment have dominated the Western Christian imagination since the debates of the thirteenth and fourteenth centuries in Europe.[2] The first, and more traditional view, is that of the universal judgment of all people at the end of the current age. This involves the resurrection of the dead to their bodies and a divine judgment on all humanity. The second is that of individual or particular judgment immediately after death. The second view has dominated popular Christian imagination. N. T. Wright observes, "It has been assumed in Western Christianity that the ultimate aim is to leave this present world and to 'go to heaven.' Even the word 'resurrection' itself, which in the first century always referred to new bodily life, is seen by many as denoting its opposite, namely disembodied immortality."[3] This view either reduces the importance of the material component of human identity, or, in extreme cases, obviates it.

For many Christians, the universal corporeal judgment at the end of time became, and remains, such a postscript to the already proclaimed judgment decreed upon death, that the categories of final resurrection and judgment have become a footnote to postdeath judgment in many strains of Christian reflection. Rare is the student who arrives in my introduction to theology class who knows that the resurrection of the body and the reconstitution of the cosmos are the final hopes of Christian faith. Instead, the belief in a personal "heaven" has replaced the confidence that all virtue and evil will be put on display before the whole world, that all hidden things will be disclosed, and all wrongs put right.

The replacing of universal resurrection and public, universal judgment by an immediately postdeath judgment and spiritual reward, has many causes. The early Christian hope in the resurrection of the body, taken from its original Jewish roots, was almost immediately complimented by Greek Platonic spiritual concepts. Indeed, in Judaism itself before Christianity, such ideas appear to be present.[4] However, it is clear from the New Testament and from the witness of early debates between Christians and their pagan detractors, that the question of the resurrection of the body at the end of time was central to Christian belief.[5] For these early writers, the body-soul pairing made up the identity of the human person. Thus, for a person to be truly brought back to life, body and soul must be reunited. However, this focus changed when the Aristotelian hylomorphic view of identity was applied to humanity by Thomas Aquinas.[6] Aquinas, not without controversy, proposed that human identity rested within the soul as the form of the body. But this form, far from being in a dependent relationship with the matter which it shaped, had its own rational substance, and thus could survive the destruction of its material partner. Hence, human identity, far from being that which was made up of both body and soul, became an entirely spiritual matter.

This position was not, as mentioned above, received without controversy. Indeed, elements of Thomas's view were condemned in Paris in 1277.[7] However, these condemnations were repealed, and Thomas's view started to gain ground.

The proclamation of *Benedictus Deus* in 1336 by Pope Benedict XII, is perhaps one of the greatest contributors to the replacing of resurrection with a heavenly spiritual afterlife in the Western imagination. The document, which was promulgated with full apostolic force, proclaims the souls that die in a state of grace, or who do not die in mortal sin and go through purification, see God soon/immediately after death.

after the passion and death of our Lord Jesus Christ have seen and see the divine essence by intuitive vision, and even face to face, with no mediating creature, serving in the capacity of an object seen, but divine essence immediately revealing itself plainly, clearly, and openly, to them, and seeing thus they enjoy the same divine essence, and also that from such vision and enjoyment their souls, which now have departed, are truly blessed and they have eternal life and rest[.][8]

With *Benedictus Deus*, no future blessing is held back from the spirits of the dead. No added joy comes to them by the resurrection of their bodies. Indeed, the resurrection has become superfluous, a footnote to the doctrines of last things. The dead will rise to receive good or ill in the flesh because their deeds have been done in the flesh. There is no sense here that the essential nature of humanity is a psychosomatic unity, nor that earth is humanity's true home. Instead, we see a strong platonic pull toward the spiritual home of humanity being a nonmaterial reality.

Space here forbids tracking the development of these ideas in detail through the intervening centuries. However, the general view of the spiritual destiny of humanity is evident in the context of the origins of the modern Anglophonic ghost story. The idea of spiritual destiny underwent a significant change in the imagination of Anglophonic culture in the eighteenth century, at least partially under the influence of the writings of Emmanuel Swedenborg and the practice of Franz Mesmer. Swedenborg wrote twenty-eight volumes in his life, claiming direct revelation from God about the state of reality, spirits, and the Last Judgment. He proclaimed that the Last Judgment had already taken place in the spiritual world. Mesmer, on the other hand, contributed the practice of mesmerism, or what would be later called hypnotism, which would become one of the main means of contacting spirits in the religious practices of the Spiritualists.[9]

This rise in Spiritualism sets the stage for the modern Anglophonic ghost story. I will argue here that the ghost stories that have arisen from this context betray several concerns that are addressed by the Christian belief in the resurrection of the body, the Last Judgment, and the reconstitution of the cosmos and are therefore out of step with their immediate context of Spiritualism. By both owing their innovation to Spiritualism and by being out of step with it, I contend that ghost stories in the Anglophonic Victorian and post-Victorian periods host several concerns that are in tension with Spiritualism but not with traditional Christian psychosomatic anthropology.

In the initial part of the discussion I will consider the basic problem of the tension between the ghost story and both an anthropology that locates human identity in the nonmaterial (spirit anthropology) and materialism, which locates human identity in the material world. As Empiricism was also prevalent at the time of the birth of the ghost story, it is appropriate to consider how the ghost story is out of step with this intellectual movement as well. However, the focus on this work is the relationship between the ghost story, its spiritualist origins, and its Christian affinities.

I will conclude by pointing to those places where the ancient Christian belief in the resurrection of the body and the universal Last Judgment function to answer the concerns of the ghost story.

ANTHROPOLOGIES AND SPECTERS

The Victorian era, as a transitional period for Anglophonic ghost stories, moves the ghost from a warning or educating figure into the role of a central actor.[10] This period of change for the ghost may have many causes, including the burgeoning spiritualist movement in tandem with the failed belief in the essentially dual nature of humanity's identity as psychosomatic being. But the ghost as it functions in the Victorian and post-Victorian period is distinct from the older and more universal fear of the dangerous remnants of the dead. The malevolent and dangerous ghosts of Japanese and other Asian cultures are perhaps well known as examples. But the European ghost was, in the ancient world, often a similar danger. Take, for example, the ghost of Lycas or Polites, who appears in a legend of the Greek boxer Euthymus. The ghost is the remnant of one of Odysseus's men who raped a girl at the town of Temesa. He was killed by the locals and his wicked ghost remained, killing residents of the area. When they decided to leave, the Oracle at Delphi "forbade them to leave Temesa and told them to propitiate the ghost."[11] They did this by building him a temple and offering him the most beautiful virgin as his wife each year. Not only does the visitor Euthymus exorcise the ghost and save the girl on his travels through Temesa, but he does so by defeating it in physical combat. One can hardly imagine a Victorian ghost being laid low by a left hook and solid uppercut. A change has occurred in the nature of the ghost, as well as the anthropology that produces such a being. That change in anthropology is a move from a generally material view in which the essential person is lost at death, leaving only a kind of shade that dwells in the halls of hades or haunts the earth, to a spiritual standpoint in which the spirit is the essential person.[12] The Greek ghost is still earthy; the Victorian ghost is "spirit."

These two perspectives are, broadly speaking, the two main perspectives of human identity.[13] The material view sees the earth and its cosmos as humanity's natural home. The spiritual view sees the transcendent, divine, or simply nonmaterial as the most proper environment for humans. The material view understands humanity's problems primarily as those that confront us day to day and may see our mortality as the ultimate difficulty for humanity. The spiritual view sees the day-to-day problems of our life as distractions from our ultimate concerns, and views death as a transformative event.

One of the defining elements of the ghost story is that it blurs the line between these two views. Often the spiritual view is primarily espoused, for the spirits of people are destined to move on to the "next life" or to enter some form of rest, but they are bound by their concerns of this life, either due to their own guilt or regret, or because of the misdeeds of others. In other words, the ghost is often held back from realizing its spiritual transformation by unresolved earthly business. The concerns for earthly reconciliation, justice, or even, as we shall see, the desire that one's plight should be turned from private and hidden matters to public ones, are all deeply resonant with the older, more biblical concern for physical resurrection and final public judgment. Those things, which were promised in scripture, and for a long time in the imagination of the Church, lost their potency as a spiritual Christian anthropology won out. However, the human need for those desires to be met did not disappear with the shifting popular theological landscape.

Again, I am not here making the claim that the modern Anglophonic ghost story was the conscious or even sole product of human invention to fill the gap left in the imagination of a Christianized world. However, the ghost story as developed in the growing vacuum of belief in the resurrection of the flesh demonstrates the commitment that the concerns for justice regarding human life do not die along with the concerned parties. Within the framework of both the materialistic and spiritualistic understandings of humanity, justice is either a social utility or a passing concern. For the materialist, justice is not a transcendent good that all temporal goods are measured against. Instead, justice is a social norm defined mainly by utility and consensus. [14] When a person dies, the concept that they might still deserve justice is either a logical inconsistency, or simply a fanciful way of saying that emotional needs of the living are still a going concern when it comes to things that happened in the dead person's life.

For the spiritualist, the concerns of a past life are an incongruity. If this world is not ultimately our home, then the idea that unresolved issues of love or justice should keep the spirit in the fleshly realm are not congruous with the idea that, in the end, all of us will simply transcend the physical and enter the spiritual. The spiritual transcendence that death offers is belied by the fact that the dead might be unquiet.

The Victorian and post-Victorian construction of the ghost demonstrates a basic Christianized understanding of our relationship to and dependence on our physical world while acknowledging that human identity is not merely physical. Within this ghost tradition, we see then, if one will pardon the expression, a specter of the Christian dedication to a bipartite humanity of soul and body forming a whole person, with neither element able to claim the absolute and final identity of a human.

This Christian view of the human being essentially functions, at least within the Western Christian Tradition, as a middle ground between the classical Hebraic, Greek, and Germanic[15] views of humans as finite beings who may leave posthumous psychic ruminants but do not finally continue on everlastingly within the sphere of this or another world, and the spiritualized views of various forms of Platonism. This middle way does not originate within Christianity, but instead appears within Enochic Judaism within The Book of the Watchers at some point in the fourth or third centuries BC.[16] This novel view of the destiny of humanity, or at least of part of humanity, was the idea of the resurrection at the end of the current age. In the resurrection, the dead would be raised to judgment and restored to a perfected world.

The category of the resurrection then functions within the community that formed around the man Jesus of Nazareth as an interpretive lens for the events that followed his death. The insistence of those early Christians upon his physical rising, as opposed to a simple disappearance/assumption,[17] initiated the long Christian theological reflection upon the place of the body in human identity.

The modern ghost exhibits the commitments of a Christian anthropology that is essentially confounding to the materialist or purely spiritualist construction of human identity. However, for the Christian the remnant of a human life calling out for justice, or exhibiting an enduring malevolence, is essentially congruous. For, within most Christian anthropology, death is a nonessential element of human existence. Indeed, it is not only nonessential, but the result of error and evil. The world has been deeply wounded, and humanity's relationships to the world and its creator are wounded.

Indeed, one can find striking resonances with the modern ghost story within the biblical text itself. I am not here concerned with the often considered "witch of Endor" and her summoning of the spirit of Samuel. Instead, we can find the basic ghost story structure in place in the Genesis story of Cain and Abel.

> Then the Lord said to Cain, "Where is your brother Abel?" He said, "I do not know; am I my brother's keeper?" And the Lord said, "What have you done? Listen; your brother's blood is crying out to me from the ground! And now you are cursed from the ground, which has opened its mouth to receive your brother's blood from your hand." (Genesis 4:9–11, NRSV)

Here we have injustice done to a person, a crying out by the "blood" of the slain person, and a curse that will now follow the man who has done the evil. I'm not suggesting that the Cain and Abel story is itself a ghost story, but only that the basic outline of the modern ghost story is both familiar to a Christianized audience and congruous with its anthropology of justice taking place within the realm of the living, not merely for the sake of social propriety but for the person who is now dead.

This concern for justice in the realm of the living is one which, for the majority of Christian history, was addressed by the doctrines of the resurrection of the dead and the Last Judgment. On the last day all evil would be judged and put right. That there was a deep concern for a more advanced understanding of the marriage of justice and mercy during the nineteenth century is without doubt. Reforms abounded in the areas of mental health, gender, political justice, and theology. The Victorian period is replete with an awakening desire in the hearts of many that the old belief that the love of God would overcome all human evil and restore all things and persons to a state of goodness, even to the remotest and most unrepentant sinner. Preachers and teachers like Frederick William Farrar, George MacDonald, and Thomas Erskine of Linlathen, among many others, taught that God's love would overcome all sin and that all people would be saved from their sins and hell in a universal reconciliation.

That it is also a moment of creative innovation with regard to the world of fiction is also without doubt. And the modifications to the ghost story are, at least in part, a result of the intersection of revolutions in justice, theology, imagination, and the burgeoning art form of the novel.

To substantiate the resonances between the ghost story and Christian concerns for an earthly, psychosomatic theater for temporal and terrestrial justice, I will next consider several major themes in popular ghost fiction. Following this, I will look at their connections to the Christian concern for the resurrection and the Last Judgment.

THE CONCERNS OF THE GHOST STORY

Unresolved Injustice

Perhaps the most common trope of the gothic ghost story is the theme of unresolved injustice. Margaret Oliphant's "The Library Window,"[18] Susan Hill's *The Woman in Black*,[19] Peter Medak's *The Changeling*, and countless other ghost stories exhibit this core plot point. In this perhaps most popular version of the ghost story, the dead haunt the living world because they have died either as a result of some great injustice, or they died before they could put an injustice right. Their haunting may be an attempt to bring the perpetrated evil to light, perhaps to give those left behind peace, or merely so that their story might be heard. Or, the haunting might be malicious, as with Susan Hill's titular *Woman in Black*, Jennet Humfrye. In this version of the story, the malicious haunting is also the result of unresolved injustice for which the vengeful spirit will not be propitiated.

While some exceptions may be pointed to, the resolution to the haunting in cases of unresolved injustice is not that someone should go to jail or suffer punishment. Instead, the essential resolution to ghost stories of this kind is that hidden things should be revealed. Hidden bodies are found, secrets are told, and evil deeds are disclosed.

That is not to say that all such ghost stories either have or require resolutions. Some simply relate the tales of figures who appear as the result of personal tragedy. Such tales are the bread and butter of the ghost tour industry, and the substance of many late-night college dorm discussions. Of the four institutions of higher learning that I attended as a student, two had prominent ghost stories that I was aware of.

It may be that we find this need for resolution in many ghost stories coming from the meeting of two genera: the first being the story of the unquiet dead that we find in European tales such as the stories of Viga-Styr and Thorgunna in *Eyrbyggja's saga*, an Icelandic tale composed in perhaps the mid-thirteenth century,[20] and the second being the developing form of the contemporary novel. In any case, the idea of unresolved injustice, either overt, such as murder, or natural, such as the death of a child or the ending of romantic love through sickness, is perhaps the most common trope in ghost stories.

In Margaret Oliphant's "The Library Window," an unnamed young female narrator visits her aunt and day by day observes a young man in a window across the street. She sees with great clarity the young man working always on his writing. The story ends when her now obsessive watching of the young man is brought to its conclusion with the revelation that he is the ghost of a young author murdered by her ancestors because they heard of their sister's obsession with the man. Some women of the family, though not all of them, are haunted by the man's ghost, reenacting both the obsession and the failure to consummate the love.

In Susan Hill's *The Woman in Black*, Jennet Humfrye haunts Eel Marsh House beyond the Nine Lives Causeway because her child was taken from her and subsequently died, suffocated in a bog. She is dead, her sister who took the child is dead, and the child is, of course, dead. From the strict materialist or spiritualist views, this should end the matter. But, instead, Humfrye haunts the house and surrounding town, killing off children in vengeance. Her wrong cannot be made right by the simple reclamation of her child's body. Instead, others must suffer.

The 1980 movie *The Changeling*, directed by Peter Medak, tells the tale of a man who has suffered the loss of his wife and child, only to find himself living in a house haunted by the ghost of a murdered boy. The boy's identity was stolen, and he seems to want both the truth to come out and revenge on the young man who was given that identity. We see once again the desire for evil to be put right, and some sense of balance restored. However, we can also observe here a trope in which the person who is addressed by the ghost has themselves suffered great loss. *The Changeling*'s end suggests that, after terrible secrets have been exposed, and the man who lived a stolen life, though it was unknown to him, has died, the ghost of the boy is now at peace. Here again we see the direct reliance on the spiritualist origins of the ghost story, as communication with the spirit is accomplished through trance and a personal communion. In a chilling scene, a medium is able to receive information from the spirit world, as Swedenborg claimed, and uses a hypnotic state to induce the communication. Here, automatic writing is used as the device of communication, a medium used in Spiritualism.

In these examples, as well as others such as Richard Matheson's *A Stir of Echoes*,[21] the dead attempt to right the wrongs of their earthly existence. Each ghost wants its wrongs seen, and perhaps experienced by others. Some great injustice has been done to them, and neither the material nor spiritual anthropology of detachment after death suffices to answer their plight.

Personal Moral Evil

Along with the innocent and wronged ghost, we also find the ghosts of the wicked haunting the world in literature and film. To consider this version of the ghost story, I will look at two stories: Richard Matheson's *Hell House*,[22] and Susan Hill's *The Mist in the Mirror*.[23]

Matheson's *Hell House* is one of the clearest examples of a haunting due to a man's personal evil and spite and has a direct influence on Stephen King's own work with the Overlook Hotel in *The Shining*, which I will discuss below.

Hell House echoes the basic plot of Shirley Jackson's *The Haunting of Hill House*. A researcher, Dr. Lionel Barrett, gathers a team to investigate supernatural occurrences at the Belasco House in Maine. The house is widely reputed to be haunted due to debauched and unnatural acts that took place under the supervision of the house's architect and founder, Emeric Belasco. The researchers undergo numerous psychic and physical attacks in the house during their week-long stay. Barrett's team includes both a spiritual medium and a physical medium. Florence Tanner, the spiritual medium, like Mrs. Montague in Jackson's *Hill House*, demonstrates the continued use of the spiritualist tradition that gave birth to the ghost story and the debt owed to Mesmer and Swedenborg. Spirits may be communicated with through particular means, including trances. While Mattheson's Florence uses traditional séance settings, Jackson had Mrs. Montague use the Planchette, another tool of Spiritualism. Mattheson's story concludes with the discovery of Belasco's body entombed in a room in which he died of thirst. His proud and malevolent spirit is finally overcome by the mockery of one of the researchers.

In *The Mist in the Mirror*, Hill explores the idea of personal moral evil surviving a person's death in more than just one location. The posthumous figure of Conrad Vane haunts the main character of the novel and draws him ever onward toward both revelation and horror. Vane's personal moral evil is so great that it seems to taint every place he goes, and the characters in the novel are convinced that his evil's potency remains to do harm even after his death.

The concept of great personal moral evil as a cause of haunting suggests a permanence of human choice, and its ability to stain the world in a way that a material understanding of humanity would find hard to explain, and a spiritual understanding cannot. The sense that a person's evil might have a kind of substance of its own, lent reality by human will and action. Understood as a social or psychological pattern, an individual's moral evil might remain after their death. However, with figures like Belasco and Vane, the evil does not rest in such mundane realities. Instead, their evil is, for lack of a better term, supernatural. It clings to the world not in recognizable mundane patterns, but in spiritual form to haunt and potentially do mental, emotional, and spiritual harm to those who cross its path.

Memory and Justice

In stories, ghosts may remain for their own justice, or they may remain because they have put themselves out of a right relationship with reality through their moral evil. But ghosts may also remain as figures tied to the memory of characters in a story.

In Dan Simmon's *A Winter's Haunting*,[24] the main character, Dale Stewart, confronts the ghosts of his childhood, which haunt him for good and ill. Dale has not remembered the traumas of a single summer that left his brilliant friend Duane McBride dead and his life changed. Duane and other specters haunt Dale, not that they might be put to rest, but that Dale might have rest. The novel functions as a kind of "Hegelian" synthesis of memory and fact. And it emphasizes one of the essential elements of the whole ghost story phenomenon regarding the question of justice: memory.

In the 1993 video game, *The 7th Guest* by Trilobyte games, the player enters a haunted mansion and is trapped within until they can solve the mystery of how six people were murdered years ago. The ghosts of the unjustly murdered play out the night of their deaths, revealing that they were often desperate or clutching people who had been lured to the mansion under the promise of a reward, in a manner like the *House on Haunted Hill* (1959/ 1999). The game's story brings the player into the house in order to witness the events of that night, to solve the mystery of who the seventh guest was, and to escape the house. Once more, memory functions in concert with the ghosts of the past.

In the movie *The Awakening*, Florence Cathcart debunks séances and other spiritualist claims. She is called to a boy's school where a ghost has been seen. Cathcart disbelieves in the ghost until she's confronted, not only with its reality but her memory of both the school and the specter. Her history is tied up in the ghost, and the tragedy that took place in the building that used to be her house.

Susan Hill's *The Small Hand*,[25] functions in a similar mode. The ghost of a child, drowned, draws a man into first a sense of wonder and then horror. The story turns on the fact that the child's death is intertwined with the man's own history, and memory must be roused by visiting a house with an overgrown garden before resolution can be found.

In each of these situations, the actor in the story is intimately involved in the events leading to the haunting. The past has gone wrong, and the haunting draws the person back to relive what has gone wrong. Here, especially the spiritual view of humanity is deeply challenged. Far from transcending the past, characters are called back not only into memory but into physical locations which form important parts of their past and identities. There is not only a spiritual element to memory in these hauntings, but a geographic connection to memory, loss, and rectification.

The Haunted Place

Another common trope in the ghost story is the location that has suffered some kind of trauma and becomes haunted. This is distinct from the idea of a single haunting due to unresolved injustice or personal moral evil in that the location itself has become a place of more than one of the unquiet dead. There are distinct stories, unique tragedies, and a kind of perpetuation of sorrow due to the tainting of the location. Here, the focus is less on the individual spirit, but on the place and its own dread countenance.

Perhaps the most famous haunted house in America was, at least at one time, the house at 112 Ocean Avenue, Amityville, Long Island, NY. The book by Jay Anderson, *The Amityville Horror*,[26] that was turned into a series of movies and received a remake in 2005, told the story of the Lutz family that moved into the house after a mass murder performed by Ronald DeFeo in 1974. The Lutz family allegedly experienced paranormal events that eventually drove them from the house. The dramatized versions of the story depict all manner of hauntings including those by Native Americans who were tortured on the site of the house.

The movie *I Am the Pretty Thing that Lives in the House* expresses the same sense of a haunted place due to the losses that have occurred in the same location. However, with Osgood Perkins's slow-moving ghost story, one haunting precipitates the other tragedies that result in a haunted place. In the end the distinction between the ghosts in the house and the house itself blurs.

Of all horror fiction, however, perhaps the most renowned haunted location, given that it has received treatment by two of the greatest geniuses of their respective crafts in the twentieth century, is The Overlook Hotel. Stephen King's novel, *The Shining*,[27] and Stanley Kubrick's film of the same name, present distinct, but resonant images of The Overlook, a Colorado hotel haunted by a parade of malevolent ghosts. Here we find the idea of personal moral evil that results in a haunting, as in Richard Matheson's *Hell House*, which King has cited as a major influence on *The Shining*, writ large. However, it is the place that is evil, the hotel itself is wrong, and it perpetuates the wrongs done within it such that the spirits remain and haunt the halls.

Larger even than The Overlook Hotel is the town of *Silent Hill*. Depicted in a series of video games by Konami, comic books, and novels, Silent Hill is an entire town haunted by the ghosts of personal moral evil, memory, and unresolved injustice. The ghosts of the town largely stem from the guilt of those who visit the town, and yet the town itself is largely responsible for the hauntings. Silent Hill is, like Derry, Maine, or Weeping Cedars, New York, a place of complexly intertwined evil. It is the haunted house on a grand scale, a physical place where creation has gone wrong.

JUSTICE IN THE FLESH

Having looked at several of the main tropes of the ghost story, we can distinguish material, nonmaterial spirit, and ghostly anthropologies. The ghostly anthropology is one in which the identity of a person transcends the material world, and thus is like the nonmaterial spirit anthropology. However, the ghost is still deeply concerned with the matters of the world, and thus does not conform strictly to a nonmaterial spirit anthropology, which transcends the world after death. The two anthropologies, nonmaterial spirit and ghost, are, in fact, at odds with each other. For the concerns of human life in unresolved injustice, personal moral evil, memory, and the corruption of physical locations, should all be able to be simply pushed aside in a nonmaterial spirit view of humanity's identity. Instead, the ghost story maintains that all these elements remain important and cry out to be put right, much the way that Abel's blood cries out from the earth.

The Christian doctrine of the resurrection of the body, the recreation of the cosmos, and the Last Judgment all take these concerns seriously. The Last Judgment functions to not only pronounce punishment on evil but to make all hidden things known and to right all wrongs. It is in the public declaration of deeds in the Last Judgment that the hidden things that ghost stories are so often concerned with will be made known. All will see the horrors that have been done, and all will see that a mighty justice has come to address them. The ghost story's desire that someone, anyone, should bear witness to evil will not only be met but met in tremendous super-abundance. Not just anyone will see and know what has been done, but all will see and know.

The question of personal moral evil is one that is addressed by the Last Judgment in one of two ways. The more dominant tradition deals with personal moral evil by identifying it with the person who performed the evil and sending both into one of two kinds of destruction, either an everlasting torture or a final destruction. The less dominant tradition distinguishes the person from their moral evil and casts the evil into destruction and restores the person to their essential goodness. In both cases, the personal moral evil of a person is taken seriously and not merely forgotten as it must be in a purely spiritual anthropology, which must consider the activities of the material world as inconsequential and to be transcended.

The recreation of the cosmos is meant to put all things right in the physical world and to reclaim for God and purified nature those places where great evil has been done. The concern that the world must be remade takes seriously the fact that human evil has scarred the creation. This concern is expressed as early as the story of the Garden of Eden. That human beings, by their free will, can poison the creation and permanently mar it certainly rings true after the establishment of places like Bergen-Belsen and Dachau. How the scarring of creation will be addressed in the new cosmos is unclear to us. It may be that the old scars are wiped away, or it may be that they remain but as trophies of God's victory over evil, just as the scars of the crucifixion remain on Christ's body.

Perhaps the most insightful reflection on heavenly memory comes from C.S. Lewis's *The Great Divorce*, in which Lewis insists that heavenly life works backward through the memory of a person (as does hellish life) so that the person who is in heaven may understand themselves to always have been in heaven. Such a process would be the unmaking of the ghostly memory and its ability to haunt the world. Insofar as human memory is a physical component and relates us strongly to the physical world and identifies us within time and space, here too does the physical resurrection and the remaking of the cosmos play a central role. In a spiritual anthropology, memory must be overcome, or forgotten, loosening us from the concerns of the material world. But the physical reconstitution of the human person in the material world for Christianity is the means to cleanse and reclaim memory as a central element of the human experience.

At each point, then, Christian hope for the reunification and purification of the human being in spirit and body neither passes over the concerns of the ghost story nor rejects them. Indeed, to some great degree the original Christian construction of the final hope, drawn from preexisting Jewish concepts, that God should raise us from the dead, put all things right, and make all things known, is the answer to many of the concerns expressed in ghost stories. The old construction of anthropology and eschatology says to every ghost, "be still, and wait on the Lord, for He is coming in mighty strength and will make all things known and all things new."

NOTES

1. One particular thread of some ghost stories, the spectral romance, will not be considered here. Though perhaps much can be made of the "spiritual" sense of love that rejects all physical impulses. See, for example, Mankiewicz, *The Ghost and Mrs. Muir,* 1947.

2. Bynum, *The Resurrection of the Body.*

3. Wright, "Death, Resurrection, and Human Destiny in the Bible," in Marshall and Mosher, *Death, Resurrection, and Human Destiny,* 3–24.

4. See Nickelsburg, *Resurrection, Immortality, and Eternal Life.*

5. The question occupied the thought of Athenagoras and Justin Martyr in the second century, setting the stage for Augustine's extensive consideration of the question in *The City of God,* which became the standard discussion throughout the medieval period.

6. Aquinas, *Summa Theologiae,* I.76.

7. Bynum, *The Resurrection of the Body,* 271.

8. Benedict XII, *Benedictus Deus,* 530.

9. See, for example, McLaughlan, *Re-imagining the 'Dark Continent,'* 165ff. McLaughlan also addresses other forms of mesmerism in fiction.

10. Freeman, "The Victorian Ghost Story," in Smith and Hughes, eds., *The Victorian Gothic,* 93.

11. Russell, "Greek and Roman Ghosts," in H. R. E. Davidson, ed., *The Folklore of Ghosts,* 193.

12. Spiritual here is distinguished from spiritualist. Spiritual means seeing the primary identity of human beings as residing in a nonmaterial component that is released or "set free" upon death. This viewpoint is, broadly speaking, common to Plato, certain strains of Hinduism, and Thomistic Catholicism. The spiritualist position is more specific and represents a particular historical religious expression that cannot be subsumed under these viewpoints.

13. This is, of course, excluding views that see human identity as an illusion.

14. That justice must be a social construct in a purely material world appears prima-facia to be the case, as no transcendent justice could exist in a purely material reality. See, for example, Copan, "Grounding Human Rights," in *Legitimizing Human Rights.* See, as well, Watkin, *Difficult Atheism,* 206ff.

15. The classical Hebraic view being that of Sheol, which is simply the state of being dead, despite poetic descriptions. See Papaioannou, *Geography of Hell* and Tromp, *Primitive Conceptions,* for understandings of death in the Old Testament. The Germanic view, as far as we understand its representation in the admittedly late recordings of Snorri Sturluson, depicts a temporary continued existence for warriors until their final "Second death" at Ragnarök when all things will be destroyed and remade.

16. For the dating of the Book of the Watchers, see Nickelsburg, *1 Enoch 1.*

17. That is not to say that there was not a strain of assumption theology in the earliest Christians that may be represented within the theoretical document of "Q." For this theory, see Smith, "Revisiting the Empty Tomb," 123–37.

18. Oliphant, "The Library Window," 1–30.

19. Hill, *The Woman in Black.*

20. H. R. Ellis Davidson, "The Restless Dead: An Icelandic Ghost Story" in Davidson, ed., *The Folklore of Ghosts,* 155–75.

21. Matheson, *A Stir of Echoes.* Here as well the relics of Spiritualism remain, as the protagonist is exposed to an apparition through mesmerism.

22. Matheson, *Hell House.*

23. Hill, *The Mist in the Mirror.*

24. Simmons, *A Winter's Haunting.*

25. Hill, *The Small Hand.*

26. Anson, *The Amityville Horror.*

27. King, *The Shining.*

WORKS CITED

Anson, Jay. *The Amityville Horror*. Upper Saddle River, NJ: Prentice Hall, 1977.

Aquinas, St. Thomas. *Summa Theologiae*. Translated by Fathers of the English Dominican Province. Westminster: Christian Classics, 1981.

Augustine, St. Marcus Dodds, trans. *The City of God*. Peabody: Hendrickson, 2011.

Benedict XII. *Benedictus Deus*. In *The Sources of Catholic Dogma*, by Henry Denzinger, translated by Roy J. Defarrari. Fitzwilliam, NH: Loreto Publications.

Bynum, Caroline Walker. *The Resurrection of the Body in Western Christianity, 200–1336*. New York, NY: Columbia University Press, 1995.

Copan, Paul. "Grounding Human Rights: Naturalism's Failure and Biblical Theism's Success." In *Legitimizing Human Rights: Secular and Religious Perspectives*. Burlington, VT: Ashgate, 2013.

Freeman, Nick. "The Victorian Ghost Story." In *The Victorian Gothic: An Edinburgh Companion*, edited by Andrew Smith and William Hughes. Edinburgh: Edinburgh University Press, 2012.

Davidson, H. R. Ellis. "The Restless Dead: An Icelandic Ghost Story." In *The Folklore of Ghosts*, edited by H. R. E. Davidson. Cambridge: D.S. Brewer, 1981.

Hill, Susan. *The Mist in the Mirror*. London: Sinclair-Stevenson, 1992.

———. *The Small Hand*. London: Profile Books, 2011.

———. *The Woman in Black*. London: Hamish Hamilton, 1984.

King, Stephen. *The Shining*. New York: Doubleday, 1977.

Matheson, Richard. *A Stir of Echoes*. Philadelphia, PA: J. B. Lippincott & Co., 1958.

———. *Hell House*. New York: Viking Press, 1971.

McLaughlan, Robbie. *Re-imagining the 'Dark Continent' in fin de siècle Literature*. Edinburgh: Edinburgh University Press, 2012.

Nickelsburg, George W.E. *1 Enoch 1: A Commentary on the Book of 1 Enoch*, Chapters 1–36; 81–108. Minneapolis, MN: Augsburg Fortress Press, 2001.

———. *Resurrection, Immortality, and Eternal Life in Intertestamental Judaism and Early Christianity*. Cambridge, MA: Harvard University Press, 2006.

Oliphant, Margaret. "The Library Window." *Blackwood's Edinburgh Magazine* 963 (January 1896): 1–30.

Papaioannou, Kim. *The Geography of Hell in the Teaching of Jesus*. Eugene, OR: Pickwick Publications, 2013.

Russell, W. M. S. "Greek and Roman Ghosts." In *The Folklore of Ghosts*, edited by H. R. E. Davidson. Cambridge: D.S. Brewer, 1981.

Simmons, Dan. *A Winter's Haunting*. New York: William Morrow, 2002.

Smith. Daniel. "Revisiting the Empty Tomb: The Post-Mortem Vindication of Jesus in Mark and Q." *Novum Testamentum* Vol. 45 (April 2003): 123–37.

Tromp, Nicholas J. *Primitive Conceptions of Death and the Nether World in the Old Testament*. Rome: Pontifical Biblical Institute, 1969.

Watkin, Christopher. *Difficult Atheism: Post-Theological Thinking in Alain Badiou, Jean-Luc Nancy and Quentin Meillassoux*. Edinburgh University Press, 2011.

Wright, N. T. "Death, Resurrection, and Human Destiny in the Bible." In *Death, Resurrection, and Human Destiny: Christian and Muslim Perspectives*, edited by David Marshal and Lucinda Mosher. Washington, DC: Georgetown University Press, 2014.

FILMOGRAPHY

The 7th Guest. Trilobite Games, 1993.

The Awakening. Directed by Nick Murphy. London, UK: BBC Films, 2011.

The Changeling. Directed by Peter Medak. Los Angeles, CA: Chessman Park Productions, 1980.

The Ghost and Mrs. Muir. Directed by Joseph Mankiewicz. Los Angeles, CA: 20th Century Fox, 1947.

I Am the Pretty Thing That Lives in the House. Directed by Osgood Perkins. Los Gatos, CA: Netflix, 2016.

The Shining. Directed by Stanley Kubrick. The United Kingdom: Hawk Films, 1980.

Chapter Eight

Who's Afraid of the Big Bad Wolf?

Two Models of Christian Theological Engagement with Lycanthropy

Michael Asher Hammett

In 1692 in Swedish Livonia (what is now modern-day Estonia), a highly unusual trial occurred in which a man, Thiess of Kaltenbrun, faced charges of lycanthropy at the local court in Jürgensberg. The eighty-six-year-old man was not initially to be tried himself; his presence was needed as a witness to a church robbery, but his local reputation as a werewolf preceded him. In response to the charges of engaging in the demonic crime of lycanthropy, which would imply some consort with the Devil, Thiess of Kaltenbrun offered a bold response—he openly admitted to having engaged in lycanthropy, but said that he engaged in true shapeshifting in service of God. Thiess claimed that he and several companions were benevolent werewolves and "hounds of God," who transformed into wolves and ventured down into hell to engage in combat with the Devil and his witches. His interrogators believed that he had been deluded into a pact with the Devil. Ultimately, he was sentenced to be flogged and banned for life from Jürgensberg for seeking to turn people away from Christianity.[1]

Historical cases like this in Christian Europe were not necessarily uncommon. In the fifteenth and sixteenth centuries, there were certainly a number of trials in which individuals were accused of the crime of lycanthropy. Between 1540 and 1620, over 30,000 accusations of lycanthropy surfaced in France, and eventually the charge of lycanthropy was subsumed into the broader charge of witchcraft.[2] In these cases, the accused would be charged with having made a deal with the Devil, where in exchange for an unguent, coat, or belt buckle that granted the wearer the perceived ability to transform from a human into a wolf, the wearer would pledge allegiance to the Devil, and once utilizing the device, would wreak havoc through the form of property crimes, deviant behavior, and especially violence, including the murder of livestock and children.[3] However, the case of Thiess of Kaltenbrun differs from the norm in that the accused did not admit to committing a crime against God; rather, he claimed that his lycanthropy was performed in God's service and for His greater glory.

These historic cases provide an interesting parallel with our own modern moment. The fascination with lycanthropy and other forms of shapeshifting has continued well into the modern era with no signs of abating.[4] Just as popular culture phenomena such as *Twilight* provide fodder for discussion among workplaces and internet message boards, the cases described above in Christian Europe typically circulated as the topic of public discussion and entertainment, with attention paid to demonological treatises and tabloi-desque trial pamphlets alike.[5] Modern fascination may be less rooted in tangible, immediate fear over the threat of wolf attacks, but the fact remains that such modern popular culture represents a continuity with the theological debates and discussions emerging from medieval Christian Europe. More-over, this modern fascination raises numerous questions of particular interest to the Christian theologian. What are the foundational theological premises underlying the notion of physical transformation from the form of a human into that of a wolf? Is lycanthropy an acceptable idea within an orthodox Christian framework? If not, how ought the Christian theologian reconcile an orthodox theological understanding of lycanthropy with the sheer ubiquity of it, not only in fictionalized accounts but also in popular accounts claiming personal experience?

In this chapter, I will seek to historically and theologically untangle the issue of Christian engagement with lycanthropy. I will first explain two primary Christian responses to lycanthropy: skepticism and critical accep-tance. Based on these two paths of response, I will outline two distinct models of lycanthropy in Christian thought and discuss the ways in which they populate historical theological accounts. Finally, I will turn to modern popular culture and see whether we can understand two specific were-wolves—Remus Lupin in the Harry Potter series and David Kessler—as reflecting these two Christian models of lycanthropy. In the process, I hope to illuminate some broader lessons for Christian theological engagement with elements of popular culture.

LYCANTHROPY: TWO RESPONSES, TWO MODELS

The first question is a fairly benign one at its face—what is lycanthropy? Lycanthropy can be defined fairly simply as the experience, either actual or delusory, in which one is transformed out of their human form into that of a wolf and exhibits the corresponding behaviors. In modern popular culture, this transformation typically exhibits natural causes, or supernatural causes exhibiting natural features.[6] Modern popular culture more often treats lycanthropy as by definition a literal, physical transformation without question. Historic Christian theologians, however, engaged in a complicated debate over the very nature of such a transformation that questions the very premise of lycanthropy at the outset—whether physical transformation into animal form is even possible in a Christian framework. The perception of this initial premise sets the stage for the two potential responses to the notion of lycanthropy: skepticism and critical (or qualified) acceptance.

Skepticism and Christian Objections to Lycanthropy

The skeptical Christian response to narratives of lycanthropy rejects the notion that anybody can possibly physically transform from their human form into that of an animal. This response, favored by Western theologians from Augustine onward, did not wholly disregard the notion that the boundary between human and animal bodies was fluid. Historically, notions of the malleable nature between man and animal permeate the ancient world. Christian interaction with notions of such fluidity go back to the very beginning (a very good place to start) when Adam and Eve converse with the serpent in the Garden of Eden.[7] The notion that one's physical form was not fully limited by the scope of nature was not unfamiliar to Christian culture, nor was the idea of a fluid boundary between humans and animals; however, there is a crucial skepticism of physical forms of transformation.

There are three key factors that form the orthodox Christian rejection of physical transformation in lycanthropy. The first objection is that it challenges and rejects God's sovereignty and unique creative power. The problem with the various accounts of transformation in antiquity and the Middle Ages is that there is typically no indication that they occur by God's direct power, and it is often indicated that they occur via demonic forces. Accounts such as those described by Augustine, in which the sorceress Circe "transformed the companions of Odysseus into beasts" and the "Arcadians who, chosen by lot . . . were there changed into wolves, and lived in the desolate parts of that region in the company of similar wild creatures"[8] cannot occur in a framework without God's authority. Rather, demons "can achieve nothing by means of any power belonging to their nature . . . except what God permits." However, while Satan holds dominion over the earth, he does not possess the sovereign power of God to create and form matter. To suggest that people can, via a contract with the devil or a demon, actually physically transform from their human form into animal form is to suggest that the Devil has true creative power to cede God's sovereignty over the world. Such physical transformation of the body must occur then not by God's intervention, but by demonic or diabolic intervention. Lycanthropy is thus rejected by most medieval Christians, in part, because it challenges God's unique power to create, shape, and form matter. This rejection most articulately emerges in the canonical rejection of lycanthropy, the *canon Episcopi*. In this obscure passage of canon law, the author writes that he who "believes that anything can be made, or that any creature can be changed to better or to worse or be transformed into another species or similitude, except by the Creator . . . is beyond doubt an infidel."[9]

While the first objection to physical lycanthropy is theocentric, the second rejection of lycanthropy is primarily anthropocentric. Medieval and early modern Christians rejected the notion of physical lycanthropy because it threatened the importance of Christian anthropocentrism. Medieval theology took quite seriously the importance of Genesis 1, in which humanity is not only created as the apex of God's creation, but also in which humanity is given dominion and responsibility over the earth and all other living creatures. The mindset that challenged the physicality of lycanthropy was one in which humans are the pinnacle of God's creation and charged with the care and subjugation of the natural world.[10] Because humanity is created in the image of God, transformation out of human form into that of an animal would considerably diminish the human authority over the created order and serve as an affront to the image of God—if the image of God can be dissolved by transformation into animal form, then it appears less distinctive and important to understanding the uniqueness of humanity among God's creatures. The notion of human transformation into animal form is thus considered theologically suspect because it both undercuts humanity as the pinnacle of God's creation and challenges the creation of animals specifically for the use of humans. The maintenance of proper bounds between humans and animals was crucial to maintaining the dignity of humanity.[11]

Similar notions to this are evident when we consider Enlightenment notions of the human condition—while Enlightenment philosophers and thinkers certainly challenged the metaphysical distinction between humans and animals and affirmed humanity's place in nature, philosophers of the Enlightenment also still tended to affirm a natural hierarchy, with humans existing beyond the level of mere beasts and retaining a certain dignity reserved to humanity. Thinkers like Denis Diderot and Jean-Jacques Rousseau tended to challenge the distinctions between humanity and animals and suggested a more materialist view of humanity as the "happy outcome of chance combinations of matter." But naturalists like George-Louis Leclerc, Comte de Buffon, in his *Discourses*, presented a picture of humanity as necessarily and metaphysically in a privileged state separate from that of animals, a distinction that most Enlightenment thinkers declined to challenge in favor of affirming the unique dignity and position of humanity. Despite eventual shifts as a result of naturalist thought, the impact of Christian theological anthropo-centrism on a broader cultural level in the West may be evident in the En-lightenment affirmation of humanity's unique status.[12]

Related to but distinct from the anthropocentric argument is the third ratio-nale for the rejection of lycanthropy: physical lycanthropy is theologically sus-pect because it threatens the fixity of the species. Christian theologians were certainly not unfamiliar with the notion of a fluid boundary between humans and animals. The European context for much of the formative Western theological tradition is littered with allusion to and acceptance of a more porous boundary between species. However, theologians tended to fundamentally reject this porosity. To accept this porous boundary, and thus the possibility of transfor-mation from human form into animal form, is problematic because it sug-gests that the created order can shift seamlessly from God's original intent. Human transformation would not only challenge the image of God in human-ity, but it would also disrupt the hierarchical structure of creation. A human, created in the image of God, should not be able to switch to animal form because it subjects humans to the status of animals as subject to animals—humans cannot exist in this ambiguous, liminal state in which they both have authority over animals and are subjugated by humans.[13]

The theological response is perfectly intelligible in its rejection of physi-cal transformation; however, most of the writers discussing this responded actively to accounts of lycanthropy around them. How, then, does this skepti-cal view of lycanthropy explain the experiences relayed by people who claimed to actually take lupine form? The explanation lay in broad contours of what may be called the diabolical model of lycanthropy.

The Diabolical Model

The diabolical model of lycanthropy ultimately explains lycanthropy with reference to the actual capacity of demonic power. True physical transforma-tion is only possible through God's creative power. However, while demons and the Devil are unable to physically shape or mold matter, they are able to impact the human senses and delude human perception of events to perceive a greater capacity of demonic power than is actually possible. Demonic power, at its core, is not actual power but consists of varieties of tricks and illusions. For instance, fifteenth-century demonologist Johannes Nider ex-plains away the account in Exodus, in which Pharaoh's sorcerers seem to create snakes out of nothing, with reference to the delusory power of de-mons. Demons only create animals with "God permitting," and even then cannot make perfect animals, but imperfect animals. When Pharaoh's sorcer-ers seem to create snakes, it is actually demons traveling around the world quickly, compiling seeds (*diversa semina*) into new species in a deceitful attempt to display the same creative powers as God.[14] In the same way, demons cannot actually transform people from their human form into animal form, but they can only delude human senses. In attempting to demonstrate creative power in lycanthropy, demons only offer what Augustine refers to as a "great mockery perpetrated by the demons."[15]

Once we acknowledge that demonic power, which in the skeptical mind-set is the primary source of lycanthropic experiences, we must answer exactly how these delusory experiences happen. The skeptical response provides two broad categories of response to lycanthropy—those who acknowledge lycanthropy as delusion, and those who view diabolical intervention less in delusion and more in naturalistic features in the world.

The first category in the diabolical model argues that lycanthropy is a delusory experience. God grants power to spirits, demons, and the Devil, but the power is limited to powers which are utilized deceitfully. Demons cannot physically transform a human into animal form, but they can cause the human to perceive that they transform into a wolf by deluding the senses. Regarding the notion of transformation, Augustine specifies that demons lack the capacity to create real substances but can only change their appearances; thus, Augustine explains that rather than an actual transformation, "a man has a phantom which, in his thoughts or dreams, assumes various forms through the influence of circumstances or innumerable kinds . . . with wondrous speed, it takes on shapes which are like material bodies, and it is this phantom, I believe, that can . . . be presented in bodily form to the senses of others, when their physical senses are asleep or suppressed." The body of the man is still alive but asleep with senses "suspended in a torpor far deeper and heavier than that of normal sleep," while the phantom "may appear to the senses of others as being embodied in the likeness of some animal." To Augustine, the burdens are thus borne by demons, while men are deceived into believing that they bear the burdens themselves.[16]

This explanation is echoed by seminal demonological and theological texts of medieval Christianity. The German Catholic clergy Heinrich Krämer, in his 1486 treatise the *Malleus Maleficarum*, provides an in-depth defense of the existence of witches, during which he discusses the issue of bodily transformation. In a section entitled, "Can witches use the art of trickery and deception to change people into animal shape?" Krämer responds that witches cannot affect such a change because the animal does not exist in reality; thus, there is nothing for the senses to apprehend. The way the deception works, then, is that typically, the "visible shapes of animals" flow "because of the operation of evil spirits, to the organs of interior senses . . . [which] is what happens in a dream." When wolves "snatch adults and children out of their houses and eat them; and they run all over the place with great cunning, and cannot be hurt or captured by any skill," Krämer responds that while it is possible that they are merely an illusion, it is also possible that they are simply real wolves that are possessed by evil spirits, or that "they are roused to action . . . without workers of harmful magic doing anything," or as "an illusion created by workers of harmful magic."[17] These workers of harmful magic may also delude people into seeing witches in the guise of animals. He references an account by Gervase of Tilbury in which a laborer one day was chopping wood when he had to forcefully repel off three large cats who were "biting and ripping the clothes between his legs." Later, however, the man is arrested for "inflic[ting] wounds on three highly respectable women of this city, with the result that they are lying in their beds, unable to get up or move." The man gave his account of what had occurred, and everybody realized that what had happened was the work of an evil spirit, in which three witches attacked him while an evil spirit created the illusion that the women had transformed into cats and "obliged to attack the laborer."[18]

The arguments of the *Malleus* are echoed elsewhere by other fifteenth- and sixteenth-century demonologists, including Johannes Nider. In his magnum opus *Preceptorium Divine Legis*, Nider answers the question "Whether by the work of demons transformations can be made of people into beasts and wolves." Nider's answer is that demons only delude human senses, but those natural transformations within creation can be achieved using demonic operations using the same materials.[19] The eminent preacher Geiler von Keyserberg's later use of Nider in his sermons in 1507 *Die Emeis* show a similar response. Particularly in his sermon on "On the Unholden, or the Witches." Geiler answers whether witches can "transform men into wolves, pigs, or birds?" writing that "You must not believe that any man can be transformed into a wolf or a pig, that this is merely a ghost, or an appearance deceiving the eyes or created in the imagination." Werewolves are not people at their heart, but are actual wolves "which eat women and children," and filled with a lust for human flesh by any number of natural and supernatural factors.[20] Moreover, Christian judges utilized these arguments in understanding cases of lycanthropy. By the early seventeenth century, French judge Henri Boguet argued that a physical lycanthropic transformation would be impossible, as it would require the Devil to perform a miracle in the witch who had made a pact with the Devil; however, he could make witches believe that they had transformed into werewolves and still incite them to cause damage and kill, and they deserved to be executed for their intentions.[21] Protestant theologians such as Lutheran Jakob Heerbrand argued similar points. He wrote in *De Magia Disputatio* that while Satan is powerful, he cannot "transform people and their limbs and appearances into other ones, such as animals or werewolves . . . for he absolutely cannot create anything from nothing, which is the property of God alone."[22]

The second category argues that lycanthropy is potentially demonic, but with more immediate natural causes. Rather than suppose immediately that it must be demonic interference as explained with delusions, this line of thought suggests first that the cause of lycanthropy is medical rather than spiritual. One major thinker to embrace this perspective is Reginald Scot. As one of England's first demonologists, Scot rebukes the ideas of Heinrich Krämer and French demonologist Jean Bodin. He writes that God has given humans and animals different natures and substances, and that "therefore it is absolutelie against the ordinance of God (who hath made me a man) that I should flie like a bird, or swim like a fish, or creepe like a worme, or become an asse in shape . . . what a beastlie assertion is it, that a man, whom GOD hath made according to his owne similitude and likenes, should be by a witch turned into a beast?" So, Scot rejects the notion of a physical transformation not only as absurd but also as insulting to God's honor. His ultimate conclusion is that the transformation of lycanthropy "is (as all the learned sort of physicians affirme) a disease proceeding partlie from melancholie, whereby manie suppose themselves to be wolves, or such ravening beasts. For *Lycanthropia* is of the ancient physicians called *Lupina melancholia* or *Lupina insania.*"[23]

Protestant physician and demonologist Johann Weyer goes into considerably more depth on the issue than did Scot. His response in *De Praestigiis Daemonum* to the "Imaginary transformation of men into beasts"[24] finds the idea that people could transform into wolves to be a silly proposition. Rather, he thinks that there are far more reasonable explanations for the stories of lycanthropy arising throughout Western Europe and Scandinavia. He writes,

> If Livonia and the neighboring regions seem to have some dangerous wolves roaming about—which the people suppose to be *Lamiae*, and which are called werewolves by the Germans—these are almost certainly real wolves, stirred up for this tragic performance by a demon, who meanwhile imbues and impairs the organs of imagination of the raving "wolf-men" with the random wanderings and actions of these real wolves, so that consequently, because of their corrupted imaginations, they think and admit that they are the ones who perform these wandering excursions and activities. And from a description of the disease involved, lycanthropy, anyone can see that this task is not difficult for the Devil when he sets in motion the humors and spirits suitable for these illusions, especially in the case of persons whose brains are oft impaired by mists of black bile.[25]

So Weyer's viewpoint of lycanthropy as a disease explicitly discounts the possibility of actual transformation, attributing beliefs of transformation to the Devil, who works to set the natural processes and humors of the body into motion. Meanwhile, wolves may be stirred up to cause chaos and death, while "those who believe themselves transformed into wolves are found lying somewhere immersed in deep sleep by the efforts of the devil."[26]

Thus, the skeptical response argues that within an orthodox Christian framework, there is no acceptable way to understand lycanthropy as an actual physical transformation of the human into lupine form. But is there any orthodox way to understand lycanthropy as an actual physical transformation? For this, we turn to the second response and model—that of critical acceptance and the benevolent werewolf model.

Critical Acceptance and the Benevolent Model

The response of critical acceptance to lycanthropy first and foremost is not a rejection of the logic of the skeptical response. Critical acceptance accepts the reasoning that lycanthropy from a demonic standpoint is unacceptable, because it challenges God's sovereignty and creative power as well as attacks humanity's unique status in God's created order. However, the response of critical acceptance attempts to answer whether there might be a way in which physical transformation may still happen with the permission of God, and perhaps to God's greater glory.

The most prominent use of critical acceptance is one that argues for the possibility of actual physical transformation by God's actual power and sovereignty. This response accepts the initial premises of the skeptical response and seeks to operate within those parameters. Certainly, transformation may only occur within the purview of God's sovereignty, and it must not go so far as to demean or remove the image of God from humanity. However, if one understands the image of God not to apply to the physical human form, and only to apply to the human capacity for reason and interaction with God, then the state of human physical form is irrelevant, and transformation may be possible. So long as a lycanthropic transformation does not remove the image of God from the human, lycanthropy is both possible and acceptable within a Christian framework.

The most important example of a figure arguing for this physical transformation within a Christian framework comes from the twelfth-century British writer Gerald of Wales. In his *Topographia Hibernica*, an account of the landscape and people of Ireland, Gerald affirms the ecclesiastical line on transformation from demons as a delusion. However, he argues through his stories that God does permit people to change their outward appearance while retaining their essential human nature in a way that is not contrary to patristic teachings. One tale specifically links the transformation of lycanthropy with the Eucharist. Gerald describes a tale in which "a priest, who was journeying from Ulster . . . was benighted in a certain wood on the borders of Meath . . . lo! A wolf came up to them, and immediately addressed them." The wolf, warning the priest not to fear, informed him that he and his wife had been cursed "every seven years to put off the human form and . . . assume that of wolves." However, the wolf's wife is "at the point of death," and the wolf implores the priest to "give her the consolations of your priestly office." The priest, terrified by the human noises made by these wolves, refuses by lying, claiming to not have the viaticum on his person; in response, the first wolf pointed out where he saw the priest's viaticum and "intreated him not to deny them the gift of God . . . and, to remove all doubt, using his claw for a hand, he tore off the skin of the she-wolf . . . thus, she immediately presented the form of an old woman."[27] Gerald's description reflects not only a Christian perspective on transformation, that Christian metamorphosis changes the exterior to reveal animalistic characteristics of the human without changing the human's essence.[28]

This experience also reflects that across medieval Christian Europe, popular culture maintained records and tales of experiences with animals that ventured beyond or built upon the traditional dogma on transformation as delusory while simultaneously seeking to adapt to be dogmatically acceptable. Without rejecting the theological or canonical heritage that rejects physical transformation, Gerald of Wales affirms his account, claiming "It is, however, believed as an undoubted truth, that the Almighty God . . . when he pleases, [can] change one into another, either for vindicating his judgments, or exhibiting his divine power."[29] [30] When popular accounts meet institutional teachings, a compromise position emerges that affirms the possibility of bodily transformation without compromising the reason that makes one human.[31]

Elsewhere other accounts of benevolent lycanthropy and sympathetic werewolves emerge, embracing a more natural source of lycanthropy that offers moral lessons to humanity. The tenth-century *lais* of Marie de France reflect a desire to consider lycanthropy from a more sympathetic perspective. The *Lay of Bisclavret*, for instance, opens by defining a werewolf as "a ferocious beast which, when possessed by this madness, devours men, causes great damage and dwells in vast forest," but immediately follows it by saying, "I leave such matters for the moment, for I wish to tell you about Bisclavret."[32] Marie de France then describes the tale of a knight who is able to transform monthly into a wolf by removing his clothing. His wife follows him and steals his clothing, however, stranding him in his lupine form. However, despite his form, he is able to rejoin the king's court as a quasi-pet. Years later, however, Bisclavret sees his wife at the king's court and "tore the nose right off her face." Bisclavret's reaction reveals to the king his true identity, and the *lai* ends with his restoration to his place in the king's court and the banishment of the woman and her new husband, with many of their children retaining the wife's noseless appearance as a marker of her betrayal.[33] While the primary message of the story is misogynistic and seeks to emphasize the monstrosity of women, the secondary message one can glean is an appreciation that transformation into animal form can reside alongside the retention of human characteristics, and that restoration to human form is possible. Amid the metamorphosis, something from the human endures, indicating a stability of self and a fixity of reason alongside beastly appearance.[34]

Finally, while critical acceptance generally trends toward a benevolent model of werewolf, a select few theologians accept the possibility of both actual physical transformation and demonic intervention. This idea is embraced by Jean Bodin around 1580. Bodin, a French lawyer and demonologist of the sixteenth century, interpreted ecclesiastical tradition, specifically the *canon Episcopi*, as referring to human reason; certainly the Devil or spirits could transform the exterior part of man to resemble a wolf, but they could not transform or remove human reason when they did so.[35] In this way, Bodin situates lycanthropy in a "vision of the whole," wherein God as the first eternal cause can still grant power to one of His creatures at the second level of causation.[36] Moreover, Bodin's werewolf was no longer a product of the mind, but a real human who had used magic to turn into "fearful and threatening wild animals." Bodin's view of the werewolf was of a devouring, destructive creature—a "diabolical, demonized being," and a metaphor for the Devil.[37] In this case, God is the primary source of the transformation and maintains the image of God in the lycanthrope, but permits it not for Christian werewolves, but as part of the overall scheme in which demons seek to challenge the boundaries between species to promote disorder and deviance.

The arguments of somebody like Bodin complicate the picture of two primary responses and models of lycanthropy. Ultimately, though, the crux of these various interpretations of lycanthropy rests in a desire to situate any understanding of the natural world in God's sovereignty, power, and design. Christian responses to lycanthropy have typically been careful to affirm that whatever the motivation for lycanthropy (diabolical or benevolent), it can only happen within God's sovereign power and plan. Moreover, the explanations and accounts offered above clearly shape the framework in which modern popular culture understands and situates lycanthropy narratives. We turn now to consider two examples of these models of lycanthropy played out in popular culture.

LYCANTHROPY MODELED IN POPULAR CULTURE

Modern popular depictions of lycanthropy are abundant. However, the modern landscape is such that lycanthropy accounts no longer serve as a broader explanation for local events. The accounts described so far emerged in an era grappling with the actual threat of wolf attacks in local villages, as well as a broader fluidity in considering the human body. For the modern moment, however, the express cause of lycanthropy in most popular accounts and depictions is less likely to be a demonic deal than the transmission of lycanthropy as a disease—not from humoral theory, but from transmission via bite. And while the Enlightenment heritage of the West may have challenged the separation between humans and animals in ways veering toward more naturalism, they still tend to place humans on a pedestal as separated from animals by their capacity for reason. Despite the shift from overt diabolical narratives to more naturalistic ones, we still clearly experience the ways in which the Christian theological heritage and the heritage of Enlightenment inflect popular narratives, both in expressions of the diabolical and benevolent models.

David Kessler in *An American Werewolf in London*

The 1981 film *An American Werewolf in London* tells the story of an American traveler who, while on holiday with a friend in Britain, is attacked by a werewolf, hospitalized, and ultimately transforms into a werewolf at the full moon, causing violence and mayhem on the streets of London. Upon its release, it was revered as a cult classic, primarily regarded for its dark humor and its groundbreaking makeup effects, for which it received an Academy Award.[38] Often lost in the excitement over its pioneering makeup effects, however, is its actual engagement with the lore of lycanthropy.

It appears evident that the intent of the film is to depict a diabolical form of lycanthropy. In the process, it participates in a broader trend of Anglo-American werewolf films adopting medieval and early modern structures of lycanthropy as Satanic evil.[39] Several key signs point to the involvement of darker, diabolical forces prompting the lycanthropic episodes. The first sign we receive relates to the nature of those encountering the werewolves. David and his friend Jack both participate in several activities that demonstrate their penchant for vice throughout the films. As David and his friend Jack are hitchhiking across the Yorkshire moors, their conversation points to their general openness to various activities that, from the typical framework of the horror film genre, indicate that they are primary targets as victims for the source of evil. The casual conversation between David and Jack revolves around a desire to engage in sexual relationship, as Jack indicates his desire to seduce a woman—Debbie—when they arrive later during the summer in Rome. Later in the film, David himself actually is seduced into a fairly inappropriate sexual relationship with the nurse Alex, staying in her home and having sex with her several times upon his release from the hospital. These indications suggest that Jack and David are targets for a werewolf attack as a diabolical attack.

Elsewhere, there are very clear signs throughout the movie that the attacks in question are intended as diabolical forces. Prior to the initial werewolf attack, Jack and David enter The Slaughtered Lamb, an inn with a sign of a disembodied wolf's head attacking a lamb. The townspeople inside seem remarkably averse to conversation with outsiders, as well as unwilling to explain the ambience of the inn, as Jack and David both note the connotations of a pentagram painted on the wall, and David remarks to Jack, "It's used in witchcraft . . . as a mark of the wolf man . . . you should ask if they're using candles to ward off monsters." Upon their departure from the inn, we hear the innkeeper remark that the whole situation is "in God's hands now."

All of this points to diabolical forces at work, but none of it is particularly unique to *An American Werewolf in London*, as such tropes are common elsewhere in the realm of popular horror culture. The most important factors that can be interpreted through the diabolical model concern his actual lycanthropic experiences. At the moment of the attack, the werewolf attacks and kills Jack and attacks David; however, before the wolf can kill David, townspeople from the inn shoot and kill him. Remarkably, we see a naked man on the ground with several gunshot wounds, but no fur, claws, or any indication that this man had been transformed into a wolf. While the lycanthropic transformation is a crucial aspect of the film,[40] we never see any actual transformation from lupine form into human form. When David wakes up after the first night of transformation in London, he is naked in the wolf enclosure at the London Zoo, but in human form, without any fur or evidence of his transformation. When both the first werewolf at the beginning of the film and David at the end of the film are shot and killed, we see no evidence that they ever physically transformed into a wolf—we simply encounter their human torsos, free of fur and shot, but clearly human, almost as if an illusion of lupine form had been dispelled upon their deaths. To suppose that because we saw a physical wolf means that there necessarily was a physical transformation ignores the indications throughout the film that demonic forces are at play in the film, and are doing as demons frequently do throughout Christian demonology—causing havoc and mayhem among humans to sow the belief that there are actual werewolves in existence.[41] After all, there is no evidence of a wolf at the end of the film. We have two humans who have been killed, and in response to David's insistence that he had been attacked by a wolf, the doctor remarks that a "madman has the strength of ten," and in response to the notion that only an animal could physically commit that violence, the doctor remarks that "you'd be surprised at what a human is capable of."

The transformation sequences and lack of visual transformation back into human form is only one part of the picture, however. David's visions and encounters with Jack's ghost are even more suggestive. After the initial attack, David wakes up three weeks later in the hospital in London. During this time, we see David apparently dreaming that he is walking through the countryside. Throughout his hospital stay, he continues to experience such visions, including one in which he runs naked through the woods, attacks a deer, and eats it. Notably, following the visions where he attacks and eats an animal, he lacks an appetite when he wakes up in person, prompting Nurse Alex to force-feed him. Later, when David encounters the ghost of Jack, Jack urges him to avoid his impending transformation by committing suicide. At the first vision, Jack is decomposing but still mostly in human form; as the visions progress, however, he continues to decompose and more forcefully urges David to kill himself because the "wolf's bloodline must be severed." Such visions may very well be indicated as actually Jack; however, from a Christian theological standpoint, there are few reasons to believe that a human spirit will wander the earth following death. It is more likely that this is a malevolent spirit causing damage through the guise of a lycanthropic episode.

To be clear, the damage that David wreaks on London in the last werewolf rampage sequence is substantial and not a delusion. He attacks people in a movie theater, decapitates the inspector from Scotland Yard investigating the case, and causes several traffic crashes. However, everything described from his lycanthropic episode would be just as in place in a recounted episode from the *Malleus* or Johann Weyer. An experience *á la* Weyer is even likelier in some respects; the transmission of lycanthropy, while apparently delusory, does not occur through some demonic deal gone awry, but through a natural transmission (in this case, spread through a bite). The dream episodes may indicate a spirit stirring up actual wolves in Yorkshire or the transportation of David with the spirit to commit actual violence. The transformation sequences only display a graphic transformation from human to wolf, while the transformation back is almost instantaneous. The Christian skeptical response to *American Werewolf* in London indicates the likelihood of diabolical interference with a delusory experience of lycanthropy.

Remus Lupin in *Harry Potter*

While the dominant narrative surrounding lycanthropy in popular culture revolves around sinister forces, the last few decades have exhibited a surge in positive portrayals of lycanthropy. Whether in the case of Oz in the late 1990s *Buffy the Vampire Slayer* or Jacob in the *Twilight* series of the 2000s, more recent portrayals of lycanthropy or shapeshifting, while not rejecting the horror of such a transformation, do embrace a more positive vision of characters as werewolves. Perhaps the most significant character in this regard, and whom we might attempt to read through the benevolent model, is Remus Lupin from the Harry Potter series.[42]

Remus Lupin is introduced in the third book of the Harry Potter series, *Harry Potter and the Prisoner of Azkaban*. While Harry is under the impending threat of an escaped criminal attacking him, he returns to Hogwarts School for the year. Because of Sirius Black's escape from Azkaban Prison, dementors from Azkaban (creatures which feed on the misery and despair of humans) are employed to guard the school grounds. However, these creatures have a disproportionate impact on Harry, causing him to faint; when we first meet Remus Lupin, he fends off the dementors to protect Harry and his friends. We learn that Lupin has been hired to be a professor at Hogwarts, and he is far and away the best professor that Harry experiences in his time as a student. [43] Despite his lycanthropy, which is only overtly revealed late in the novel, Lupin is not only capable, but warm, approachable, and generally good-natured.

Lupin is consistently portrayed in the course of the series as unambiguously good. The first act that Lupin commits in the novel, apart from fending off the dementors, is a healing action. After suffering the effects of the dementor, Harry feels weak; Lupin gives him chocolate to eat to revitalize him, and "to his great surprise [Harry] felt warmth spread suddenly to his fingers and toes." [44] Elsewhere, we see Lupin's capability not only to teach effectively, but to teach with the capacity to emotionally strengthen and fortify his students. Not only does he teach them how to defeat the boggart (a creature which manifests as the deepest fears of the victim), but he also does his best to encourage his students personally. As Harry continues to struggle with the dementors, Lupin offers to teach Harry the Patronus Charm, a means of providing a protector between the victim and the dementor, and eventually defeating the dementor. [45] We consistently see Lupin act in ways contrary to what we would expect from a werewolf—he is competent as an instructor, kind to others, and consistently seeking the best not only for Harry but for his students in general. Moreover, we eventually learn that Lupin had been very close friends with Harry's parents during his own time as a Hogwarts student.

What should we make of his lycanthropy then? Can we read his benevolence in the broader model of the benevolent werewolf? The model offered by J. K. Rowling certainly appears to be in this model. The first factor that makes this the most plausible reading is that Lupin's transformations are very affirmatively physical, and not delusional. Lupin describes that he became a werewolf through a bite as a young child which causes him to transform at the full moon. Lupin's own description of his werewolf transformations indicates the physicality of it. He writes that his transformations as a youth "were terrible," and that "it is very painful to turn into a werewolf. I was separated from humans to bite, so I bit and scratched myself instead." [46] Similarly, when he transforms shortly later, Rowling gives a very physical description, in which "Harry could see Lupin's silhouette. He had gone rigid. Then his limbs began to shake . . . Lupin's head was lengthening. So was his body. His shoulders were hunching. Hair was sprouting visibly onto his face and hands, which were curling into clawed paws." [47] The description of his transformation is not dissimilar from the image we see in *An American Werewolf in London*; however, in the case of Lupin, we hear directly from Lupin about the nature of his transformations and his state both during and after his transformations.

This leads us to the next, most important factor in interpreting his lycanthropy—the ability to retain his human mind when he transforms. Lupin describes that when he first came to Hogwarts, his transformations were terrible. However, when his friends discovered his secret, they secretly became Animagi, or wizards who can transform into an animal. Lupin describes that "A werewolf is only a danger to people," so James Potter, Sirius Black, and Peter Pettigrew would spend time with him during his transformations as animals. Lupin says that "under their influence, I became less dangerous. My body was still wolfish, but my mind seemed to become less so while I was with them."[48] When he returned to Hogwarts to become an instructor, he began using the Wolfsbane Potion, made by the potions instructor, which he says "makes me safe. . . . As long as I take it in the week preceding the full moon, I keep my mind when I transform . . . I am able to curl up in my office, a harmless wolf, and wait for the moon to wane again."[49] In part, then, we might understand the benevolent model of lycanthropy as displayed by Remus Lupin as benevolent precisely because the benevolent werewolf is able to dwell in the liminal space between human and animal—exhibiting animalistic characteristics while retaining the capacity for reason.

This physical transformation sounds theoretically similar to the diabolical transformation in that it seems a horrifying event. Lupin himself says that before the Wolfsbane Potion, "I became a fully fledged monster once a month."[50] However, the insertion of these taming elements indicate that at their core, these transformations are very different and fit within the benevolent model. Whether through interaction with others during the stage or through a potion, Lupin retains the ability to maintain his human mind during his transformations. His actual transformations are horrifying, but in the context of the Harry Potter series, Lupin and others work to ensure that his transformations only affect his bodily matter and not the image of God in him, his innate capacity for reason. Moreover, in the context of the series, the fact that it is possible for people to become Animagi indicates a clear division between physical transformation and mental transformation. Those who successfully become Animagi transform their human bodies but retain their human minds. Beyond that, it is easy to read Lupin's lycanthropy in the Harry Potter universe as not merely a facet of his personality, but as a greater piece of a broader message about society. Werewolves in the Harry Potter universe are ostracized and misunderstood because of their affliction—because of their capacity for such violence and perceived lack of means to control their affliction, they are marginalized by wizarding society and stigmatized as less than human, even when the vast majority of the time they exist as humans.[51]

Clearly, then, it is very simple to read Lupin within the critical acceptance response. He clearly retains the image of God, his rational intellect, during the course of his transformations, and creates a very clear delineation between his human mind and his animal body. In the same way, Gerald of Wales insists that God can prompt these transformations for his own power. Lupin may not be a "hound of God," but he clearly retains benevolent qualities that remain within him despite his lycanthropy and bolster the argument that he fits in the sympathetic werewolf response.

CONCLUSION

The modern preoccupation with werewolves ultimately seems to carry great significance for the Christian theologian. As long as werewolves and the idea of shapeshifting permeate popular culture, theological engagement with these ideas are important. While the notion of lycanthropy is understandably rejected by modern culture, engagement with and understanding of lycanthropy narratives is important for various reasons. Christian theological engagement first helps to translate popular depictions in intelligible terms. To be able to understand popular culture in theologically intelligible ways is useful for helping navigate popular portrayals.

More importantly, untangling the theological foundations of the idea of lycanthropy illuminates not only the ways in which theology undergirds and permeates our modern era but it also reminds us of the numerous ways in which we ourselves limit the possibilities of theology in contemporary life. While lycanthropy may or may not have been an actual, physical transformation in Christian life and culture, the narratives of lycanthropy ultimately illuminate to the reader the vast possibilities available within the purview of God's sovereignty and power. Understanding elements of popular horror narratives theologically underscores the myriad ways in which spiritual forces, both benevolent and diabolical, operate within the world.

Thus, as we consider lycanthropy narratives, we do not merely understand the ways in which Christians across time have articulated their experience of spiritual forces. We come to situate ourselves within a world that is intensely theological, spiritual, and with tangible stakes and possibilities. These possibilities clarify the ways in which even horror narratives such as lycanthropy underscore the potential within God's world. Whether that potential leads to "hounds of God" or "raving wolf-men," I leave to the reader.

NOTES

1. Blecourt, "A Journey to Hell," 49–51; Donecker, "Werewolves of Livonia," 289–90.
2. Gibson, *Legends, Monsters, or Serial Killers*, 7.
3. Schulte, "She-Wolves," in Priest, ed., *She-Wolf*, 39.
4. One has only to look to the abundance of depictions of the supernatural in popular culture, ranging from the long-running series *Supernatural* to pop-culture phenomena *Harry Potter* and *Twilight*.
5. Often as the only major records of such trials, pamphlets and broadsheets were both problematic and crucial in forming the public perception of these trials. One particularly notable pamphlet told the story of Peter Stubbe, who admitted to being a werewolf and having committed numerous violent and deviant crimes, including murder and cannibalism; the pamphlet recounts the confession of his murder of animals, women, and at least fourteen

children as a werewolf, as well as the gory details of his execution, where he was executed on the wheel, had his skin torn apart with hot pincers, had his limbs broken, was beheaded, burned, and had his head placed with a wolf's skin on a pike at the site. See "A True Discourse Declaring the Damnable Life and Death of One Stubbe Peter, a Most Wicked Sorcerer, Who in the Likeness of a Wolf Committed Many Murders, Continuing This Devilish Practise 25 Years, Killing and Devouring Men, Women, and Children Who for the Same Fact was Taken and Executed the 31st of October Last Past in the Town of Bedburg Near the City of Collin in Germany," in Van Otten, *A Lycanthropy Reader*, 69. See also Gibson, *Legends, Monsters, or Serial Murderers*, 58–61.

6. Steiger, *Werewolf Book Beings*.

7. Genesis 3:1–24 (NRSV).

8. Augustine, *City of God*, 841–42.

9. "Canons of the Council of Ancyra," translated by Henry Percival, from *Nicene and Post-Nicene Fathers, Second Series*, Vol. 14, edited by Philip Schaff and Henry Wace. Gratian in the *Decretum* attributes the canon *Episcopi* to the Council of Ancyra. See Gratian, *Decretum Magistri Gratiani*, in Freidberg, ed., *Corpus Iuris Canonici*, C. 26 Q. 5 c. 12, columns 1030–31.

10. Genesis 1:26–28 (NRSV).

11. Thomas, *Man and the Natural World*, 36–41.

12. Guichet and Nicholson-Smith, "From the Animal of the Enlightenment," 72–74.

13. Thomas, *Man and the Natural World*, 36–41.

14. *Preceptorium divine legis venerabilis fratris Johannis Nider de ordine predicatorum* (Basle: Berthold Ruppel, c. 1470), image 67, Precept 1, Ch. 11, Q. 7. http://eeb.chadwyck.co.uk.ezproxy.cul.columbia.edu/search/displayItemFromId.do?ItemID=fra-bnf-rlr-00001231-001&DurUrl=Yes.

15. Augustine of Hippo, *The City of God*, 841.

16. Ibid., 843–44.

17. Krämer, *Malleus Maleficarum*, 88–90.

18. Ibid., 156–58.

19. *Preceptorium divine legis,* image 67, Precept 1, Ch. 11, Q. 7–8. http://eeb.chadwyck.co.uk.ezproxy.cul.columbia.edu/search/displayItemFromId.do?ItemID=fra-bnf-rlr-00001231-001&DurUrl=Yes.

20. Geiler von Kaysersberg, *Die Emeis*, in Hansen, *Quellen und Untersuchungen*, 284. Kaysersberg clearly borrows from Nider; even the name of Kaysersberg's compilation of sermons, *Die Emeis*, translates roughly to the same name as Nider's treatise *Formicarius*—the Ant Hill or Ant Colony. Ibid. See also selections in Kors and Peters, eds., *Witchcraft in Europe*, 237; Gould, *The Book of Werewolves*, 263–64; Van Otten, 104–5.

21. Boguet, *Discours de Sorciers*, (1602), 110–11, 118–19.

22. Heerbrand, from *De Magia Disputatio*, 10.

23. Scot, *The Discoverie of Witchcraft*, 118–25.

24. Weyer, *Witches, Devils, and Doctors*, 192.

25. Ibid., 193.

26. Ibid.

27. Gerald of Wales, *Giraldus Cambrensis*, 79–81.

28. Salisbury, *The Beast Within*, 143–44.

29. Gerald of Wales, *Giraldus of Cambrensis*, 84.

30. Raudvere, "Trolldómr," in Jolly et al., eds., *Witchcraft and Magic in Europe: The Middle Ages*, 102–3. While theologians and demonologists tend to focus on issues in the Holy Roman Empire or Britain, the Scandinavian heritage of shapeshifting accounts becomes significant in the development of lycanthropy trials in Europe by the late sixteenth century, as many of the known trials occur in Swedish Livonia. See also Blecourt, "The Werewolf, the Witch, and the Warlock," in Rowlands, ed., *Witchcraft and Masculinities*, 196; Dillinger, "Species, Phantasia, Raison," 149; and Metsvahi, "Estonian Werewolf History," Blecourt, ed., in *Werewolf Histories*, 205–8.

31. Similar tension resides around other popular beliefs and institutional response or repression, such as with popular belief in fairies and changelings in the British Isles. Richard Green overstates his case regarding the repressive Middle Ages (or, as he unfortunately uses, the

"Dark Ages," but he does aptly point out that local superstition in thirteenth-century Britain was opposed and mocked in pastoral literature, but without much discipline to repress such beliefs. See Green, *Elf Queens*, 48.

32. France, *"Bisclavret,"* in *The Lais of Marie de France*, 68.

33. Ibid., 71–72.

34. Salisbury, *The Beast Within*, 145. See also Bynum, *Metamorphosis and Identity*, 29.

35. Dillinger, "Species, Phantasia, Raison: Werewolves and Shape-shifters in Demonological Literature," in Blecourt, ed., *Werewolf Histories*, 60.

36. Bodin, *On the Demon-Mania of Witches*, 122–28. See also Jacques-Lefevre, "Such an Impure, Cruel, and Savage Beast," in Edwards, ed., *Werewolves, Witches, and Wandering Spirits*, 186.

37. Schulte, *Man as Witch*, 21–23.

38. Steiger, *Werewolf Book*, 10.

39. Walter, *Our Old Monsters*, 185–86.

40. David Naughton, the actor portraying David Kessler, underwent a rigorous training regimen to prepare himself for his nude transformation scenes from man into wolf, and the visceral nature of the transformation sequence allows the viewer to participate in the graphic, painful, horrifying transformation from human to wolf. See Steiger, *Werewolf Book*, 10–12.

41. Cameron, *Enchanted Europe*, 42–49.

42. There is much to glean from the entire Harry Potter series as a whole regarding the interaction of Christian theology with popular culture; however, for simplicity of focus on the lycanthropy element, I will only deal with *Harry Potter and the Prisoner of Azkaban*, as it offers more substantive engagement with lycanthropy than the rest of the series.

43. An analysis of Lupin's pedagogical practices concludes that we see effective implementation of practical education, along with the use of Socratic instruction to encourage not only dialogue, but also a democratic spirit of inclusion among his students. His pedagogy stands in marked comparison to his peers at Hogwarts, who range from incompetent and dangerous (Hagrid) to cruel (Severus Snape). See M'Balia, Russell, and Warren, "Pedagogy in Harry Potter," 186–92.

44. Rowling, *Harry Potter and the Prisoner of Azkaban*, 86. While the roles are certainly reversed, we might see a parallel here to Gerald of Wales's account, where the werewolf seeks the viaticum from a priest for spiritual edification. In this case, though, Lupin's act of giving chocolate provides a sort of spiritual and physical healing to Harry.

45. Ibid., 257.

46. Ibid., 353.

47. Ibid., 380.

48. Ibid., 354–55.

49. Ibid., 352–53.

50. Ibid., 353.

51. Trosclair, "Fantastic Beasts or Beings, and Why Define Them?" 99–107.

WORKS CITED

Alkemeyer, Bryan. "Circe Stories: Transformation, Animals, and Natural History 1550–1750." PhD Dissertation. Cornell University, 2012.

Almond, Philip. *England's First Demonologist: Reginald Scot and 'The Discoverie of Witchcraft.'* London: I.B. Tauris, 2011.

Ankarloo, Benkt, Stuart Clark, and William Monter. *Witchcraft and Magic in Europe: The Period of the Witch Trials*. Philadelphia: University of Pennsylvania Press, 2002.

Apps, Lara, and Andrew Gow. *Male Witches in Early Modern Europe*. Manchester: Manchester University Press, 2003.

Augustine of Hippo. *The City of God against the Pagans*. Edited and translated by R. W. Dyson. Cambridge: Cambridge University Press, 1998.

———. *De Doctrina Christiana*. Edited and translated by R. P. H. Green. Oxford: Oxford University Press, 1995.

————. *On Eighty-Three Diverse Questions*. In *Witchcraft in Europe, 400–1700: A Documentary History*, 2nd ed., edited by Alan Kors and Edward Peters. Philadelphia: University of Pennsylvania Press, 2001, 43.

Bauer, Gillian Nelson. "The Werewolf's Closet: Clothing as Prosthesis in Marie de France's Bisclavret." In *The Treatment of Disabled Persons in Medieval Europe*, edited by Wendy Turner and Tory Pearman. Lewiston: Mellen, 2011.

Blécourt, Willem de. "A Journey to Hell: Reconsidering the Livonian Werewolf." *Magic, Ritual, and Witchcraft* 2, no. 1 (Summer 2007): 49–67.

————., ed. *Werewolf Histories*. New York: Palgrave Macmillan, 2015.

Bodin, Jean. *On the Demon-Mania of Witches*. Translated by R. Scott. Toronto: Centre for Reformation and Renaissance Studies, 2001.

————. *De la démonomanie des sorciers*. Paris: Jacques du Puys, 1580.

Boguet, Henri. *Discours de Sorciers*. 1602.

Broedel, Hans Peter. *The Malleus Maleficarum and the Construction of Witchcraft: Theology and Popular Belief*. Manchester: Manchester University Press, 2003.

Bynum, Caroline Walker. *Metamorphosis and Identity*. New York: Zone Books, 2001.

Cameron, Euan. *Enchanted Europe: Superstition, Reason, and Religion, 1250–1750*. Oxford: Oxford University Press, 2010.

Canon Episcopi. Translated by Henry C. Lea. *Materials Toward a History of Witchcraft*. Philadelphia: University of Pennsylvania Press, 1939.

Chaney, Jayne. "Our Animal Kindred: Affinitive Anthropomorphism in Medieval and Early Modern Literature." PhD Dissertation. Lexington: University of Kentucky, 2013.

Clark, Stuart. *Thinking with Demons: The Idea of Witchcraft in Early Modern Europe*. Oxford: Oxford University Press, 1997.

Crane, Susan. *Animal Encounters: Contacts and Concepts in Medieval Britain*. Philadelphia: University of Pennsylvania Press, 2013.

Daston, Lorraind, and Gregg Mitman, eds. *Thinking with Animals: New Perspectives on Anthropomorphism*. New York: Columbia University Press, 2005.

Davidson, Jane, and Bob Canino. "Wolves, Witches, and Werewolves: Lycanthropy and Witchcraft from 1423 to 1700." *Journal of the Fantastic in the Arts* 2, no. 4 (1990): 47–83.

Davidson, Jane. *Early Modern Supernatural: The Dark Side of European Culture, 1400–1700*. Santa Barbara, CA: Praeger, 2012.

Deane-Drummond, Celia, and David Clough, eds. *Creaturely Theology: On God, Humans, and Other Animals*. London: SCM Press, 2009.

Donecker, Stefan. "The Werewolves of Livonia: Lycanthropy and Shape-Changing in Scholarly Texts, 1550–1720." *Preternature: Critical and Historical Studies on the Preternatural* 1, no. 2 (2012): 289–322.

Edwards, Kathryn, ed. *Werewolves, Witches, and Wandering Spirits: Traditional Belief and Folklore in Early Modern Europe*. Kirksville, MO: Truman State University Press, 2002.

Fitzgerald, Allan, ed. *Augustine through the Ages: An Encyclopedia*. Grand Rapids, MI: William B. Eerdmans Company, 1999.

Frost, Brian. *The Essential Guide to Werewolf Literature*. Madison: University of Wisconsin Press, 2003.

Fyler, John. "Ovid and Chaucer." In *Ovid: The Classical Heritage*, edited by William Anderson. New York: Routledge, 1995.

Gardenour, Walter. *Our Old Monsters: Witches, Werewolves, and Vampires from Medieval Theology to Horror Cinema*. Jefferson NC: McFarland and Company Inc, Publishers, 2015.

Geiler, Johannes von Kaisersberg. *Die Emeis, dis ist das büch der Omeissen*. Strasbourg: Johannes Grieninger, 1517.

————. "From *Die Emeis*." In *The Book of Werewolves*, by Sabine Baring-Gould, 1865. New York: Forgotten Books, 2008.

Gerald of Wales. *The Historical Works of Giraldus Cambrensis, Containing the Topography of Ireland, and the History of the Conquest of Ireland*. Translated by Thomas Forester. London: George Bell and Sons, 1905.

Gibson, Dirk. *Legends, Monsters, or Serial Murderers? The Real Story Behind an Ancient Crime*. Santa Barbara, CA: Praeger, 2012.

Gildenhard, Ingo, ed. *Transformative Change in Western Thought: A History of Metamorphosis from Homer to Hollywood.* New York: Legenda, 2013.

Ginzburg, Carlo. *The Night Battles: Witchcraft and Agrarian Cults in the Sixteenth and Seventeenth Centuries.* London: Routledge, 2011.

Gratian. *Decretum Magistri Gratiani.* In *Corpus Iuris Canonici*, edited by Emil Friedberg. Graz: Akademische Druck-Universität Verlagsanstalt, 1881.

Green, Amy. "Interior/Exterior in the *Harry Potter Series*: Duality Expressed in Sirius Black and Remus Lupin." *Papers on Language and Literature* 44, no. 1 (Winter 2008): 87–108.

Guichet, Jean Luc, and Donald Nicholson-Smith. "From the Animal of the Enlightenment to the Animal of Postmodernism." *Yale French Studies* 127 (2015): 69–83.

Guynn, Noah. "Hybridity, Ethics, and Gender in Two Old French Werewolf Tales." In *From Beasts to Souls: Gender and Embodiment in Medieval Europe*, edited by E. Jane Burns and Peggy McCracken. Notre Dame, IN: University of Notre Dame Press, 2013.

Hansen, J. *Quellen und Untersuchungen zur Geschichte des Hexenwahns und der Hexenverfolgung im Mittelalter.* Hildesheim: G. Olms, 1963.

Heerbrand, Jakob. From *De Magia Disputatio cap. 7. Exo., . . . praeside reverendo et clarissimo viro Jacobo Heerbrando, sacrae theologiae Doctore eximio, ac eiusdem in Academia Tubingensi Professore publico . . . Nicolaus Falco Salueldensis . . . respondere conabitur.* Tübingen, 1570. Translated and annotated by Euan Cameron, 2006.

Hoorens, Vera. "Why Did Johann Weyer Write De Praestigiis Daemonum? How Anti-Catholicism Inspired the Landmark Plea for the Witches." *Low Countries Historical Review* 129.1 (2014): 3–24.

Institoris, Heinricus, and Jakobus Sprenger. *Malleus Maleficarum*, vol. 2. Edited and translated by S. Mackay. Cambridge: Cambridge University Press, 2006.

Karkov, Catherine. "Tales of the Ancients: Colonial Werewolves and the Mapping of Postcolonial Ireland." In *Postcolonial Moves: Medieval Through Modern*, edited by Patricia Clare Ingham and Michelle R. Warren. New York: Palgrave Macmillan, 2003.

Kinoshita, Sharon, and Peggy McCracken. *Marie de France: A Critical Companion.* Rochester, NY: D. S. Brewer, 2012.

Kors, Alan Charles, and Edward Peters, eds. *Witchcraft in Europe, 1400–1700: A Documentary History.* Philadelphia: University of Pennsylvania Press, 2001.

Krämer, Heinrich. *The Malleus Maleficarum.* Edited and Translated by Peter Maxwell-Stuart. Manchester: Manchester University Press, 2007.

The Lais of Marie de France. Translated by Glyn S. Burgess and Keith Busby. New York: Penguin Classics, 1999.

The Lais of Marie de France. Translated by Robert Hanning and Joan Ferrante. Grand Rapids, MI: Baker Books, 1995.

Lecouteux, Claude. *Witches, Werewolves, and Fairies: Shapeshifters and Astral Doublers in the Middle Ages.* Translated by Clare Frock. Rochester, VT: Inner Traditions, 2003.

Levack, Brian. *The Witch Hunt in Early Modern Europe.* New York: Longman, 1987.

Mann, Jill. "From Aesop to Reynard: Beast Literature in Medieval Britain." In *Marie de France: Poetry*, edited and translated by Dorothy Gilbert. New York: W. W. Norton and Company, 2015.

Martin, Christian. "Bodin's Reception of Johann Weyer in *De la Démonomanie des Sorciers*." In *The Reception of Bodin*, edited by H. Lloyd, 117–36. Leiden: Brill, 2013.

M'Balia, Thomas, Alisa LaDean Russell, and Hannah Warren. "The Good, the Bad, and the Ugly of Pedagogy in Harry Potter: An Inquiry into the Personal Practical Knowledge of Remus Lupin, Rubeus Hagrid, and Severus Snape. *Clearing House* 91, nos. 4/5 (Summer 2018): 186–92.

McCracken, Peggy. *In the Skin of a Beast: Sovereignty and Animality in Medieval France.* Chicago: University of Chicago Press, 2017.

Nider, Johannes. *Formicarius*, Argentoratum (1516). Digitale Sammlungen, images 161–62. http://daten.digitale-sammlungen.de.ezproxy.cul.columbia.edu/~db/bsb00009662/images/.

———. *Preceptorium divine legis venerabilis fratris Johannis Nider de ordine predicatorum.* Basle: Berthold Ruppel, c. 1470.

Otten, Charlotte F., ed. *A Lycanthropy Reader: Werewolves in Western Culture*. Syracuse, NY: Syracuse University Press, 1986.

Priest, Hannah, ed. *She-Wolf: A Cultural History of Female Werewolves*. Manchester: Manchester University Press, 2015.

Pyle, Andrew Scott. "Bestiality, Sexuality, Aggression: The Track of the Werewolf in French Literature." PhD Dissertation. Atlanta: Emory University 2012.

Rowlands, Alison, ed. *Witchcraft and Masculinities in Early Modern Europe*. New York: Palgrave Macmillan, 2009.

Rowling, J. K. *Harry Potter and the Prisoner of Azkaban*. New York: Scholastic, 1999.

Salisbury, Joyce. *The Beast Within: Animals in the Middle Ages*. London: Routledge, 2011.

Schulte, Rolf. *Man as Witch: Male Witches in Central Europe*. Translated by Linda Froome-Döring. New York: Palgrave Macmillan, 2009.

Scot, Reginald. *The Discoverie of Witchcraft*. Edited by Montague Summers. London: J. Rodker, 1930.

Steiger, Brad. *The Werewolf Book: The Encyclopedia of Shapeshifting Beings*. Canton, MI: Visible Ink Press, 1999.

Summers, Montague. *The Werewolf*. New York: University Books, 1966.

Thomas, Keith. *Man and the Natural World: A History of the Modern Sensibility*. New York: Pantheon Books, 1983.

———. *Religion and the Decline of Magic*. New York: Charles Scribner's Sons, 1974.

Trosclair, Lauren Elizabeth. "Fantastic Beasts or Beings, and Why Define Them? Examining Racial Ideology Towards Magical Creatures and Social Hierarchies Within J. K. Rowling's Harry Potter Series." Master's thesis. Lafayette: University of Louisiana at Lafayette, 2018.

Walter, Brenda S. Gardenour. *Our Old Monsters: Witches, Werewolves, and Vampires from Medieval Theology to Horror Cinema*. Jefferson, NC: McFarland Company, 2015.

Ward, Renee Michelle. "Cultural Contexts and Cultural Change: The Werewolf in Classical, Medieval, and Modern Texts." PhD Dissertation. Edmonton, Canada: University of Alberta, 2009.

Weyer, Johann. *De Praestigiis Daemonum*. 1560. *Witches, Devils, and Doctors in the Renaissance*. Edited by George Mora, and translated by John Shea. Binghamton, NY: Medieval and Renaissance Texts and Studies, SUNY-Binghamton, 1991.

———. *De Praestigiis daemonum, et incantionibus ac veneficiis, libri V*. Basle, Johannes Oporinus, 1563.

FILMOGRAPHY

An American Werewolf in London, DVD. Directed by John Landis. New York: Universal Studios, 1981.

Chapter Nine

Endings That Never Happen

Otherness, Indecent Theology, Apocalypse, and Zombies

Jessi Knippel

Zombies don't think or compassionately save humanity, and Latin American women from the barrio don't do theology, especially sexually indecent theology. From the beginning, Gwen, the main character in *i-ZOMBIE*, and Marcella Althaus-Reid, a Latin American theologian, present intersectional identities that challenge stereotypes and notions of what is, and isn't, possible for one in their positionality. In doing so, they offer a dynamic counter to the zombie genre and typically held notions of theology. Together they challenge and complicate readings of apocalypse, salvation, and white heteronormative patriarchy. So what do a cognitive-functioning female zombie from a graphic novel and a queer feminist liberation theologian have in common? The presentation and celebration of otherness, the embodiment of diversity in spaces that are often dominated by a narrow lens of the straight, white Western male, and counterreadings of apocalypse, of course! The graphic novels of *i-ZOMBIE* and the Indecent Theology of Marcella Althaus-Reid, when placed together, offer a contrast to both the patriarchal individualistic white male dominance in Western theologies and the media, specifically comic books/ graphic novels within the zombie subgenre.

> In essence, mainstream comic books derive from a socially constructed world in which White males, both consumers and producers, create, promote, and reinforce a world in which men are placed in positions of power. Thus, in many mainstream comic worlds, female characters are often relegated to subservient roles in which they are depicted as sexual objects, as needing protection, or are presented as secondary characters used to enhance the storyline of their male counterparts. [1]

In much of what is considered mainstream or normative theology, the female identified voice holds a similar position to feminine representation in the zombie genre, which is to say, mainly absent. This reality, that theology is the realm of men (especially white Western men) is easily seen in a quick search of top theological texts or the top one hundred Christian books, where the most common author demographic is white men.[2] Additionally, much of this theology has also been used as to justify violence in many forms, as theologian Miguel De La Torre says,

> Eurocentric Christianity is a political ideology responsible for more enslave-ment, more death and more misery than any other worldview throughout re-corded history.[3]

The exception to this dominance is texts that fall under the categorization of contextualized or intersectional theologies such as feminist, black, or queer theologies. Often feminism and other forms of otherness are treated as addi-tions to the theological enterprise instead of a central and normative lens through which to vividly and dynamically engage the core message of Chris-tianity. For example, the violent gang rape, dismemberment, and subsequent misleading call to war that takes place in Judges 19 was not named for the gang rape it was until Phyllis Trible dubbed it a "text of terror" in her 1984 monograph.[4] Too often, all other readings of the text beside those of (white) straight-powered male are set apart as contextualized or some other moniker that distinguishes it as "other." Then, the Western-centric male perspective is just "theology" with no qualifying adjective. So our discourse subtly estab-lishes the Western white straight male perspective as the normative lens through which theology is encountered.

This centering of male normativity affects every aspect of mainstream theology and genre fiction as it focuses on the experiences of straight white powerful men. Therefore, the apocalypses that are constructed within these areas represent a view that seeks to uphold this normativity and prolong this group's continued power and control. Primary to this worldview is the myth of retributional and redemptive violence, the idea that through further vio-lence peace is possible. Not only is this notion problematic because it leads to an ongoing cycle of retaliatory violence, for "those who take the sword will perish by the sword,"[5] but it also casts those who are not empowered men in a submissive role, only capable of gaining salvation through masculine aid. While seeming to be powerful, this worldview is incredibly fragile and re-quires constant upkeep through the assertion of dominance and power. This worldview's ephemeral nature can be seen when placed in conversation with the perspectives of those present in *Indecent Theology* or *i-ZOMBIE*, which not only hold differing positionalities but are also asking different questions that lead to radically opposite forms of engagement with apocalypse and the subsequent remaking of the world. The questions *Indecent Theology* and *i-ZOMBIE* ask lead away from destructive apocalypses and retaliatory violence toward an apocalypse that never happens and a self-sacrificial nonviolent restoration that absorbs into itself the destructive evil.

MONSTER HERE, MONSTER THERE,
I SEE MONSTERS EVERYWHERE

i-ZOMBIE, the 2011 graphic novel by Chris Roberson and Michael Allred, stands in sharp contrast to the typical individualistic and male-driven zombie narrative popular in this genre. Featuring a female lead and her diverse "Scooby Gang," *i-ZOMBIE* represents a unique and dynamic way to use and tell zombie tales. Roberson and Allred's novel centers on Gwen Dylan, a twenty-something woman living in her hometown of Eugene, Oregon and working as a gravedigger. Gwen entered this line of work after becoming a member of the living dead, *a zombie*. Gwen chose to be a gravedigger post-transformation because it provides her with "ethical," that is, nonmurderous, access to the human brains she needs monthly to remain "passing" as human. Without this timely consumption, Gwen risks becoming a traditional zombie, one of the staggering hordes. In addition to brain consumption, Gwen's zombification has left her with gaps in her memory about her preliving dead life. She is aided in the uncovering and solving of this mystery by two friends who make up her "Scooby Gang." Gwen's "Scooby Gang" consists of Eleanor (Ellie), the ghost of a young woman who died in the 1960s, and Scott "Spot," a were-terrier who works in the IT department of an old folks' home. As the narrative moves along, the Scooby Gang encounters a variety of other characters including: a paintball-running band of art-history-graduate-students-turned-vampires, a secret government monster-hunting agency, a centuries-old monster-hunting organization, and rogue monsters trying to control the apocalypse who wish to usher in the monster for their own selfish gain. Gwen's mission (and reason for becoming a monster),[6] which, in the end, is to stop the coming global destruction of the earth via a soul-sucking Lovecraftian creature from another dimension named Xitlau, that is, an apocalypse, is revealed through interactions with these various entities. She is convinced by John Amon, another revenant, to take on this salvific mission. Amon, as a representation of the typical individualistic powered male savior figure, is unable to see a way to defeat Xitlau that will not result in the sacrificial death of many. This is in part because he has been willing to sacrifice others to extend his life, finding ways to justify their deaths. It is the intersectional vision of Gwen's character makeup and her desire to save others that leads to her ability to see broadly and creatively enough to think of another means of defeating the world-destroying monster. In this series,

Gwen and her friends, along with many of the other characters within the narrative, embody and represent a diversity of humanoids, with wildly varying sexual, gendered, racial, and spiritual identities. It is through this diversity that the authors diverge from the white-male-savior narrative to tell a different kind of apocalypse and zombie narrative that encompasses a completely new way to encounter an end of the world.

Gwen is a revenant, a rare zombie-like creature that retains a close connection to humanity along with the strengths and skills of a zombie, because unlike other creatures, revenants retain both an oversoul and undersoul.[7] In the world of *i-ZOMBIE* most of the "monstrous" creatures are either ruled by their oversoul or undersoul. However, without a serving of brains once a month, the revenant risks going all "mindless and shambling"[8] and becomes a full-fledged Romero-esque zombie, rather than a reanimate who can pass as human. The revenant's diet has at least one side effect: she retains the memories and associations of the dead person. As readers, we see the memories visualized through Gwen's paintings or clues illustrating who the dead person was, to help solve their mystery and bring them rest. It also transpires that Gwen is able to piece together her own memory gaps and discover her salvific mission because of the memories she encounters while consuming the brains of others.

The diversity of otherness is presented in the story in various ways, the first being that the central character is a woman: a real, complicated, dynamic woman. That reality in and of itself is a rare one for the genre. For many zombie storytellers that one case of alterity (feminized) would be enough. Even then in the instance where there is a female lead in the genre they rarely resemble actual living, breathing women and live more in the realm of male fantasy than actual womanhood.[9] But for the creators of *i-ZOMBIE* this minor incarnation of otherness is not enough. Roberson and Allred have filled their story with characters that represent various forms and images of otherness. Not only are the characters in the story racially diverse, but several characters are diverse in their sexuality as well. Out of this "Scooby Gang" Gwen is the only one who might even remotely be considered heteronormative, given her relationship with Horatio, who happens to be a monster-hunter. The rest are quite inventively diverse. Scott, over the course of the narrative arc, embraces both his identity as a gay man (who marries Gwen's brother Gavin) and a were-terrier, and navigates the eventual coming out process to his friends and family about who he is.[10] Ellie, given her ghost status, can only connect physically with her love interest, the zombified Francisco, through the physical body of another. This leaves the couple with becoming a consensual trio as their only avenue for connection. Their first trio is with the twice-reanimated vampire Claire and then, later on, with the vampire Tricia, Gwen's best friend from her human life and Francisco's girlfriend when they were humans. All of the relationships and the people in them, minus characters like Claire who are, by nature, inherently selfish and self-centered, are presented as good. The only time these alterities are quantified as bad or negative is through the characters' own prejudice or self-criticism. Francisco, Horatio, Tricia, Kennedy, Diogenes, and many other characters all embody the diversity of races and nationalities present in humanity. Their diversity represents the hope of a just and equitable community.

One of the overarching strengths of the graphic novel is the agency of Gwen as a character. She chooses to become a revenant and she chooses to become the savior of her family, friends, hometown, and ultimately, the world. She enters into her zombie state with her eyes open, taking the path to monsterdom so she can assist in the salvation of the world. Gwen's agency comes from her embrace and guidance of positionality, not rejection of it. Although when the reader encounters Gwen, in what is revealed at the story's end to be the middle part of her story, she has lost the memories of how she became a revenant. Even without her memories as to how and why she is a monster, Gwen's character traits of self-agency, compassion, wisdom, and openness, and the need to do something to bring peace for those whose brains she consumes, are still very present. Gwen also embodies wisdom, thoughtfulness, compassion, and openness even when her perspective of her situation is challenged or changed, unlike many of the male lead characters in this genre who often represent constructed notions of white-male power that lack self-awareness and these other traits. It is less about knowing the answers and more about asking the right questions.[11] Much of theology and the white-male-driven zombie narratives function like John Amon in *i-ZOMBIE* in that they are only able to conceive of one way to deal with the approaching threat: preemptive violent action. Their position and privilege allow for very narrow and limited solutions to the issues at hand, and like Amon they are willing to sacrifice the few for the sake of the many because for them those who are sacrificed, "their lives are meaningless."[12] Gwen stands in contrast to this limited lens of privilege; through the utilization of her intuitive and compassionate nature as well as drawing from her community's knowledge and experience, she is able to approach and process a different way to engage with the coming apocalypse. Ultimately, Gwen is able to bring a more dynamic and less destructive and violent solution to the world-consuming monster because of her community and positionality. In a genre that typically positions women as reacting to the situation around them instead of engaging in self-agency (see *Planet Terror* or *Dawn of the Dead* [1978]), Gwen becomes a truly empowered female lead.

The uniqueness of her as a female versus a male lead is shown in the ways in which she reacts to the various situations she finds herself in. For example, Gwen (unlike other revenants, John Amon or Kennedy) feels an obligation to bring peace to the deceased whose brains nourish and sustain her. She does not take lightly the cycle of life in which she is enmeshed, but rather goes out of her way to seek peace for the dead. Similar to certain indigenous tribes,

Gwen takes only what she needs and refuses to commit harm to the living for her survival. Even as a monster, Gwen continues to represent the ideal of care for the other, goodness, and in the end, self-sacrificial love. Gwen stands in contrast to other male characters in this genre, specifically because even as the story becomes more and more desperate and horrific, Gwen still seeks to be open and compassionate unlike, say, Rick Grimes in both versions of *The Walking Dead* who moves from openness and compassion toward a hard suspiciousness as the series progresses.[13] It is also in her act of salvation that Gwen stands starkly against the "action hero" motif of the genre. John Amon, the revenant mummy who is the catalyst for Gwen's transformation and a guide into the aspects of being a revenant, tells her there is no other way to stop Xitalu but her taking the souls of those around her and then feeding her soul-gorged self to the otherworldly beast. Yet, in the aftermath of Amon's soul being absorbed into the creature, Gwen moves beyond her flawed teacher's vision and realizes that Xitalu, "might be from another universe, it might be giant, but it's no different from the souls we carry around inside us. And if I can absorb one soul. I can absorb another."[14] In fact Gwen is the only one able to absorb the creature ensuring its destruction, because unlike other monsters, her status as zombie-revenant means that she does not get "possessed by the souls" she takes in, rather she "digests them."[15] By digesting the creature, Gwen saves all those who would have lost their lives either through Amon's solution or the creature's destruction of the earth. The downside to Gwen's solution is that it means she has become a transcendent creature who can no longer remain on the same plane as the earth and all those she loves. Through her act of consumption, she becomes something which could destroy those she loves and therefore must leave. It is this final act of the narrative, the apocalypse doesn't come, or rather doesn't bring utter destruction, which holds the biggest reversal of the typical genre arc. In almost every other zombie/zombie-apocalypse narrative, the contagion and destruction ushers in a new way of life that either is the end to humanity or the adaptation of humanity to a zombie existence. In fact, this reality of the narrative is so strongly held that it is one of the key elements of Romero's rules, there is no cure for the zombie.[16] And yet in the *i-ZOMBIE* narrative, while zombies continue as figures within the community, there is no end of humanity or adaptation to a zombie-dominant culture. There is a new, more just, and equitable form of life where monsters and humans live together. The apocalypse becomes an unveiling of the hidden so that all may be free to be themselves within the community. In the post-apocalypse context of *i-ZOMBIE*, Gwen's Scooby Gang sets up an organization to help those previously considered "monsters" to enter into the broader cultural community. In creating this space for those seen as other, the community allows space for all to be free to live into their true selves.

HERSTORY: DR. MARCELLA ALTHAUS-REID'S
INDECENT THEOLOGY

Marcella Althaus-Reid was born in Rosario, Santa Fe, Argentina in 1952 and died in Edinburgh, Scotland, February 2009 after a battle with cancer.[17] During her time as a scholar and practitioner Althaus-Reid created a new form of embodied theology, which she called "Indecent Theology," which continues to transform and inspire theological conversations around the interplay of sexuality, economics, and power.[18] Althaus-Reid identified as a married bisexual feminist liberationist theologian, with connections to the Metropolitan Community Church, the Quaker Church/Meeting (Religious Society of Friends Scotland), United Methodist Church, and the Catholic traditions of her native Argentina.[19] A self-described daughter of the poor barrios, Marcella challenged her cultural tradition, which said women shouldn't study theology by earning a bachelor's degree with a focus on liberation theology from the renowned "Instituto Superior Evangelico de Estudios Teologicos (ISEDET) seminary in Buenos Aires, studying with scholars such as Jose Miguez Bonino and J. Severino Croatta."[20] She was trained for ministry by the United Methodist Church of Argentina via the "conscientation" method[21] developed by Paulo Freire in his work *Pedagogy of the Oppressed.*[22] With this background and education Althaus-Reid worked for many years in the poor communities of Buenos Aires via church-sponsored social and community projects.[23] It was through this work that she was invited to Scotland to work on similar projects which eventually led to her entering and gaining a PhD in 1994 from St. Andrews University of Scotland in liberation, feminist, and queer theologies.[24] After graduating from St. Andrews, Althaus-Reid took a lecturer position at the University of Edinburgh, eventually leading to her appointment in 2006 as professor of contextual theology at the New School, where she became the first female theology professor in the school's history and the second woman to hold an academic theological position in Scotland.[25]

During the fifteen-year period between the completion of her degree at St. Andrews to her early death, Marcella Althaus-Reid wrote prolifically, including *From Feminist Theology to Indecent Theology* (which reveals her transition from her training as a liberation theologian toward a more broad and inclusive theology), *Indecent Theology: Theological Perversions in Sex, Gender, and Politics*, and *Queer God*. In all of her work, Althaus-Reid begins with the same style[26] of liberation theology, specifically the call for divine preference for the poor and marginalized. Indecent Theology pushes beyond Liberation Theology and its entanglement with the patriarchal project. While working in the intersectionally marginalized communities that birthed Liberation Theology, Althaus-Reid found that for all its challenges to certain forms of power, Liberation Theology lacked the robust intersectional lens to critique the roots of patriarchal colonial powers present in the church as institution. "Indecent Theology represents both a continuation of Liberation Theology and a disruption of it."[27] As a project, Indecent Theology builds on the above-mentioned aspects of Liberation Theology but pushes beyond it, challenging the dominant lenses of male clerical privilege and acceptability constructions that isolate those who are doubly and triply marginalized under oppressive structures of sexism, homophobia, and economic power. Therefore Althaus-Reid begins and centers theology in the experiences of these doubly and triply marginalized people.[28] It is a theology that begins with holistic embodied experiences of marginalized people opposed to institutional structures or a statement of beliefs to affirm. Althaus-Reid does this through the means of narrative and story, a common element of Latin American theology traditions. For example, *Indecent Theology* begins with a conversation around the holistic experience of lemon vendors of the barro, how their embodiment cannot be separated from their experience of theology and religion, countering the way that most white Western male-oriented theologies are constructed along binary spaces. She says,

> Writing theology without underwear may be punishable by law, who knows. An act of gross indecency such as that of the prostitute woman described by Mexican novelist Josefina Estrada seems to be, in the words of the policeman, an action against the moral order of the country. Yet an Argentinian feminist theologian may want to do, precisely, that. Her task may be to deconstruct a moral order which is based on a heterosexual construction of reality, which organises not only categories of approved social and divine interactions but of economic ones too. The Argentinian theologian would like then to remove her underwear to write theology from a feminist honesty, not forgetting what it is to be called a woman when dealing with theological and political categories.[29]

In essence, Althaus-Reid states that one's whole embodiment and intersections of marginality are what gives greater depth and insight into the theological and biblical experiences. In this theological rubric, queer theory and experiences function in a twofold manner: first, as one of the marginalized communities centered in *Indecent Theology*; secondly, *Indecent Theology* takes figures and narratives from the biblical text and places them in reading that highlights their radical nature, undermining the history of their domestication within a patriarchal colonialist interpretation. Marginalized female experiences are also highlighted for similar reasons. By centering these marginalized peoples' experience, *Indecent Theology* roots itself in the awareness that theology must be connected to whole embodiment, and that if it is not connected, embodiment theology often can directly harm those it claims to be working for. Althaus-Reid unpacks this reality by discussing how Catholicism came into Latin America via colonialism as its agent. She speaks of how the metanarrative and grand worldview of European Colonial Christianity was imposed upon the people of the Americas, which problematically ruptured their own worldview through abusive forms of authoritarianism and religio-cultural domination.[30] The entry of Catholicism (and other forms of Christianity) for those in the Americas was a form of apocalyptic event, a world-shattering interaction that almost completely or completely destroyed their worldview and ways of life. Much like the Xitalu figure in *i-ZOMBIE*, the Western colonial brand of Christianity came, conquered, and utterly erased what had been there before, absorbing everything in its path. *Indecent Theology* seeks to engage in a "resurrection from below." Althaus-Reid describes this as a resurrection of justice, one that has strategy and time limits, that demands action.[31] It demands that the trauma and destruction of colonialism, capitalism, patriarchy, and Christianity be named and addressed. Yet it also goes beyond that, she says that resurrection from below,

> is not about the resurrection of the dead from tombs and ashes, but the resurrection *de abajo*, of the people who are oppressed and die different sort of deaths every day: the death of hopes and dreams, and of rights and love and lust. . . . I said elsewhere that people live and die in community, but also resurrect in community. . . . When Jesus died, in a sense a whole community died with him; with the death of the presence of that friend amongst them, of intimate relations with Jesus which were now gone, death took from them someone who was the witness of their lives.[32]

In the enactment of a resurrection from below, there comes the possibility of rebirth. This rebirth is marked by new worlds and ways of being that take seriously a radically inclusive notion of the divine that holds radical alterity, and intuitive and cultural knowledge, as a counter to destructive abuses, and abuse cycles of power and dominance in culture and religious context. It is also the rebirth that is seen in the post-apocalyptic world of *i-ZOMBIE*, where those who were once denied life because of their otherness are now brought into the community. A community that is birthed through and out of the characters connection with Gwen, the salvific figure.

BINARIES AND DUALISM: APOCALYPTICAL AND ZOMBIE IMAGINATION NARRATIVES AND THEOLOGIES

Cultural narratives and apocalyptical imaginations are nothing new. Carol Newsom writes in her introduction in the Kelly J. Murphy and Justin Jeffcoat Schedtler edited book *Apocalypses in Context: Apocalyptic Currents Throughout History* that the genre's origin can be seen as far back as the second millenium BCE in the Bronze Age Near Eastern context.[33] Newsom highlights the emergence of certain genre elements like "pronounced dualism, the notion of strongly marked temporal periods culminating in the victory of good over evil—as derived from Persian Zorastorian ideas."[34] These are also common elements within the zombie genre as well. She goes on to note that these core elements then get infused into Jewish and then Christian modalities of the apocalyptic imagination and narratives.[35] From there, the apocalyptic imagination grows and transforms as it builds through cultural and communal interactions and experiences.[36] Yet, Newsom also says that while the tropes and characters of the genre carry on throughout history, there is a distinctive shift in the way in which the modern understanding of apocalypse shifts.[37] One of the main reasons for this is the proliferation of Christianity's influence and normativity in Western culture, thereby affording its apocalyptic imagination a place of cultural dominance.[38] Specifically, the apocalyptical narrative and imagination found in the final text of the New Testament, the Revelation of St. John. Interpretations of this text have become the orienting notion of apocalypse in the Western context.[39] While Revelation has been a challenging text throughout Christian history, with Martin Luther famously wanting to keep it out of the canon because of the difficulty of its genre and interpretation, overall within the scope of Christian history it was not prioritized or overly analyzed. The apocalypse was something that would eventually happen but was in the realm of things that belong to God. Yet since the 1850s, the apocalyptic vision of Revelation has grown in popularity within the Western context, specifically the American. Indeed, within the American context it has taken on a primary importance in the defining Evangelical-Fundamentalist faith structures. Additionally, the broad inclusion of dispensational theology within the Christian and cultural context via texts such as Hal Lindsey's *The Late Great Planet Earth* and films like *A Thief in The Night* also helped to make a specific and violent reading of the apocalypse a normative understanding. In this cultural milieu,

> the Apocalypse becomes something more than a mobilizing motif of popular evangelism or a gnawing angst among everyday people. It marks a deep gulf between the existing temporal order and the most strongly alienated and antagonistic of its inhabitants (*or those who perceive that they are alienated*).[40]

This gulf often includes the desire for vindictive violence aimed at those institutions and persons who are perceived to be the instigators of the alienation and antagonism. Returning to Newsom, in her understanding the contemporary secular (and religious)[41] reading of apocalypse differs from earlier religious settings in that it removed the focus on "mysteries revealed" for an emphasis on "the dualistic struggle between sharply defined good and evil and on the destruction of all that is familiar and cherished."[42] She continues, saying that "in the contemporary imagination, 'apocalypse' is almost equivalent with 'disaster' or 'catastrophe.'"[43] This reading of apocalypse is often the central element of the zombie versions. Zombie apocalypses represent unexpected and unexplained disruptions of "normative" life, such as war, global economic collapse, technological fears, natural disasters, epidemics, or the like, which are outside the scope of human control. Where, in spite of all human knowledge and advancements, these manifestations of apocalypse leave humans at the mercy of the unknown and unexpected.

> Not only is the normal life within the imagined storyworld of zombie texts disrupted, but the metaphor of the zombie often works in fiction—and, more broadly in popular culture—to disturb real world "norms" or assumptions about humans and human society, particularly what we or it are capable or incapable of doing.[44]

This is in part because the constructed encounter is a good-versus-evil binary. In this set up, the narrators are, almost always, clearly good and the hero(es), and those who are against them are evil. In dualistic structures there is little space for nuance, dynamic, or creative engagement with otherness, or the situation at hand. This binary thinking is in part why apocalyptic imagination often sees violence as a necessary means toward reordering and reconstructing the world. Additional to the myth of necessary and redemptive violence, Western apocalypse and zombie narratives often include an individualistic male savior.

INDECENT THEOLOGY AND *I-ZOMBIE* FINDING LIFE IN AND AFTER THE APOCALYPSE

The *i-ZOMBIE* narrative and *Indecent Theology* stand in sharp contrast to the typical constructions of the apocalypse and post-apocalypse life. In their imaginative construction, encounters with apocalypse, salvation, and resurrection bring the formation of a new and broader reaching community—truly good news. It is the end of the world as it has been known, but it is the end of the world that upholds and recapitulates trauma and abuse, prejudice and shame. No longer do people (and monsters), who are considered other and therefore unhuman under the old ruling order (white, Western, patriarchal, individualistic), have to hide their truth and true nature. Rather, the apocalypse opens up the door for all people to dwell within the salvific community. It is the act of the unveiling and world-changing actions of the apocalypse that allow for this change. Gwen's actions in *i-ZOMBIE*, especially her dynamic and creative consumption of the creature, which is threatening the earth with extinction, leads her community (in a similar manner as Christ's followers after his resurrection) to seek to carry on her actions. They work to help those who were seen as "other" previously integrate and become part of the community, taking up the mantle of salvation and resurrection. Bearing witness to the radically inclusive vision of the world, postapocalypse. In this way, the *i-ZOMBIE* narrative aligns with Indecent Theology, for in each the resurrection and hope is found in the context of the postapocalyptic community and what is created therein.

In the scope of Indecent Theology, the community is the centering point of all aspects of life and death connected to notions of apocalypse, salvation, and resurrection. This is because Indecent Theology is rooted in the experiences of marginalized and oppressed people, specifically Latin American women. This community's experiences are forged in a history of political unrest and oppression, a living apocalypse as it were. Theirs is a worldview that seeks to find "a belief in life amid death squads" and counts crosses and resurrections as a means of remembering and bringing forth those who were lost to the ongoing horror;[45] it is a theology for those who are seeking to find a new world in the midst of apocalyptical circumstances. Theirs is a theology of memory,[46] where the community bears witness as a means of calling forth justice thereby naming the world as it should be, not how it is currently. During an ongoing apocalypse, Indecent Theology calls forth, through the community, the world as it should be for all, filled with flourishing, justice, and equity. Apocalypse in *i-ZOMBIE* and *Indecent Theology* bring about the radical resurrection and salvation of the world. It is not the erasure of all that is known and familiar but a deeper rooting into those elements of the here and now that allow for all to find equity and care to flourish. It is a revelation and a reorientation of the world that is marked by radical inclusion. Therefore, *i-ZOMBIE* and *Indecent Theology* in their apocalyptical imagination counter the destructive elitist survivalist notions of apocalypse present in typical zombie narratives and contemporary apocalyptic visions both religious and secular that fear otherness and seek its destruction through the destruction of the world as we know it. Instead, they offer a vision of a postapocalyptic world in which all can find connections and place.

NOTES

1. Tammy S. Garland et al., "Gender Politics," 60.
2. See these lists as examples: https://www.goodreads.com/list/show/19595.Top_100_Christian_Books_By_Worldview_Institute_ and https://www.librarything.com/list/9960/all/Church-Times-100-Best-Christian-Books https://www.amazon.com/Best-Sellers-Kindle-Store-Systematic-Christian-Theology/zgbs/digital-text/158432011.
3. De La Torre, *Burying White Privilege*, 23.
4. Trible, *Texts of Terror*, 65–91.
5. Matthew 26:52 (RSV).
6. Chris Roberson et al., *IZombie Repossession*.
7. In the context of the *i-ZOMBIE* mythology, all humans have both an undersoul and an oversoul, whereas "monsters" have one or the other (with the rare exception of Gwen and John Amon who are revenants, the living dead who retain both over- and undersoul but need to consume human elements of life force to remain so). For example ghosts, like Ellie, have only the oversoul which holds the memories and personality of the dead versus a poltergeist which only have an undersoul that consists of only appetite and emotion or vampires, which are

bodied creatures that only have a oversoul versus zombies that are bodied creatures which only have a undersoul.

8. Chris Roberson et al., *IZombie Death to the World*.

9. A good example of this is Alice, the main character in the *Resident Evil* film saga who resembles an idealized soldier/assassin more than a realistic woman.

10. Roberson and Allred, *i-ZOMBIE: Repossession*.

11. Althaus-Reid, *From Feminist Theology to Indecent Theology*, 61.

12. Roberson and Allred, *i-ZOMBIE: Repossession*.

13. Hamilton, "Simulating the Zombie Apocalypse."

14. Roberson and Allred, *i-ZOMBIE: Repossession*.

15. Ibid.

16. Scott, M*onsters and The Monstrous*, 1.

17. Cooper, "Remembering Marcella Althaus-Reid."

18. Ibid.

19. Ibid., and Gross-Shore, "So Get your High Heels on for Liberation, and Walk!'"

20. The Lesbian, Gay, Bisexual, and Transgender Religious Archives Network Biography of Marcella Althaus-Reid.

21. A key concept in Freire's approach is *conscientization*, meaning the ways in which individuals and communities develop a critical understanding of their social reality through reflection and action. This involves examining *and* acting on the root causes of oppression as experienced in the here and now. This goes beyond simply acquiring the technical skills of reading and writing. It is a cornerstone to ending the culture of silence, in which oppression is not mentioned and thereby maintained.

22. The Lesbian, Gay, Bisexual, and Transgender Religious Archives Network Biography of Marcella Althaus-Reid.

23. Ibid.

24. Ibid.

25. Ibid.

26. In the opening of her first book, *From Feminist Theology to Indecent Theology*, she speaks of how her "training," via Paula Freire and his *Pedagogy of the Oppressed* model, describes it as a style (indicating a fluidity, flexibility, and openness in how the work is done that is ongoing and rooted in the community and context one is in) rather than training (which indicates a completeness and authoritative hierarchy model).

27. Althaus-Reid, *Indecent Theology*, 5.

28. Althaus-Reid, *From Feminist Theology to Indecent Theology*, 11.

29. Ibid., 2.

30. Ibid., 12.

31. Ibid., 121.

32. Ibid., 122.

33. Newsom, "Foreword," *Apocalypses in Context*.

34. Ibid., x.

35. Ibid.

36. Ibid.

37. Ibid.

38. Ibid.

39. Ibid.

40. Italics in original. Hall et al., *Apocalypse Observed*, 6. Note that his quote reveals that the Christian/Religious Right in the U.S. context often sees itself as persecuted and alienated from the broader culture and therefore desires apocalyptical intervention even when, as at the time of this writing in 2019–2020, it actually holds a space of political and cultural power.

41. While the coming of Christ is given lip service within contemporary conversion theologies the actual focus when infused in cultural imagery primarily focuses on sharp definitions of good and evil and the threat of destruction of the familiar as a means of conformity and conversion to the Religious Right worldview.

42. Newsom, "Foreword," *Apocalypses in Context*, xi.

43. Ibid.

44. Hamilton, "Simulating the Zombie Apocalypse in Popular Culture and Media," 45.
45. Althanus-Reid, *From Feminist Theology to Indecent Theology,* 114.
46. Ibid.

WORKS CITED

Althaus-Reid, Marcella. *From Feminist Theology to Indecent Theology: Reading on Poverty, Sexual Identity and God*. London: SCM Press, 2004.
———. *Indecent Theology: Theological Perversions in Sex, Gender, and Politics*. New York: Routledge, 2000.
Balaji, Murali, ed. *Thinking Dead: What the Zombie Apocalypse Means*. Lanham, MD: Lexington Books, 2010.
Beal, Timothy K. *Religion and Its Monsters*. New York: Routledge, 2002.
Comentale, Edward P., and Aaron Jaffee, eds. *The Year's Work at the Zombie Research Center*. Bloomington: Indiana University Press, 2014.
Cooper, Thai. "Remembering Marcella Althaus-Reid." *Political Theology* 10, no. 4 (2015): 758–59.
Davis, Wade. *The Serpent and the Rainbow: A Harvard Scientist's Astonishing Journey into the Secret Societies of Haitian Voodoo, Zombies, and Magic*. New York: Touchstone, 1985.
De La Torre, Miguel A. *Burying White Privilege: Resurrecting a Badass Christianity*. Grand Rapids, MI: William B. Eerdmans Publishing Company, 2019.
Garland, Tammy S., Nickie Phillips, and Scott Vollum. "Gender Politics and *The Walking Dead*: Gendered Violence and the Reestablishment of Patriarchy." *Feminist Criminology* 13, no. 1 (November 2016): 59–86.
Hall, John R., Philip D. Schuyler, and Sylvaine Trinh. *Apocalypse Observed Religious Movements and Violence in North America, Europe and Japan*. New York: Taylor and Francis, 2005.
Hamilton, Patrick. "Simulating the Zombie Apocalypse in Popular Culture and Media." In *Thinking Dead: What the Zombie Apocalypse Means*, ed. Murali Balaji, 48–54. Lanham, MD: Lexington Books, 2010.
The Lesbian, Gay, Bisexual, and Transgender Religious Archives Network Biography of Marcella Althaus-Reid, https://www.lgbtran.org/Profile.aspx?ID=234.
Kearney, Richard. *Strangers, Gods and Monsters: Interpreting Otherness*. London: Routledge, 2003.
Kordas, Ann. "New South, New Immigrants, New Women, New Zombies: The Historical Development of the Zombie in American Pop Culture." In *Race, Oppression, and the Zombie: Essays on the Cross Cultural Appropriations of the Caribbean Tradition*, edited by Christopher M. Moreman and Cory James Rushton. Jefferson, NC: MacFarland & Company Publishers, 2011.
Newsom, Carol A. "Foreword." In *Apocalypses in Context: Apocalyptic Currents through History*, edited by Kelly J. Murphy and Justin Jeffcoate Schedtler. Minneapolis, MN: Augsburg Fortress Publishers, 2016.
Roberson, Chris, Mike Allred, Laura Allred, and Todd Klein. *IZombie: Dead to the World, UVampire, Six Feet under and Rising, Repossession*. New York: DC Comics/Vertigo, 2011.
Scott, Niall. *Monsters and The Monstrous: Myths and Metaphor of Enduring Evil*. New York: Rodopi, 2007.
Sutton, Matthew Avery, *American Apocalypse: A History of Modern Evangelicalism*. Cambridge, MA: Belknap Press, 2014.
Trible, Phyllis. *Texts of Terror: Literary-Feminist Readings of Biblical Narratives (Overtures to Biblical Theology)*. Minneapolis, MN: Fortress Press, 1984.
Zombie Wikia, http://zombie.wikia.com/wiki/Revenants; http://zombie.wikia.com/wiki/Romero_zombies.

Part IV

Readings in Theology
and the Horror Film

Chapter Ten

"Do I Look Like Someone Who Cares What God Thinks?"

Exploring Narrative Ambiguity, Religion, and the Afterlife in the Hellraiser Franchise

Mark Richard Adams

Despite its title, Clive Barker's 1987 horror classic *Hellraiser* does not depict what many would consider a traditional representation of Hell and the demonic, nor does it, as many presume, overtly explore Christian mythology as its primary theological mythology. The use of the term "mythology" in this context is not intended to emphasize the etymological source word "myth," as in "untrue." Instead, I draw on its other use as a term to describe a specific group or collection of foundational stories that usually address the human condition and seek to explore aspects of human nature. I will discuss both "Christian mythology" and "the *Hellraiser* mythology" throughout this chapter, meaning the narratives and themes that are understood to be part of these particular frameworks. Though *Hellraiser* draws on the themes of classic narratives like Dr. Faustus and utilizes certain religious iconography, the narratives' primary interests lie elsewhere, with themes of queer community, alternative sexuality, and transformative bodies being at the forefront of the films. I will not argue that such themes cannot be understood in a religious context, but rather that these themes are not inherently Christian, nor the sole concern of religious followers.

The Hellraiser films, especially the first two, make use of different cultural symbols and imagery as signifiers, but these are not exclusively Christian and are used for their visual impact more so than their narrative importance. The Hellraiser franchise, in its first decade or so, presents a more agnostic view of religion, although as I will discuss further on, this quickly begins to change. I argue that it is the films' very title, utilizing the semantically loaded word "hell," that works to heavily imprint Christian ideology onto the film and, in doing so, fundamentally alters the direction and vision of the entire franchise over the next three decades. I will argue that the Hellraiser franchise presents a conflicted narrative space, where ideas of religion, spirituality, and damnation often contrast or even conflict with Lovecraftian themes of cosmic horror, explorations of sadomasochistic pleasure, and queer monstrosity. Having said that, I will also look at different historical religious influences on the horror genre, in general, and question to what extent certain themes can be said to be inherently Christian. I will be using close textual analysis to look at the narratives of the Hellraiser franchise, primarily the first two films, to explore how these films depict the mythology of the series. Approaching it from what could be termed an agnostic perspective, I will analyze how the films depict and use themes often associated with religious horror, but without presuming that God or Heaven, in Christian mythologic terms, exist. I contend that the mythology established in the first two films is its own unique narrative, which nevertheless draws on traditional Christian iconography and rhetoric, but does not use them to depict a biblical Hell or demons, and God himself is notable for His absence. However, the Hellraiser sequels engage with the question of religious narratives in varied and often contradictory ways, a result of the different approaches by the writers and directors who brought their own ideas to the narratives. Religion is rendered unstable within the Hellraiser franchise, which continuously reinvents and contradicts itself. Rather than a singular fictional mythology, *Hellraiser* is caught between offering up its own unique theological narrative and adhering to a Christian perspective, albeit one filtered through its own aesthetics. I will be addressing the depiction of the Cenobites, "demons to some, angels to others," and the depiction of their world, generally referred to as the Labyrinth and ruled over by a gigantic floating diamond referred to as Leviathan, "the God of flesh, hunger, and desire." I generally segregate the first two *Hellraiser* films from the other entries in the franchise, as they were produced by largely the same production teams in quick succession in the United Kingdom and before control of the franchise began to move further away from those who originated it. This movement away from the original contexts of the franchise's creation further destabilizes its narrative trajectory, and the different voices who would go on to work on the franchise bring their own spiritual beliefs to how they approach the material. This exploration will serve to illustrate how the evolution of the Hellraiser franchise can be mapped to both the changing attitudes of its creators and audience, and the changing engagement with religious ideas and themes within wider cultural contexts.

DEMONS AREN'T REAL, THEY'RE PARABLES, METAPHORS

Religion has been a dominating force for societal and cultural control in the Western world, with religious leaders holding huge political power and sway in the affairs of countries, while churches would be the focal point for local communities. While religious beliefs cannot be said to be monolithic, their importance in culture is such that their influence on the texts, stories, and media produced from these societies cannot be simply dismissed. Joel W. Martin suggests that in order to "understand religion in a contemporary Hollywood film . . . assume it is important to understand the religious traditions informing the cultural context in which the film was made and viewed."[1] Secularism is an increasingly dominant feature in contemporary Britain, and secular humanist approaches to morality and thought suggest that religion is not required to explore universal themes. However, the fact remains that historical contexts tie religion to certain themes in such a way that it is arguably impossible to explore them without opening the text up to Christian interpretations. I would argue then, that a text that does not incorporate direct references and representations of Christian mythology, such as the appearances of Lucifer, or God, cannot be said to be an inherently religious narrative. Rather, it is the audience's own interpretation of the messages, and their reading of the narrative presented, that renders the text religious, in their perspective. Martin suggests scholars of religion will "examine the film to see if traditional religious teachings or values are present. If any common forms of expression normally associated with religion are present, if religious symbols are being invoked, and so on."[2] A secular humanist approach, however, might see these same themes as universal, and not inherently religious in their exploration, and may look at the evocation of religious symbols as representative of our cultural past, or even in some cases, a criticism and rejection of traditional religious values, depending on their use within a film's narrative. Horror, often dealing with notions of good and evil, and death and punishment, is a genre that has particularity drawn influence from religious ideology of the contemporary era in which it was written.

The work of H. P. Lovecraft remains some of the most influential horror fiction of the previous century, directly inspiring numerous film adaptations, as well as video games, comics, and expanded narratives written by later writers. Indirectly, the tone, aesthetic, and themes of his work, often termed as "Lovecraftian" have inspired all manner of science fiction and horror narratives. *Hellbound: Hellraiser II* directly builds on Lovecraftian tropes in order to construct its depiction of Hell, something I shall discuss further on, and offers a depiction of the afterlife that is distinct from Christian orthodoxy. However, Lovecraft's work itself draws influence from the historical and religious contexts of his upbringing, and Neil Syme argues that despite his "professed atheism, however, his weird mythos has a distinctly Calvinist flavour."[3] Instigated by John Calvin, central to his doctrine "is the conception of original sin, the notion that due to Adam's temptation mankind is inherently depraved."[4] Calvinism proposed that God has already selected those chosen for Heaven, and no action of man could in any way influence or change this, and that any goodness within man was from God. Syme explores how Calvinism took hold in Scotland, and eventually spread to the new world where it would leave a mark on America's cultural identity. He argues that this "long historical and geographical influence of Calvinism . . . has seen writers identify and develop a number of horrific potentialities from within the theology."[5] He identifies Christopher Marlowe's *Dr. Faustus* as an early example of fiction locating "a sense of the horror in the doctrine of Calvinism,"[6] but goes on to identify Robert Louis Stevenson, and through its spread to the new world, eventually Stephen King and H. P. Lovecraft. Syme further argues that Calvinistic predestination suggests "God lacks not only the inclination, but the ability to redeem, a deity either bound by his own rules or simply cold and unempathetic."[7] It is in this latter half that the connections between Calvinistic ideology and Lovecraft's mythos, with its "unsettling notion of a divine entity that is uncaring, unfathomable and effectively inhuman or alien," becomes clear.[8] Syme states that Lovecraft's stories "form a metaphysics of evacuated mysticism which ironically mirrors the indifference of the Calvinist God and the apocalyptic destiny of humanity."[9] Texts cannot be separated from their cultural contexts, and the case of Lovecraft and Calvinism illustrates how theological ideas can permeate stories which may not deliberately seek to convey a particular religious lore. As a franchise, *Hellraiser* draws both on Lovecraftian and Faustian influences, but doing so does not ground the narratives in any singular religious doctrine. Rather, this reflects the ongoing anxieties, fears, and cultural contexts that often drive the horror genre forward.

Contextualizing *Hellraiser*, and the franchise it spawned, is important in analyzing how it approaches religion, and perhaps more accurately, spirituality. Created by Clive Barker and based on his novella *The Hellbound Heart*, it was produced in England, by a British production team, financed by Hollywood money. Barker's own interests and history, and his upbringing in a family composed of both Catholics and Protestants, informed his own interest in the Bible and spirituality. This duality of positions perhaps goes some way to explaining the shifting, negotiable interpretations of the otherworldly and the demonic across Barker's work and his interest in gothic traditions that often highlight the monstrous. In exploring Barker's use of the gothic and Faustian pacts, Sorcha Ní Fhlainn describes Barker's "renunciation of any theological influence" and argues it is his embrace of the gothic that "opens Barker's fiction up to more complex, feminine, and queer readings."[10] Ní Fhlainn suggests that "Barker makes use of Faustian themes in order to "explore the corrupting nature of desire and the twisted path toward the sublime."[11] However, Barker's work tends to combine "borrowed traits from fantasy and horror, yet his journeys are not about reinstating the patriarchal order but rather transcending it."[12] Barker is part of a gothic tradition, and his work tends to celebrate the wonders of the supernatural and even horrific, rather than shy away from or condemn them. Ní Fhlainn suggests he embraces "the monster and the outcast, refuting the reinstatement of normality in favour of wonder."[13] This siding with the outcast, also attributable to his own queer identity, and embrace of the potential visions found within the darkness would be rendered more problematic were his worlds founded on the moral absolutism associated with traditional depictions of Heaven and Hell. Barker is less interested in punishing sinners, and more inclined to ask what drives them on, and what possible sights they might see when they cross the threshold between worlds. While the franchise would develop with influences from other writers, directors, and producers, the first film draws in many of Barker's concerns and themes found in his wider body of work. While I am not attempting to make auteurist claims at this stage, I do think it is important to understand *Hellraiser* as stemming from Barker's common interests and gothic themes. The queer gothic of Barker opens his texts up to multiple readings, and while initially creators with stronger links to him, such as *Hellbound, Hell on Earth*, and *Bloodline* writer Peter Atkins, would embrace some of the more gothic, Lovecraftian elements, the further the film texts were removed from Barker, the more they embraced traditional moralistic notions of Hell and sin.

Horror and religion have interwoven often, and both utilize themes that reflect the anxieties, concerns, and ideologies of the cultures and societies around them. However, a secular humanist view might suggest that these themes explored in horror narratives are not inherently Christian or religious but reflect the human condition in itself. Lovecraft attempted to build his own mythology but could be argued to reflect Calvinistic ideas of an apathetic God, even if not by intent. Barker's own work and history demonstrates a negotiated engagement with Christian mythology, where he draws on gothic traditions and Faustian storytelling, in order to create new and transcendent texts that break away, rather than reinforce, patriarchal order. The first two *Hellraiser* films fit perfectly into this narrative, of both drawing on rhetoric and iconography of Christianity, but also rejecting them in favor of original mythological worldbuilding. I will work now to illustrate both how this is initially achieved, and also how time and numerous sequels work to undermine this and draw the franchise back toward a more consistent and recognizable Christian narrative of demons, angels, sin, and punishment.

DEMONS TO SOME, ANGELS TO OTHERS

Central to most religious horror narratives is the representation of the demonic, whether through possessed victims or physical representations of demons themselves. *The Exorcist* (1973) is perhaps the most famous demonic possession narrative, and one that birthed a genre which often repeats its iconography and aesthetics such as in *Abby* (1974), *The Evil Dead* (1981), *The Exorcism of Emily Rose* (2005), *The Last Exorcism* (2010), and many others. Demons within film, when not possessing human bodies, are often depicted either as frighteningly monstrous or near indistinguishable from an ordinary human, the latter especially useful in narratives which see Lucifer attempting to tempt an unsuspecting mortal. Monstrous depictions of the demonic can be found in horror films such as *Evil Dead II* (1987), *Pumpkinhead* (1988), *The Church* (1989), *Children of the Corn III: Urban Harvest* (1995), *Insidious* (2010), and *Sinister* (2012), and these more horrific entities often attempt to control and manipulate human agents, though rarely directly possess them in the same way as in *The Exorcist*. The most notable horror franchise to feature both demons and angels in human form begins with *The Prophecy* (1995) starring Christopher Walken as Gabriel, seeking to win a second war in Heaven, and notable for its heavy use of religious mythology for its storyline. Other films taking this approach include *The Devil's Advocate* (1997), *Constantine* (2005), and *Drive Angry* (2011). Perhaps due to the relative lack of costs in this approach, it has also been utilized extensively by horror and fantasy television narratives such as *Charmed* (1998–2006), *Supernatural* (2005–2020), and *Good Omens* (2019). A fourth category of the demonic is an amalgamation of these, whereby the ordinary human is transformed, through either a successful possession or the granting of powers from a true demon, into a demonic entity themselves. Angela from *Night of the Demons* (1988) and Freddy Krueger of *A Nightmare on Elm Street* (1984), both fit this category, if not initially, then by revelations in later films of their respective franchises, and it is this approach that is also generally taken within the Hellraiser franchise. The demonic in *Hellraiser* is best represented by the Cenobites, and more specifically, their spokesperson and franchise icon, Pinhead. Initially presented without explanation in the original film, *Hellbound: Hellraiser II* expands on their backstory to reveal the Cenobites as having been human once, who long ago solved the Lament Configuration and were transformed into their current forms through mutilation and torture. However, while they may be representative of the demonic it is initially very ambiguous as to whether we could call them demons, and their role and objectives are very detached from traditional Christian depictions. This does change throughout the franchise's many iterations, but I shall begin by addressing how they are depicted in the initial two films, which established them as cinematic horror icons.

While the name "Cenobites" has become largely synonymous with the horror icons, giving them a separate identity from simply being demons, it is in itself a religious term that carries certain implications in how to best view them. Patricia MacCormack explains how the term, traditionally written as "coenobite," "refers to religious or monastic figures which are collective, from the Greek *koinobios*, 'to live in a community' . . . figures whose definition is premised on their being multiple."[14] In a typical example of the film's lack of subtly, ninth entry *Hellraiser: Revelations* (2011) includes an awkward scene where a character looks up "cenobite" in a dictionary, identifying them as "a member of a religious order." However, until this postmodern, self-referential moment the franchise has largely avoided addressing "Cenobites" etymological origins, if indeed they use the label at all. The community aspect is appropriate however, especially in the first two films, before Pinhead becomes a more central figure, and the other Cenobites repositioned as his subordinates. While the beginnings of this can be seen in *Hellbound*, where Pinhead alone seems to control the supernatural chains that attack various characters, the film still retains the communal nature of the Cenobites. Pinhead is certainly the spokesperson of the group and has a level of authority because of this, but the Cenobites still function as a collective group, toward the same goals. The multiple is therefore contracted into the singular, with Pinhead and the Female using "each other's mouth to speak, literally, they speak in tongues."[15] In their first full appearance in *Hellraiser*, both Pinhead and The Female Cenobite (Grace Kirby) finish each other's sentences; "But if you cheat us" begins The Female, "we'll tear your soul apart" concludes Pinhead. MacCormack suggests that "their sentences are formed of relay interjections, rather than a single speaker orientating single sentences and thus expressing singular, volitional and dividuated meanings."[16] The plural of "we" is also used as the primary descriptor by all the Cenobites, with the only use of "I" from Pinhead coming when he decides to agree to Kirsti's offer of leading them to Frank. The Female suggests "perhaps we prefer you," but here Pinhead uses his authority as spokesperson to state "I want to hear him confess himself." The instant continuation of dialogue from the Female and the return of the plural renders it a moment of internal deliberation within the collective mind. MacCormack sees this as further reflecting a contradictory state of being, where they speak from multiple mouths but in one voice, further reflective of the ambiguity seen in their embrace of pleasure and pain, good and evil, coercion and seduction, and ultimately opposing the unified monotheism of one true Word of God.[17] The Cenobites are a queer collective community in *Hellraiser* and *Hellbound*, and with Pinhead yet to stand apart as the franchise's monstrous icon, they remain a detached, otherworldly force that challenges traditional ideology and morality, rather than active participants within it.

So far, I have addressed the Cenobites as a community, drawing on Mac-Cormack's work to position them as a collective force that is both plural and also folded into a singular force. I now aim to address directly their own identities and how the franchise struggles to reconcile their statements in the first two films with more Christian-inspired ideas of the demonic. As a word, "Cenobite" has become associated with the specific entities seen in the Hellraiser franchise, but even within the films, references to this name tend to be inconsistent, and many of the later sequels have avoided it altogether, substituting the more generic "demon." The Cenobites first properly introduce themselves to Kirsty after she solves the Lament Configuration in her hospital room. The conversation what follows gives rise to the famous dialogue, "Demons to some, Angels to others," a line referred to in publicity and reference material ever since. While this does reflect the contradictory nature of the Cenobites, it is not helpful in discerning who they are to themselves, as it is a statement regarding how others see them. To see them as demonic is not difficult as, while they lack a traditional iconography of hooves or horns, they are coded as Other, and their seemingly violent imagery of bodily mutilation and nonconformitant leather apparel marks them as oppositional to a heteronormative, patriarchal culture. However, it can be argued that it is many of these same features that work to also depict them as angelic, or indeed, Christ-like in their representation. The bodies of the Cenobites themselves are queered, while Uncle Frank acts as a vampire throughout the first film, a role that is inherited first by Julia in *Hellbound*, and then Pinhead himself in *Hell on Earth*. The franchise has strong connections to the vampire genre, and Rachel Mann's work on the queer vampire in horror offers up an alternative perspective from which to view the Cenobites. Mann argues that the vampiric body "a body transformed beyond the human realm into the realm of the monstrous and horrific" has a queerness due to its Otherness, bestowed through its damaged and transformed state.[18] Christ's body is problematized by not being the "mere heteronormative, white male body of patriarchal fantasies" but instead reflecting the same process through which the vampire returns to life after death.[19] Thus Mann finds an inherent queerness in the figure of Jesus Christ, who is both human and divine, but also upon his rebirth, carries the signs of his death. Mann describes how "his risen body bears all the marks of torture and crucifixion" and that he carries "in his body the representations of violation as well as signalling new transformed power."[20] As strong as Mann's argument is in dealing with vampire fiction, the description of Christ's body maps better still onto the Cenobites, who are transformed, empowered, queered, and reborn through their own suffering. As humans who have undergone a transformation and now bear these wounds in eternal life, the Cenobites evoke not demons, nor even angels, but Christ and God Himself. The bodies of the Cenobites further remain sights of contradiction and negotiation, as they are neither demon nor angel, and they are also simultaneously both.

In the hospital, confronted by the Cenobites for the first time, Kirsty asks them clearly "Who are you?" and it is their own answer, their self-identification that should be considered. The full reply given to Kirsty by Pinhead is that they are, "Explorers, in the further regions of experience. Demons to some, Angels to others." The most famous segment of this dialogue is simply a clarification of how others choose to interpret their appearances. In answering Kirsty's question, Pinhead identifies them first and foremost as "explorers" and that their primary interest is in "experience," tying into Frank's quest for "an experience beyond the limits." The Cenobites later claim that they "have such sights to show you." This challenges the audience's perceptions of both the demonic and angelic, but also of good and evil, further disrupting monolithic binary notions associated especially with institutional religion. Where distinct references to Christian mythology occur in *Hellraiser* it is in every occasion a comment made by the mortal characters. Only the moment where the Female Cenobite replies, "We can't, not alone" to Kirsty's angered cry of "go to hell" having the Cenobites even obliquely acknowledging a traditional Christian framework. While *Hellraiser* is steeped in religious imagery and iconography it remains the purview of the human characters and, even then, is often set aside or rejected. Larry clears Ludovico Place of his deceased mother's statues of Christ, telling Julia they "mean nothing" to him. Later on, a pair of nuns ignore Kirsty as she flees from the house, while a statue of Christ falling out of a closet nearly gives the location of Kirsty away to Frank at the film's climax. Frank himself appears to be the most religious character, both referencing divinity on several occasions ("please God, help me") and having a crucifix among his belongings. However, this all remains essentially disconnected from the Cenobites, who refuse to be bound by human interpretation of their behavior and images, but instead maintain their identities as explorers, described further in the original novella as "theologians." Their infamous line of "we have such sights to show you" is as much a promise as a threat, and the experiences offered by the Cenobites are such that even as Frank flees them, he ultimately still craves to return, licking his lips and smiling as they rend his flesh apart at the film's conclusion. The Cenobites are a plurality, a community in constant conversation and negotiation, which positions them not as opposed to religious doctrine, but set aside from it, and interested more in their own explorations of experience than with human concerns of morality, sin, punishment, or damnation. This presentation of the Cenobites only lasts for the first two films, and even *Hellbound* begins the process of equating them closer to the demonic, much more freely utilizing the term "Hell" to describe the Cenobites' reality. Yet despite this, *Hellbound* also takes the audience directly into a vision of Hell that does not map onto any particular biblical vision and draws more from both eighties fantasy films and fairy-tale narratives.

WHEN YOU'RE DEAD, YOU'RE FUCKING DEAD

The Cenobites' world is barely glimpsed in the first *Hellraiser* film,[21] while the novella describes only a province that looks akin to "vast black birds caught in a perpetual tempest." This all changes in *Hellbound*, which, as the title suggests, takes the action directly into the Cenobites' world, revealing a vision of Hell which owes far more to the gothic, fairytales, and eighties fantasy than it does to the fire and brimstone of traditional depictions. Hell, in this case, is a vast and seemingly endless stone labyrinth that descends downward and features rooms occupied by those claimed by the Cenobites, who are tortured in ways designed specifically for them. At the very top of the Labyrinth are endless stone walkways and a dark sky where a vast gray diamond rotates, black light pouring out from it. This is identified as Leviathan, a name for a sea serpent in the Bible, but used here as a deity that rules the Cenobites' world, and the closest thing to the devil that can be found in the film. The Labyrinth is seen to entice people into it, to torture and torment, but the film rarely frames this as a form of punishment for its characters and, as I will demonstrate, Hell here also appears to offer assistance for some occupants, and transformation and transcendence for others.

One of the driving motivations for Kirsty to explore the Labyrinth in *Hellbound* is to try and find and rescue her father, Larry, who was murdered by Frank at the climax of the previous film. The rules by which life and death operate in the Hellraiser franchise are not only loosely defined but tend to change as the series progresses toward more Orthodox representations of Christianity within its mythology. When the Cenobites come for Frank at the opening of the first film not only do they tear him apart but they themselves then close the box, taking his organic body with him back to their world, implying a continued connection between body and soul. If, as MacCormack argues, the Cenobites offer transformation rather than destruction, then it logically follows that they offer a form of immortality where the soul does not leave the body. This ties closely with the first two Hellraiser films, which emphasize a difference between the Cenobites' world, and any form of true death, although this is not without some ambiguity itself. Kirsty enters Hell to find her father but eventually finds the message asking for help, which she believed to be from Larry, was actually from Frank who intends to rape Kirsty. Confronted with Frank, Kirsty breaks down, crying for her father at which point Frank epitomizes the themes of *Hellbound* in telling her, "grow up. When you're dead, you're fucking dead." This outright rejection of the afterlife, however, comes from a character not known for his trustworthiness or theological knowledge, leaving the decision as to whether to accept this message with the audience themselves. The unreachable nature of Larry in itself also does not predispose the series to rejecting eternal life, however, but merely places him, and the true afterlife, outside the reach of the Cenobites and their world. Just as Heaven, God, and those who have died are outside the tactile reach of those with faith, so it is here that Larry's death, as opposed to Frank's un-death, has put him beyond the purview of Kirsty, even within the fictional horror landscape. Whether this is the case or not, however, it does put greater emphasis on the Labyrinth as a physical realm inhabited by those brought there by the Cenobites, rather than as a destination for those who have died any form of natural death.

The visualization of Hell cannot help evoking the classic eighties fantasy *Labyrinth* (1986), but this is primarily because both films are drawing on fairy tales as their source material. Just as Sarah embarks on a quest to rescue her baby brother from David Bowie's Goblin King, and learn of responsibility and adulthood, so Kirsty follows a similar trajectory. She journeys to the Labyrinth to seek out her deceased father only to realize he is unreachable, and in accepting his loss, finds the maturity to take help from Tiffany, confront the Cenobites, and ultimately reach adulthood. *Hellbound* is often not subtle with this narrative, and the film's driving principle is set out from the very beginning when Detective Ronson implores Kirsty to tell him what happened in the first film, demanding "and this time no demon fairy tales," Kirsty responds, "Fairy tales? Sometimes they come true, Detective. Even the bad ones." When the returned Julia confronts Kirsty, she recognizes her changing role in the narrative: "They didn't tell you, did they Kirsty? They've changed the rules of the fairy tale. I'm no longer just the wicked stepmother. Now I'm the evil Queen. So come on. Take your best shot, Snow White."

Brigid Cherry argues that "the representations of strong femininity and female sexuality are shared between Kirsty as a strong female hero and Julia as a monstrous femme fatale" and that Kirsty "bears many points of overlap with the heroine of the fairytale."[22] *Hellbound*'s fairy-tale narrative is built around Kirsty's own ascent to adulthood, including acceptance of her father's death, and at the climax she literally steals the skin from Julia to wear as a disguise. By wearing this skin, she is able to distract Channard, and, in doing so, Kirsty reclaims representation of female sexuality from Julia and completes her maturity into adulthood. This fairy-tale narrative is played out hand-in-hand with a scientific narrative that equates the Labyrinth with the mazes and pathways of the mind. Just as Kirsty's journey is toward adulthood, Channard seeks the Labyrinth for knowledge and transformation ("I have to see, I have to know"), and his obsession with the occult and unlocking hidden knowledge is framed as a scientific pursuit. Rather than taking a more obvious route of positioning scientific reason in opposition to religious doctrine, *Hellbound* instead equates psychiatry with gothic fairy tales, in order to thematically focus on the transformation of its character, whether into adulthood as with Kirsty, or into a Cenobite as with Channard. Despite the labeling of the Cenobites' world as "Hell" in the dialogue, *Hellbound* has little interest in tying this to Christian orthodoxy, but rather emphasizes its metaphorical potential for scientific exploration and psychological development.

The Labyrinth and the Cenobites are ruled over by Leviathan, an entity that is more a geometric shape than an organic creature, evoking the indifferent Old Gods of the Lovecraft mythos but one who is given voice and intent through Julia. She tells Channard it is "the God that sent me back. The God I serve in this world and yours. The God of flesh, hunger, and desire. My God. Leviathan. Lord of the Labyrinth," and later states, "it wanted souls and I brought you." In an unused, earlier draft of the script, Leviathan was in fact depicted as a large jellyfish-like entity wielding tentacles, one of which eventually attaches itself to Channard when he comes a Cenobite, much like the final film. Leviathan is framed not as a demon or the devil, but within the pantheon of Lovecraft's Old Gods, which, as I have discussed previously, are reflecting a Calvinist reading of Christian lore. However, *Hellbound*'s depiction of Hell, and the idea of Leviathan as the God of the Cenobites, very much disappears from the *Hellraiser* film mythology, aside from fleeting references, once the series begins to move away from its British gothic roots and toward Hollywood. The third and fourth films, both written by *Hellbound*'s Peter Atkins, retain a sense of thematic continuity. *Hell on Earth* takes great efforts to position its depiction of Pinhead as an aberration from the previous films, an unambiguously evil entity separated from his human half by events in previous installments. *Hell on Earth* deals in themes of redemption, the horror of war, and a sense of catharsis in blaspheming toward a God that remains noticeably absent from the text, with the franchise's first onscreen priest telling the protagonist that "demons aren't real, they're parables, metaphors." While *Bloodline* sees the series embrace a more traditional good-versus-evil dynamic, emphasizing a duality between darkness and light, and also evoke the aesthetic of eighteenth-century spiritualism and occult rituals, it remains ambivalent about the authority or existence of God Himself. When the series left cinemas to the ignominy of direct-to-video releases, the inconsistency within the franchise increased, as numerous creative voices were able to place their own perspectives into the texts. Peter Atkins would not write another sequel, and Barker would have less and less influence, so the series began to reflect both the beliefs of those making the films but also their personal interpretations of the *Hellraiser* mythology itself.

THERE IS NO GOOD . . . THERE IS NO EVIL
. . . THERE IS ONLY FLESH

The attack on the World Trade Center on September 11, 2001 impacted all aspects of culture and society, not just in America, but globally, and as is often the case, the horror genre particularly began to pick up on changing fears and preoccupations. A direct connection to this event and the shifting changes in the horror genre have been questioned, with Laura Mee suggesting that many of the apparent allegories identified are often wider conventions of the horror genre, and often fleeting and inconsequential in the narratives themselves. Mee suggests films of this era are generally not directly, or deliberately, associating themselves with the events of 9/11, but rather that images and themes that play on the American public conscious are manifested more as ambiguous metaphors and references.[23] Barker himself has suggested that audiences have turned to the horror genre as one way of dealing with the changing situations within the world:

> The burning Twin Towers have appeared in front of us as living, vital images that say, "Be afraid—be very afraid." And how do you deal with that in your daily life? One of the ways you take hold of the things that frighten you is to grasp as you grasp the nettle, very tightly, so it doesn't sting. Horror is a debased form, but people are seeing movies and reading books in unprecedented numbers because it's speaking to our anxiety.[24]

Barker embraces the fantasy genre more in this era, beginning to write his children's series *Abarat* and appearing to embrace a greater moral dualism as well, saying "I think in a weird way the worlds of fantasy are purer worlds than the worlds of what we'll loosely call realistic fiction. You can see distinctly where good and evil lie. You can see how the moral landscape is shaped."[25] The changes in the Hellraiser franchise in the post-9/11 world do not reflect a deliberate repositioning of the series themes, but a general reflection of changing public consciousness, especially in regards to religion and ideas of good and evil. While Barker's influence and input in the Hellraiser films at this stage was minimal, his authority as an auteur figure would become more prominent in the next decade, influencing the franchise's public perception through the 2010 *Hellraiser* comic series, and then *The Scarlet Gospels* novel. I have already discussed the Faustian aspects of *Hellraiser*, while Barker's *The Damnation Game* sees a demonic figure making bargains to claim people's souls, but Mamoulian is an allegory for Lucifer rather than a literal embodiment. When Barker addresses the conflict between older, pagan Goddesses and the singular patriarchal God, Hapexamendios, in his novel *Imajica*, the narrative world is once again an allegorical one of his own creation, and it concludes with the death of the ultimately villainous God. However, Barker's work in the twenty-first century becomes more overtly

Christian in tone, moving away from just using the theological themes to explore his own created mythologies, to writing narratives set within a Christian tradition, where Lucifer, Hell, God, sin, and punishment are all existing characters and places, albeit ones filtered through his usual ideological concerns and imaginings. The Hellraiser franchise seems to increasingly follow this path, and following the publication of *The Scarlet Gospels*, a book that sees Pinhead engage in an airborne brawl with Lucifer, the film sequel *Hellraiser: Judgment* also turns to the Bible, God, and angels as central players in its narrative. While Barker's wider work is outside the scope of this chapter, I argue that both his work and the Hellraiser franchise itself transitions from allegorical depictions of theological ideas set within their own mythological framework to more literal interpretations of Christian doctrine, filtered through the iconography associated with both Barker and *Hellraiser*'s brand identities.

The first film in the franchise to overtly engage more with Christian themes of morality and sin would be 2000's *Hellraiser: Inferno*, directed by Scott Derrickson. (Derrickson would go on to explore some similar ideas in *The Exorcism of Emily Rose* [2005]). The scripts for both of these were cowritten with Paul Harris Boardman, whom Derrickson describes as a skeptic.[26] The two of them felt that by writing together they could give different perspectives on the material. This idea feels born out in *Inferno*, which constantly seems to be in a process of negotiation between its morality play story and the existing Hellraiser franchise. *Inferno* follows the story of Joseph Thorn (Craig Sheffer), a corrupt detective who cheats on his wife with sex workers, uses recreational drugs, beats his informants, and steals from evidence, all generally in the pursuit of his own gratification. On the surface the film acts as a morality play as Thorn slowly realizes that, after solving the Lament Configuration in the first act, he has in fact been transported to Hell where he will relive his own sins over and over, concluding that "I have faced my own demons and now, the only thing I know for certain, is that I must live with them, forever." Chess is used as a motif to present good and evil, and Thorn is said to have been playing against himself as the two sides of his personality have been in conflict. However, these moral absolutes are subverted by the film's narrative trajectory, that removes the possibility of redemption even as Thorn has decided to change his ways, and through the impact of the audience's cultural awareness of the wider franchise. Thorn shows the Lament Configuration to his psychiatrist Dr. Gregory (James Remar), who has seen it before and is able to explain the backstory of the franchise to him:

> It's called the Lament Configuration. It appears in occult literature here and there throughout the centuries. . . . You open it. They come for you. And they

tear you apart. Some call them Cenobites. Others call them Demons and say they take you to Hell.

A binary dynamic is set up here between the creatures summoned as Cenobites or demons. While this is not as direct as the original identification of the Cenobites as "demons to some, angels to others," discussed previously, it does articulate the same idea that their identities reflect how other people view them. Here, the "angel" option has been removed, and the film offers up a choice between "Cenobite" and "demon," but notably does not instantly equate the two as the same thing. Viewers with an awareness of the franchise as a whole will know they are indeed Cenobites, rather than simply "demons," destabilizing the idea that *Inferno* unequivocally shifts the franchise's paradigm to a Christian framework. Rather, reflecting Derrickson's wider body of work, *Inferno* works to negotiate contrasting theological positions and encourages the audience to engage with metaphysical discussions.

If *Inferno* has an ambiguous reconciliation between its more overt Christian themes and the previous entries in the Hellraiser franchise, then it is 2018's *Hellraiser: Judgment* that fully embraces a deliberate shift into Christian mythology. The film follows a police investigation into a serial killer whose murders evoke the Ten Commandments, a clear reference to the religious thriller *Se7en* (David Fincher, 1997), with the perpetrator eventually being revealed as corrupt Detective Sean Carter (David Carney) attempting to drive people back to the Bible. This is "sin ordained by Heaven," as Hell is warned to release Sean to continue his work and encourage people to become more religious, in an effort by the filmmakers to lend God a sense of moral ambiguity. For the first time in the franchise an angel appears, named Jophiel (Helena Grace Donald), depicted as an ordinary woman dressed in white. She is presented as having evicted Adam and Eve from the Garden of Eden, is shown as having authority over Hell and the Cenobites, and acts as a representative of God. *Judgment* relishes its depiction of Christian iconography, featuring angels, numerous biblical quotations from a variety of characters, including Pinhead (Paul T. Taylor) on several occasions, a character having a crown of nails inserted into their forehead, and continuous discussions of sin, judgment, and the punishment of the guilty. There is an enthusiasm in removing the traditional ambiguity of religion within the franchise, with some irony in its breaking this taboo to do something that was previously beyond the limits of the series, more so even than Barker himself had in *The Scarlet Gospels*. *Judgment* concludes with Pinhead refusing to obey God and using the traditional hooks and chains to destroy Jophiel. God punishes Pinhead by turning him human, leaving him a rambling homeless man on earth. *Judgment*'s depiction of God has aspects of Calvinistic ideology as God remains distant and disavows any redemption for Sean, but otherwise the film deliberately sets out to foreground elements of Christian orthodoxy and specific notions of good and evil as binary opposites. *Judgment* reflects growing anxieties in culture and engages with religious concerns about increased secularism, but its messages remain somewhat confused. Its attempts to both overtly use elements of Christian mythology, while also maintaining themes associated with *Hellraiser*, render it a destabilized and incoherent text. By attempting to close down the ambiguity of the Hellraiser franchise, *Judgment* is rendered both mythologically confused in its narrative messages and philosophically less profound that it aspires to be.

While *Inferno* and *Judgment* stand as the two films most heavily imbued with Christian mythology, it is important to be aware of how this change evolves across the ten films that currently make up the franchise. It is not a direct evolutionary trajectory but rather a negotiated transition between positions, shifting from film to film primarily motivated by the interests and preoccupations of their respective filmmakers. Gary Tunnicliffe wrote both *Revelations*, evoking the core themes and mythology of the first two films and emphasizing the Cenobites as explorers, and also *Judgment*,[27] in which he seems to have drawn influence from the release of *The Scarlet Gospels*. It would be remiss to ignore the influences from Eastern mysticism archetypes, stemming from the Chinese puzzle box that originally inspired Barker, or the philosophical discussions of both *Hellbound* and *Deader*. As I have demonstrated, even when the franchise does directly address Christian mythology, it is not in a straightforward or necessarily orthodox manner, remaining open for interpretation from different theological positions.

CONCLUSION: "WE HAVE SUCH SIGHTS TO SHOW YOU"

While I have tended to focus on Christianity as the primary religious reference point, this is only because it has in many ways become the default assumed mythological position for the Hellraiser franchise, which as I have shown, reaches its apotheosis in *Hellraiser: Judgment*. However, I argue that the Hellraiser franchise is best understood as a destabilized space of religious ambiguity, which offers up the potential for varied theological readings and interpretations. I have offered potential humanist readings primarily to help dispel these presumptions of specific intentional interpretations of the franchise narratives, and I have sought to emphasize how the first two films especially have little interest in representing any religious orthodoxy on screen. That this has changed reflects both a wider change in culture and in audience perceptions of the franchise, as well as changes in Barker's own work and worldview which have come concurrently with a greater emphasis of auteurist principles of his authority over the franchise's mythology. This was cemented in the traditional Hell presented in *The Scarlet Gospels*, and its positioning of Pinhead in opposition to Lucifer, battling over the dominion of

Hell itself. I reject both this claim to authorial authority and any thought that this might bind the Hellraiser franchise to a single theological outlook. The myriad interpretations of Hell, the afterlife, and the demonic in the film, books, comics, and other media, only work to increase the semiotic density of the franchise, rendering it a site of religious debate and exploration.

Rather than a weakness, the franchise's ambiguity and often contradictory approaches allow the series to be interpreted from various viewpoints, many of which have only been touched on briefly here. I would argue that this ambiguity may go some way to explaining its continuing appeal, as the franchise can be many different things to different people, with even the lower-budget sequels having their fans. For some, the Lovecraftian elements might hold the most interest, others may be drawn by the themes of sadomasochistic pleasure, while yet others may find entertainment in a depiction of the classic struggle between good and evil. For many people, religious belief itself is a deeply personal thing, fueled by their own convictions and personal moral codes, formed in part through their interpretation of the Bible and Christian doctrine. There is an inherent ambiguity in the Hellraiser franchise that perhaps reflects the ambiguity of religion in general, where mythology is interpreted in ways that serve the needs and beliefs of the individual. The continued fascination with a franchise that has languished in low-budget, direct-to-video ignominy for a quarter of a century illustrates its potential for exploration, from other scholarly fields including that of theology. It is at its core the theological ambiguity, and the franchise's potential to mean many things to many different people, that continues to imbue it with a broad appeal and offers a sight for continued debate and discussion within a fictional mythological landscape.

NOTES

1. Martin, "Introduction," 5
2. Ibid.
3. Syme, "Headlong into an Immense Abyss," 26.
4. Ibid., 15.
5. Ibid.
6. Ibid., 17
7. Ibid., 18
8. Ibid., 17
9. Ibid., 27
10. Ní Fhlainn, "Devil and Clive Barker," 209–10.
11. Ibid., 209.
12. Ibid.
13. Ibid., 211.
14. MacCormack, *Cinesexuality*, 86.
15. Ibid., 87.
16. Ibid., 86.
17. Ibid., 86–87.
18. Mann, "Let the Queer One In," 81.

19. Ibid.

20. Ibid., 81–82.

21. When Kirsty solves the Box she enters a long stone corridor, thick with webs and stretching on seemingly forever. Julia's visions of the Cenobites shows them against stones walls, marked with occult symbols. Otherwise little else is seen of the spaces they inhabit.

22. Cherry, "Beauty, Pain, and Desire," 121.

23. Mee, *Reanimated*, forthcoming.

24. Hutson, "Seven Questions."

25. McIntyre, "Hellraiser No More?"

26. Scott Derrickson, on the *Emily Rose* DVD audio commentary.

27. Tunnicliffe also directed *Judgment* himself, having been unavailable to do so for *Revelations*.

WORKS CITED

Barker, Clive. *Abarat*. New York: HarperCollins, 2002.

———. *The Hellbound Heart*. Chicago: Dark Harvest, 1986.

———. *Imajica*. New York: HarperCollins, 1991.

———. *The Scarlet Gospels*. New York: St. Martins Press, 2015.

Cherry, Brigid. "Beauty, Pain, and Desire: Gothic Aesthetics and Feminine Identification in the Filmic Adaptations of Clive Barker." In *Clive Barker: Dark Imaginer*, edited by by Sorcha Ni Fhlainn, 110–25. Manchester: Manchester University Press, 2017.

Greenaway, Jonathan. "Reconfiguring Gothic Anti-Catholicism: Faith and Folk-Horror in the Work of Andrew Michael Hurley." In *Horror and Religion: New Literary Approaches to Theology, Race and Sexuality*, edited by Eleanor Beal and Jonathan Greenaway, 159–78. Melksham: University of Wales Press, 2019.

Hutson, Matthew. "Seven Questions." Interview with Clive Barker. *Psychology Today*, April 2009.

MacCormack, Patricia. *Cinesexuality*. Surrey, UK: Ashgate Publishing, 2008.

Mann, Rachel. "Let the Queer One In: The Performance of the Holy, Innocent and Monstrous Body in Vampire Fiction." In *Horror and Religion: New Literary Approaches to Theology, Race and Sexuality*, edited by Eleanor Beal and Jonathan Greenaway, 77–94. Melksham: University of Wales Press, 2019.

Marsden, S. "Horror and the Death of God." In *Horror and Religion: New Literary Approaches to Theology, Race and Sexuality*, edited by Eleanor Beal and Jonathan Greenaway, 119–36. Melksham: University of Wales Press, 2019.

Martin, Joel. W. "Introduction: Seeing the Sacred of the Screen." In *Screening the Sacred: Religion, Myth, and Ideology in Popular American Film*, edited by Joel W. Martin and Conrad Eugene Oswalt, Jr., 1–12. Boulder, CO: Westview Press, 1995.

McIntyre, Gina. "Hellraiser No More?" Interview with Clive Barker. *Dreamwatch* 101 (February 2003). http://www.clivebarker.info/ints03.html

Mee, Laura. *Reanimated: The Contemporary American Horror Film Remake*. Edinburgh: Edinburgh University Press, 2020.

Ní Fhlainn, Sorcha. "The Devil and Clive Barker: Faustian Bargains and Gothic Filigree." In *Clive Barker: Dark Imaginer*, edited by Sorcha Ní Fhlainn, 208–29. Manchester: Manchester University Press, 2017.

Ostwalt, Conrad Eugene, Jr. "Hollywood and Armageddon: Apocalyptic Themes in Recent Cinematic Presentation." In *Screening the Sacred: Religion, Myth, and Ideology in Popular American Film*, edited by Joel W. Martin and Conrad Eugene Oswalt, Jr., 55–64. Oxford: Westview Press, 1995.

Sharrett, Cristopher. "The Horror Film in Neoconservative Culture." In *The Dread of Difference: Gender and the Horror Film*, edited by Barry Keith Grant, 253–78. Austin: University of Texas Press, 1996.

Stanley, Richard. "Dying Light: An Obituary for the Great British Horror Movie." In *British Horror Cinema*, edited by Steve Chibnall and Julian Petley, 183–95. London and New York: Routledge, 2002.

Syme, Neil. "Headlong into an Immense Abyss: Horror and Calvinism in Scotland and the United States." In *Horror and Religion: New Literary Approaches to Theology, Race and Sexuality*, edited by Eleanor Beal and Jonathan Greenaway, 15–34. Melksham: University of Wales Press, 2019.

FILMOGRAPHY

Abby. Directed by William Girdler. Los Angeles: American International Pictures, 1974.

Charmed. Created by Constance M. Burge. Los Angeles: Paramount Pictures, 1998–2006.

Children of the Corn III: Urban Harvest. Directed by James H. R. Hickox. Burbank, CA: Buena Vista Home Entertainment, 1995.

The Church. Directed by Michele Soavi. Rome: Secchi Gori Group Entertainment, 1989.

Constantine. Directed by Francis Lawrence. Burbank, CA: Warner Bros., 1995.

The Devil's Advocate. Directed by Taylor Hackford. Burbank, CA: Warner Bros., 1997.

Drive Angry. Directed by Patrick Lussier. Santa Monica: Summit Entertainment, 2011.

The Evil Dead. Directed by Sam Raimi. New York: Renaissance Pictures, 1981.

Evil Dead II. Directed by Sam Raimi. New York: Renaissance Pictures, 1987.

The Exorcism of Emily Rose. Directed by Scott Derrickson. New York: Screen Gems, 2005.

The Exorcist. DVD. Directed by William Friedkin. Burbank, CA: Warner Bros., 1973.

Good Omens. Created by Neil Gaiman. London: BBC Studios, 2019.

Hellraiser. Directed by Clive Barker. London: Cinemarque Entertainment BV, 1987.

Hellraiser: Deader. Directed by Rick Bota. New York: Dimension Films, 2005.

Hellbound: Hellraiser II. Directed by Tony Randel. Atlanta: New World Pictures, 1988.

Hellraiser: Inferno. Directed by Scott Derrickson. New York: Dimension Films, 2000.

Hellraiser: Judgment. Directed by Gary J. Tunnicliffe. New York: Dimension Films, 2018.

Hellraiser: Revelations. Directed by Victor Garcia. New York: Dimension Films, 2011.

Hellraiser III: Hell on Earth. Directed by Anthony Hickox. Granada Hills, CA: Fifth Avenue Entertainment, 1992.

Insidious. Directed by James Wan. Los Angeles: Sony Pictures, 2010.

Labyrinth. Directed by Jim Henson. San Francisco: Lucasfilm Ltd., 1986.

The Last Exorcism. Directed by Daniel Stamm. Los Angeles: Strike Entertainment, 2010.

Night of the Demons. Directed by Kevin S. Tenney. Santa Monica, CA: Blue Rider Pictures, 1988.

Nightmare on Elm Street. Directed by Wes Craven. Los Angeles: New Line Cinema, 1984.

The Prophecy. Directed by Gregory Widen. Century City, CA: First Look International, 1995.

Pumpkinhead. Directed by Stan Winston. Wilmington, NC: De Laurentiis Entertainment Group, 1988.

Se7en. Directed by David Fincher. Los Angeles: New Line Cinema, 1995.

Sinister. Directed by Scott Derrickson. Santa Monica: Summit Entertainment, 2012.

Supernatural. Created by Eric Kripke. Burbank, CA: Warner Bros. Television, 2005–2020.

Chapter Eleven

Ferocious Marys and Dark Alessas

The Portrayal of Religious Matriarchies in Silent Hill

Amy Beddows

Theologians have repeatedly drawn attention to the unfavorable portrayal of women in Judeo-Christian texts and practice. Feminist critics have noted that "the norm for women is absence and silence"[1] and that when women do appear in ancient scripture, they tend to be framed in binary terms as passive devotees or monstrous demons, virginal mothers or seductive whores, innocent lambs or corrupt sinners.[2] Unsurprisingly, such stereotypical depictions are in line with the patriarchal norms, which have long persisted in wider, secular society and which deem women as inferior and subordinate to men.[3] Subsequently, there have been calls for alternative theological interpretations which value and empower women.[4]

In the absence of such belief systems we have to look outside of existing frameworks for more egalitarian possibilities. This chapter will briefly consider the critical arguments regarding the role of women in religion, primarily Judeo-Christian canons, and explore the value of alternative representations as a challenge to the dominant power structures in nonsecular and secular society. It will do this through readings of the multimedia horror franchise *Silent Hill*, as a critical response to the ways that religious belief and practice can embody the social devaluation and control of women.

WOMEN AND RELIGION

In biblical texts, women are often presented in relational roles as mothers, wives, or mistresses rather than individuals with their own humanity and agency.[5] The predominant archetype is Eve and theological interpretations of

189

the Creation story often denote man as the superior being to his lesser female companion. Subsequently, Eve is blamed for humanity's need for salvation and has become a template for female wickedness which has justified the devaluation of women ever since.[6] Another archetype of female wickedness is Lilith; in Jewish mythology, she rejected a life of inequality as Adam's wife and was banished to become a demon. Although to some Lilith represents "the banished power and autonomy of woman,"[7] the warning is clear: Violate patriarchal expectations and you will be cast out as a monster.

Biblical women are often defined by and punished for their sexuality. Mary Magdalene's identity has been conflated with other "sinful" women and reduced to a sexual being who passively bore witness to Jesus's suffering.[8] Dinah (Genesis 34), the unnamed concubine of Levite (Judges 19), and Susannah (Book of Daniel 13) are all raped, dismissed, and held accountable for their violations,[9] demonstrating their low value as well as an inherent mistrust of women's words. Jezebel has become a cultural archetype for wicked and deceitful women (particularly women of color), while the Whore of Babylon is the ultimate symbolic conflation of female sexuality, evil, and the corruption of man.[10]

Even Mary, the most notable woman in Christian theology, imposes a template of passive femininity through her "perfection" for despite her role as mother of humanity's Savior, she has no influence or agency in biblical passages. The veneration of Mary also presents a restrictive expectation for women to either model her compliance or be punished as sinful Eves,[11] as well as the impossible aspirations of virginal purity *and* natural (heteronormative) motherhood.[12] This model of female purity is revered today by religious fundamentalisms that frame societal problems as the result of women neglecting "traditional" roles or asserting their sexuality.[13] Additionally, there is an absence of positive alternative representations of women to challenge these troubling stereotypes. Most notably, there is no template for a female "redemptrix" figure to "dismantle the systems of private repression and public violence," which complicates for women the messages of liberation which can still be found in religious texts.[14]

These are not merely theological concerns but have real, practical implications for women. Biblical messages of female devaluation have infiltrated many areas of society. Gender differences and the depreciation of female/ feminine traits are accepted as part of a natural order or "divine plan" and religious positions on issues of gender or sexuality are seen as indisputable "truths," even outside of nonsecular contexts.[15] The early templates of women as deceitful and seductive are still inherent today, in societal myths that justify the silencing and discrediting of women in the justice system, education, politics, health, and social policy.[16]

This is not intended as a blanket criticism of religion. While some doctrines may embolden misogyny in modern society, religious traditions can also challenge prejudicial messages. Yet addressing these imbalances is not as simple as merely adding women back into the picture of religion as this would do little to dismantle the underlying patriarchal structures.[17] Even the inclusion of female deities does not automatically challenge social status discrepancies; a female God can only have power if She speaks to the truth of oppression and vilification of women, otherwise She would also maintain the fallacy of equality.[18]

In light of these concerns, there have been calls for radical reimaginings of theological frameworks.[19] Mary Daly[20] proposed a matriarchal "counterworld" to create a new imagining of God, faith, and practice as a foundation for wider cultural change. Yet without prior examples of matriarchal or egalitarian frameworks to refer to, it is hard to imagine how such a society might function. This is where it may be fruitful to turn to fiction for creative imaginings of alternative religious communities.

MATRIARCHIES IN HORROR

The horror genre is known for exploring everyday fears and social or political issues through a fantastical and nihilistic lens.[21] It is an ideal medium for tearing down comfortable, familiar worlds to rebuild bold, new frontiers for audience consideration. Arguably, video games have even greater capacity to create immersive spaces through which to explore cultural anxieties via our control of and relation to symbolic avatars and representative environments[22] that can "embody uncomfortable truths about ourselves and our society."[23] In comparison to other media products, there is a decreased distance between the horror and the participatory player/viewer, which further encourages us to relate to the presented content.

The vulnerability and corruption of women is a common theme in horror, and these portrayals often conflate religious notions of "abjection" and impurity with the female body.[24] Horror is well-suited for exploring complex social issues such as difference, oppression, and the abuse of power within patriarchal societies—look to the number of media products addressing the witch trials of Europe and North America—yet despite the genre's potential for subverting the status quo, there are surprisingly few depictions of structures where women are centered and afforded power. The examples that do exist paint a negative picture of the prospect.

Matriarchal cults in film are often shown as a source of horror and evil hidden within wider patriarchal society. A recent resurgence in depictions of matriarchal groups in *Suspiria* (2018),[25] *Hereditary* (2018), *Midsommar* (2019),[26] and the *Paranormal Activity* franchise, most notably *Paranormal Activity 3* (2011), suggests a renewed interest (and renewed anxieties) in the prospect of female-centric societies.[27] While some aspects of these matriarchies are depicted positively, such as the sense of community and engagement with nature, they are also demarked as amoral, anti-Christian cults who torture and murder (notably male) nonbelievers in pursuit of their faiths. The horror of these societies lies in their deep contrast to the "normal" standpoint—primarily male, white, Western, Christian—against which they are clearly "other." By depicting alternative societies as a source of horror and violence, films such as *Midsommar* reinforce the patriarchal insistence that any challenges to the dominant power structures would be unnatural, immoral, and inherently damaging to humanity, especially men. This renders such depictions as interesting and refreshing but ultimately more problematic than hopeful. And with no comparable templates in reality or history, [28] this becomes the dominant viewpoint on matriarchal communities.

Another version of religious matriarchy can be found in *Silent Hill*. Ostensibly, the horror franchise appears to mirror the problematic depictions found within the above examples, yet a deeper reading demonstrates a reflection of feminist concerns over the role of women within religious societies while simultaneously presenting us with fascinating new templates of female resistance against such oppressive patriarchal structures.

SILENT HILL

Silent Hill is a psychological, survival-horror franchise which centers on the eponymous fictional town. The original video game *Silent Hill* (1999) was developed by Team Silent (part of the Japanese company Konami) and has spawned a number of game sequels, two films, and multiple novelizations. In the games, players explore the mostly abandoned town in order to solve clues and contend with the nightmarish monsters stalking the foggy streets. The twisting narratives are less coherent than typical horror games and the inclusion of "otherworlds"—when the town periodically shifts into the Fog World, a transitional realm of Darkness, and the disintegrating, nightmarish Otherworld or Nowhere—creates an unnerving and disorienting experience for players. [29] Despite the shifting realities, it is a very human world that focuses on those trapped in the town, with each title in the franchise following a new protagonist as they search for a missing loved one or uncover some truth about themselves.

This analysis will focus on the first and third games, *Silent Hill* and *Silent Hill 3*, and the film *Silent Hill* (2006, hereafter *SH*2006), due to the overlapping themes and common religious elements. [30]

Silent Hill (*SH1*) follows Harry Mason in his search for his daughter, Cheryl, following a car accident. He encounters a sinister cult, The Order, led by the fanatical Dahlia Gillespie who burned her own daughter, Alessa, as part of a failed ritual to "birth" the cult's deity. Alessa has supernatural powers and survived the burning by splitting into two: the "innocent" part of her was manifested as the infant Cheryl (whom Harry adopted), while the rest of her remained incapacitated in the town's hospital. Alessa's torture exaggerated her powers and created the darkness and monsters in the town. Harry thwarts the cult's plot and rescues the infant reincarnation of Alessa/ Cheryl, whom he raises as Heather (the protagonist of *Silent Hill 3*).[31]

In *Silent Hill 3* (*SH3*) we follow Heather Morris, a teenage girl who is lured to Silent Hill to avenge the murder of her father and discover the truth of her origins. The game is a direct sequel to *SH1*, and Heather is revealed to be the reincarnation of Alessa/Cheryl who is chosen by the cult (this time led by Claudia Wolf) as the vessel for their unborn god. Heather disrupts the ritual—by vomiting up the half-formed deity—and Claudia takes her place but dies during the birth. Heather kills the god and escapes the town.

The 2006 film adaptation covers the events of *SH1* with some notable differences. We follow Rose Da Silva, the adoptive mother of Sharon, as she searches for her daughter after they become separated in Silent Hill. Rose encounters the zealous cult, the Brethren, led by Christabella who ritually burned Alessa as a witch in an attempt to purify her "sin" (Dahlia is Alessa's mother but a minor cult member in the film). The burning split Alessa into three selves: her innocence as manifested in Sharon, the human Alessa who remained bedbound in the hospital, and Dark Alessa, the embodiment of suffering who is responsible for the monstrous otherworlds. In order to save her daughter from being burned, Rose helps Dark Alessa and adult Alessa gain entry to the church where the cult seeks sanctuary from the monsters and darkness. Alessa kills the cultists in revenge, and Rose and Sharon leave Silent Hill with the suggestion that Dark Alessa has merged with Sharon and gone with them.

RELIGIOUS IMAGERY AND THEMES

The *Silent Hill* franchise is characterized by dark, psychological imagery of torture, gory violence, and Catholic-tinged religious symbolism, with different narratives centering on sin, atonement, and retribution.[32] The shifting otherworlds are clear representations of limbo, purgatory, and hell, and the religious cult who inhabit the town feature prominently in the plot.

Silent Hill's design is an amalgamation of Western and Eastern cultural influences. This is particularly reflected in the town's theology, which blends Judeo-Christian iconographies (crosses, churches, altars) with elements of Shinto (mirrors/water as portals, realms of fog/darkness, pollution and purification), Native American, and Aztec mythologies.[33] This combination creates an interreligious picture of organized religions, yet the vast majority of aspects and symbols are coded as Christian. The immediacy of religious imagery in the games (a crucified corpse in *SH1*, Heather's memories of magic symbols and altars in *SH3*) and film (the opening scenes feature an illuminated cross and billboards with psalms) adds weight to the intentionality and relevance of these theological themes.[34]

The cult is the only functioning organization in Silent Hill. As other traditional institutions are either absent or reduced to a few individuals in *SH1* (Cybil Bennett as police, Dr. Kauffman and Lisa Garland as medical staff), religion is the dominant power in the town. The cult appears to follow a version of Christianity, yet there are some contradictions: in *SH1*, Dahlia refers to the cult as the "other church," the altar beneath the Antiques Shop is scrawled with "No God," and they worship a female deity. This suggests that Christianity has some importance, but their belief system is mixed with something more ancient (which is in line with other cinematic matriarchies). In the film, the Brethren are more clearly depicted as Christian through their language, their embellished crucifix symbol, and the biblical murals adorning their church. There is also no mention of a female deity.

Through the viewpoints and interactions of different characters, the world of *Silent Hill* presents a uniquely multifaceted picture of religious oppression of women. The Order uses indoctrination, hallucinogens, and violent sacrificial rituals to cement their belief system, and it is their unchecked religious fanaticism that has created the dark otherworlds through their persecution and murder of a young girl. The Brethren are obsessed with purifying "sin" by burning women and girls who are demarked as witches after daring to challenge the cult's control. Similar to the archetype of Eve, the persecution of witches is another form of female subjugation and scapegoating which was especially used against women who posed a threat to patriarchal authority by refusing to conform to expectations of purity and femininity.[35]

WOMEN IN *SILENT HILL*

The *Silent Hill* franchise embodies feminist criticisms of organized religion, particularly Christian fundamentalism, in three distinct ways. Firstly, it reflects and subverts the ways that theological frameworks often depict women as lesser. It highlights the fallacy of addressing gender inequality by affording power and reverence to the women living within patriarchal religious structures. Finally, it presents several compelling models of female resistance to the status quo. Subsequently, *Silent Hill* can be seen as a "dark doppelganger"[36] to the traditional, patriarchal religious systems, which have silenced and erased women for centuries.

The town is populated by complex female characters who both reflect and eschew the binary stereotypes usually available to women: Alessa and Dahlia, Heather and Claudia, Rose and Christabella. Even the dark versions of

Alessa are not portrayed as completely evil, for she protects her adult self and helps her to obtain justice against her abusers while showing mercy to other characters. The series confronts female-centric issues such as abuse, sexual agency, birth, and motherhood. The Silent Hill cults have a distinctly matriarchal structure and are consistently led by women—Dahlia in *SH1*, Claudia in *SH3*, Christabella in *SH2006*—and in *SH1* and *SH3,* their primary goal is to facilitate the birth of their female god through female sacrifice (Alessa and Heather, respectively).

At a cursory glance, the series seems to replicate some less than progressive messages. The protagonist in *SH1* is male with female characters being secondary (as is the case in the other games, aside from *SH3*), many of the monsters are crude mutations of the female form (patients, nurses, the deformed god), and the major antagonists are women (Alessa, Dahlia, Claudia, Christabella). *SH1* especially falls into typical gendered tropes with Harry as the male protector searching for his vulnerable daughter, reassuring the passive, emotional Lisa and thwarting the deceitful Dahlia and vengeful Alessa. In the film, the Brethren perpetuate many traditional patriarchal injuries against women, casting them out as "false prophets" (Dahlia) and violently punishing those who do not live up to their ideals (Alessa, Cybil, Sharon). This reinforces dominant narratives that women are inferior and deserving of retribution for societal violations.

Yet on closer analysis, *Silent Hill* does challenge these tropes. Firstly, the cults are depicted as cruel and misguided, and their violence against women is directly challenged by the protagonists:

> Rose: "That's your answer—burn anything you are afraid of, anything you can't control!"
>
> *SH*2006

> Heather: "A God born from hatred can never create a perfect paradise."
>
> *SH3*

Ultimately, the cult's cruel and persecutory religion fails them. In *SH1*, the ritual fails to birth the deity, whereas in *SH3*, the deity is weak and easily defeated. In *SH*2006, the cultists are unable to protect themselves from Alessa's vengeful punishment, and they perish within their church.

The wealth of strong and compassionate female characters in *Silent Hill* challenges the notion of women as lesser; they are not weak, emotional, or passive, and their male counterparts are not overly masculine or dominant in comparison.[37] There are no sexualized characters aside from the monstrous nurses, which can be read as exaggerated reflections of Alessa's attitude toward her supposed caregivers. Additionally, men are minor bystanders to the female-driven narratives of *SH3* as Heather's interactions with Harry,

Douglas, Leonard, and Vincent are designed to facilitate her development and confrontation with Claudia and the female god. The male characters in *SH*2006 are well-meaning yet ineffectual; Chris and Gucci are compassionate figures but remain sidelined in the real world while Rose rescues Sharon. Other male characters are relegated to voiceless cultists who are anonymized by protective mining gear and reduced to their physicality as thugs who assault the female characters at Christabella's orders. Even in the male-driven narrative of *SH1*, it is the women who have knowledge and guide Harry through the world (Cybil, Dahlia, Lisa). Cybil is a capable, trustworthy figure, and despite Lisa's emotional dependency, she is the one who exacts revenge on Kauffman. It could also be argued that while Harry is the protagonist, *SH1* is the story of Alessa.

Other notable male characters are the monstrous Pyramid Head, the retributive enforcer of societal rules (he skins a cultist for being outside the church in *SH*2006), the school janitor who abuses Alessa and is transformed into a barbed-wire-wrapped abomination, and Leonard Wolf, the abusive cultist father who attacks Heather in *SH3*. These monsters are stark representations of the violence enacted against women and girls who violate societal boundaries or are left vulnerable without male protectors. Throughout the *Silent Hill* series, male monsters often reflect the monstrous patriarchal forces of real life.[38] While the horror genre is often criticized for reveling in voyeuristic and sadistic abuses of women, *Silent Hill* condemns its violence by encouraging us to identify with female characters (particularly in *SH3* and *SH*2006), through the horrified reactions of onlookers, the nonsexualized nature of the victims, and the disfigurement or death of the monstrous abusers.

THE MONSTROUS FEMALE

As male monsters reflect different forms of violence, the feminine creatures represent the ways that women are restricted by religious and societal norms. The violent, twisted nurses embody the distorted care of Alessa's hospitalization and are a bastardization of the stereotype of women as "natural" caregivers. The shadowy Larval Stalkers in *SH1* and the burning Grey Children in *SH*2006 are ethereal childlike monsters who can be seen as personifying the violation of childhood innocence, in particular the sexual abuse and burning of Alessa. They are mostly benign and follow Harry and Rose in search of protection more than to cause harm; these creatures are frightening not because of their feminine characteristics but due to the grotesque reflections of female restriction and suffering which they represent.

The most notable female monster is the complicated character of Alessa. Despite her accused status as witch and subsequent destruction of the town, her portrayal is deeply sympathetic. Alessa is defined by her innocence[39] and shown as a gentle figure who is punished for who she is rather than what she does (in the film, it is implied that her "sin" was the illicit affair between her mother and unknown father). Her monstrousness is not inherent for it is the *act* of punishing her which creates the monster. The image of the badly burned adult Alessa emerging in the church, restricted by bloody bandages, is pitiful and saddening as much as horrifying and it complicates the division between victim and villain; as with her disfigurement of the abusive janitor, Alessa's violence against the cult can be seen as retributive and restorative.

Arguably, other monstrous females are the cult leaders, Dahlia and Christabella. Their decisive actions and lack of empathy are more typical of masculine villains, and they reject the role of fair, compassionate leader in favor of power and cruelty; in Dahlia's case, against her own daughter. Although Christabella's death is overtly sexualized—she is torn apart by barbed wire in a crude sexual assault—this violation could be intended to expose her as the cruel creator/mother of Alessa,[40] rather than commentary on the abjection of the female body or an attempt to titillate viewers.

SPEAKING OUT AND BEARING WITNESS

"Silencing is a hallmark of oppression," especially when speaking of abuse,[41] and as such, women are often omitted from theological narratives.[42] Conversely, *Silent Hill* elevates women's stories and encourages us to bear witness to their suffering. In *SH3*, we accompany Heather on her mission to avenge her father's death. Although mostly assertive, she has moments of uncertainty, and it is through her emotional colors that we experience the game. Her distress at finding Harry's body is given as much importance in an extended cutscene as the plot points which follow, enabling us to engage with her loss. At the Otherworld amusement park, she has to fight her gruesome doppelganger (the Memory of Alessa), which could be read as her symbolic resistance of the cult's bloody history against women, or her choosing to excise her personal trauma (as an incarnation of Alessa) rather than letting it define and consume her. At the end of the game, Heather decides to reclaim her identity as Cheryl. As well as an act of empowerment on Heather's part, this acceptance ultimately speaks to Alessa's resilience as she (repeatedly) survives the tortures of Silent Hill to live on through Cheryl and then Heather.

In *SH2006* we follow Rose's quest to alleviate Sharon's night disturbances, which take her to the town in search of answers. This is in contrast to Chris's initial insistence that they medicate and hospitalize her; Rose believes that rather than pathologize their daughter, the way to help Sharon is to *understand* what she is experiencing. We also bear witness to the fate of Cybil, the police officer who helps Rose search for Sharon, and although she is not as fleshed out as other characters, we are forced to watch her brutal beating and ritualistic burning through uncompromisingly graphic scenes. The women in Silent Hill are hardly passive martyrs to their fates, but the portrayal of their treatment makes us witnesses to their suffering and further subverts the notion of women as inactive, vulnerable victims of patriarchal forces. We sympathize with these characters because we descend into Silent Hill alongside them and are encouraged to engage with their losses, injuries, and dilemmas.

Most notably, we bear witness to Alessa's torments. Initially, Alessa herself does not speak of her experiences, and her story is told in other ways. It slowly unfolds through Harry (in *SH1*) and Rose (*SH*2006) as they explore the places where she was abused: the school, the hospital, the hotel, the other church. In *SH1*, we watch a shocked Lisa describe Alessa's injuries and unexpected survival. In the film, the horror is communicated through Dahlia's grief and regret at failing to protect her daughter. The scholar Amy Green compares Dahlia to Mary Magdalene, as she bears witness to the betrayal and torture of Alessa as well as her retributive resurrection in the church.[43] After Rose and Sharon leave Silent Hill, Dahlia is left behind as the only survivor who can speak of what happened. Similarly, Rose has to bear witness and tell the "truth" of the cult's cruel actions toward Alessa in order to allow her entry to the church.

In some ways, Alessa does speak. In the film, Dark Alessa communicates for her injured, adult self and forces us to witness her suffering, through visions of her immolation and painful existence in the hospital. When bed-bound Alessa rises up into the church, we witness the extent of her physical wounds and broken frame; yet her expression while slaughtering the cultists—of agony and sadness more than vengeful glee—frames her revenge as righting a wrong more than a sadistic pleasure. Like Dahlia, we are forced to confront the horror of her daughter's transformation: "What have you become?" Until this point, we have followed Rose and Sharon, but we become invested in the perverse justice of killing Christabella and the cult, and—unlike Rose and Sharon—we do not hide our eyes from it. Dark Alessa dances and revels in the falling blood, aligning us (as viewers and horror fans) with the savage, hateful part of Alessa, which makes our witnessing all the more cathartic.

ALTERNATIVE MOTHERS

Motherhood is a major theme in *Silent Hill* and we are presented with a variety of complex mothers who demonstrate that the role requires significantly more than biological birth alone.[44] Dahlia is the ultimate callous mother in *SH1*, abusing her daughter and showing similar disregard for Cheryl in fervent pursuit of her faith; she is doubly a mother to Alessa, as her violence also "births" her daughter's split selves. Her counterpart in the film adaptation, Christabella, initially appears as a compassionate, maternal figure to the Brethren but similarly deceives and tortures others to meet her own ideological ends. She tricks the naïve Dahlia into letting them purify her child. The film version of Dahlia thus represents the "failed mother" who may love her daughter but must shoulder the guilt of failing to protect her.[45] Curiously, the cult accuses Alessa of not having a father, which raises some suggestion of a virgin conception (though it is more likely that Dahlia is being damned for her sexuality, which adds to her comparison with Mary Magdalene). Another failed mother is Claudia in *SH3*, who endeavors to bring about the birth of God but dies in the process and is unable to protect her progeny from Heather's destruction.

These imperfect mothers sit in stark contrast to Rose. Green has written extensively on the comparisons between Rose and Mary, mother of Jesus; she argues that compared with Mary's subservience, Rose "represents both the sorrowful, searching mother and also the one ready to enact violence to be reunited with her offspring and to punish evildoers."[46] She is caring and sympathetic to her child as well as to Dark Alessa but is also a "violent avenger" when facing Christabella and the cult. Interestingly, Rose appears to have some Christian faith, as she prays for God's help when being pursued by the Brethren, but the necklace she clutches is a locket of Sharon, rather than a crucifix, which exalts her role as mother into something divine.

Rose also overcomes the virgin-mother dichotomy discussed by theological scholars. As adoptive mother of Sharon—and arguably of Dark Alessa, through her later absorption—she has not biologically birthed her children but cares for them more fiercely than Alessa's "natural" mother. She is willing to sacrifice herself for her child: She travels to an unknown town, is separated from her loving partner, escapes monsters, and is stabbed by Christabella, all for Sharon. She also offers her body as a vessel for Dark Alessa to enter the church, another potential allegory for motherhood. Green suggests that as a modern archetype for Mary, Rose manages the apparent contradictions between compassion, ferocity, and love that are complicated by traditional, passive images of the Holy Mother.

Moving to *SH3*, there is also the figure of the unwilling mother in Heather. After realizing that she is gestating a god-fetus (via another seemingly virginal "pregnancy"), she chooses to abort the fetus rather than carry the twisted conception to term, rejecting the cult's hateful ideologies as well as asserting her reproductive autonomy. This monstrous subversion of pregnancy and the half-formed god that emerges from Claudia illustrates the hideous abnormality that is procreation forced against the will of the mother. Heather is a bold archetype of choice and self-preservation against the venerated sanctity of selfless motherhood so often represented.

Finally, there is Alessa, the "mother of god" (Dahlia, *SH1*). To survive her suffering, she "births" her innocence into Cheryl/Sharon and her rage into Dark Alessa, and also conceives the monstrous representations of her abuse, which stalk the town in yet more versions of immaculate conception. In the final showdown in *SH1*, she is reborn as the Incubator and delivers her innocence in the form of baby Heather to Harry for protection. Her mother status comes not just from her progeny but also her mercy; she spares Rose and Sharon during the cult's slaughter and also Dahlia, whom she appears to forgive for her inaction:

> Dahlia: "Why did she not take me with the others?"
> Rose: "Because you're her mother. Mother is God in the eyes of a child."
>
> *SH*2006

The value in these varied incarnations of motherhood lies in their challenge to the notion of a single "perfect" maternal template of meekness and self-lessness. These archetypes also allow for the rejection of motherhood alto-gether, an option which is often not presented as available to women but one which elevates female humanity and agency above the ability to procreate. To reject the role of mother can be seen as an act of resistance in the face of such strident expectations and restrictive gender roles.

FEMALE RESISTANCE AND FEMALE SAVIORS

The world of *Silent Hill* provides several templates for "female power, both redemptive and terrible,"[47] which resist the patriarchal constructs that try to suppress their agency. Rose provides a loving and fierce archetype for moth-erhood that transcends patriarchal expectations and embodies female autono-my without rejecting her gender. Yet she does not attempt to control or belittle other women; she recognizes Dahlia's humanity despite her passive neglect as a mother, and she transforms from active participant to quiet observer during Alessa's revenge in the church. Her status is elevated above a purely relational role to Sharon or Chris to that of a deity: As both Rose and Cybil proclaim, "mother is God in the eyes of a child."

Cybil in *SH*2006 also represents a powerful savior through her role of selfless helper. Despite having no personal connection to Sharon, Alessa, or the town, she ends up sacrificing everything to support Rose. At first, she represents a typically masculine, patriarchal authority figure (short hair, gruff attitude, mistrust, physical aggression), but throughout the film she sheds her trappings of authority (by losing her helmet, glasses, jacket, and gun) and becomes more compassionate. Cybil's dedication to saving others is men-tioned several times by Gucci, and her last words are a plea not to spare herself but to save Sharon; she is ultimately burned for the "sin" of selflessly supporting other women and defying the religious system which persecutes them.

In the figure of Heather in *SH3*, we have a template for resistance and survival that is grounded in reality. In many ways, she is a "typical" teenage girl as evidenced by her interest in fashion, her playfulness, and sarcastic humor, yet these traits are not belittled or equated with weakness. She is streetwise and self-protective: She refuses to engage with Douglas when he approaches her at the mall—"Are you still following me, do I have to scream?"—and remains mistrustful of other characters' motivations. She also survives her trauma and loss without having to fragment or compartmentalize into monstrous versions of herself. She is thoughtful and considerate to the pain of others—she listens to the words of the Confessor (who may be Dahlia) and forgives Douglas for his role in her father's death—but vehemently rejects the cult's promises of salvation in favor of her moral beliefs:

> Heather: "Suffering is a fact of life. Either you learn how to deal with that or you go under. You can stay in your own little dream world but you can't keep hurting other people."
>
> *SH3*

As the counterpoint to Alessa, Heather chooses to resist her hate and pain rather than embrace it; yet this strength does not minimize her survival. She is a model of resistance who is strong because she *has* to be, and the action centers on her because of the cult's machinations; she does not choose to seek it out. She is also self-aware of her reality, asking, "Is that the end? I guess it's time to roll the credits" before stepping into the Darkness to return to the real world. This makes her a very human character. The scholar Ewan Kirkland points out that Heather's combination of typically feminine traits with her strength and complexity makes her a relatable figure for both female and male gamers.[48]

Although antagonist as much as protagonist, Alessa is perhaps the most interesting template of resistance as simultaneously victim, survivor, and avenger. As with Heather, the severity of her abuses is not minimized by her survival, and she is arguably the most powerful character in the series: Pyramid Head, Leonard Wolf, or the half-formed god have little weight in comparison. Her cruel actions are not reduced to simple "evil," for she embraces Dark Alessa and transforms Silent Hill out of desperation to survive rather than an intention to cause hurt:

> Dark Alessa: "When you're hurt and scared for so long, fear and pain turn to hate and the hate starts to change the world."
>
> *SH*2006

Even her existence is shown as an act of resistance, through her possession of supernatural powers. Although it is bestowed on her by others, her identity as a witch is a powerful one "beyond the good and evil of patriarchy's world."[49] In the film, Dahlia observes her "becoming," as Alessa's fragmentation allows her to marry the conflicts between honoring and protecting her innocence, valuing the justice of her rage as well as accepting the existence of her adult self. Despite all that was done to her, she retains her autonomy and her choice of transformation is an act of resistance: She was not created, she *became.*

These models of female resistance can be seen as possible saviors for women looking for "a Christ who can affirm her own personhood as woman."[50] Their subversion of both feminine and masculine traits could also provide meaning for men looking to escape the restrictions of patriarchal convention. However, as is often the case with cultural representations, it must be noted that *Silent Hill* reflects the experiences of white women, and these depictions of motherhood and female "redemptrices" are unlikely to offer significant representation or meaning for women of color.

THE FALLACY OF ELEVATING WOMEN
WITHIN A PATRIARCHY

The franchise also addresses the fallacy of empowering women within existing systems and expecting change or equity. Horror scholar Alison Lang observes that religious cults often emerge from a dissatisfaction with mainstream options for autonomy or acceptance,[51] therefore the female-centric cults of *Silent Hill* could be seen as a (problematic) reaction to the ways that women are omitted and ignored by mainstream religions. The fallacy of equality is clearly demonstrated through the cult's savage capacity for cruelty; despite their matriarchal belief system and power structure, they view women as vessels for torture and death in pursuit of their faith. The Order's female god is mostly absent, and when she does appear in *SH3*, she is fallible enough to be dispatched by a nonbeliever (Heather). As previously mentioned, female deities often support the illusion of equality and the fact that The Order's deity is never referred to as a "goddess" suggests she is just another version of the traditional male Creator. The god of Silent Hill is painted as an inversion of the God of Christianity, whose tenets are hate and destruction rather than love and forgiveness:

> Claudia: "I thank you for nurturing God with all the hate in your heart."
>
> *SH3*

The fact that the deity's existence is mostly irrelevant to the plot of the games (and absent in the film) shows that it is the blind faith and conduct of the human followers, not the underlying mythology, which is the source of evil in *Silent Hill*; this mirrors many of the caveats that criticize interpretation or practice more so than religion itself. Despite the assumption of female gentleness and compassion, Dahlia and Christabella are quick to advocate deceit, torture, and murder in pursuit of their faith. The hotel murals in *SH*2006 suggest that many women have been burned in the cult's battle against the Darkness, yet they absolve themselves of guilt by blaming the town's hellish transformation on sinners and impurity. And as discussed, the cult has no power and does not offer anything liberating or hopeful for women (or anyone), other than as a counterpoint to the versions of resistance who come up against them; the cultists live bleak, dangerous, and restricted lives within the desolate town, with little hope of salvation or reprieve.

THE COUNTERWORLD

As well as exploring individual templates for salvation and resistance, *Silent Hill* presents a version of Daly's counterworld, the radical deconstruction of patriarchal society, through its shifting reality states. As player/viewer, we witness the spreading decay of rust and rotting metal, flaking paint and ash that takes over the town, and this disintegration is most apparent within the institutions that are key sites of socialization and patriarchal control: schools, hospitals, churches. The deeper we progress through the otherworlds, the more unstable and disorienting these places become, and the reality shifts are heralded by sirens or crackling radio static, harbingers of communication failure and crumbling humanity. On a more metaphorical level, the otherworlds may also reflect the different stages of coming to terms with such a counterworld, where the Fog World represents confusion or lack of hope and the Darkness realm stands for the void of the unknown before we enter the horrific, deconstructed reality of Otherworld/Nowhere.

As well as the collapse of physical environments, *Silent Hill* explores the fracturing of the heteronormative family: Harry's wife has died and he is separated from Cheryl; Heather is orphaned and unsure of her identity; Rose, Chris, and Sharon are permanently separated. Although these splintered families and the transitions between otherworlds are both effective mechanisms for advancing plot or tension and characteristic of the series' horror aesthetic, they can also act as metaphor for the extreme upheaval of the status quo. Pursuit of a true counterworld would mean the destruction of everything patriarchal—from societies to institutions and individual families—and the results *are* horrifying. This points toward the representations of individual resistance as a more hopeful, and bearable, direction for escaping the confines of patriarchal control.

However, it is apparent that such resistance cannot come without loss. In *SH1*, Harry escapes the town with a new soul to care for but has had to leave his seven-year-old daughter behind. The events of *SH3* leave Heather facing a brave new future alone, without her family, her name, or her old identity. *SH*2006 ends with Rose and Sharon (and possibly Dark Alessa) separated from Chris in the Fog World. Yet there is also hope: Harry has Heather, Heather embraces her new identity, and Rose and Sharon seem safe and content to be with each other.

CONCLUSION

In her thorough analysis of *Silent Hill*, Green summarizes the film as a critique of blind faith more so than of Christianity.[52] However, I would argue that the series dissects and explores the ways that religion can be exploited in justification of the devaluation and control of women. Feminist theologians have long championed the need for alternative religious canons that provide value and respect to women, and perhaps such alternatives can be imagined through the exploration of subversive counterworlds in horror. With its multilayered portrayal of religion, gender roles, oppression, and retribution, *Silent Hill* fulfills these stipulations by both problematizing patriarchal structures and providing complex, relatable female-driven models of resistance. It presents a matriarchal society that imbues women with power while also demonstrating how such a system would replicate the devaluation and persecution of women; although this seems to follow the narrative set by other negative portrayals of matriarchies, *Silent Hill* explores why this would be problematic and offers more realistic feminist possibilities.

At the very least, immersive media products like *Silent Hill* can provide women with complex alternatives to the restricted options afforded through societal norms. We can aspire to be gentle and ferocious like Rose, or to recreate ourselves as an act of resistant survival like Alessa, or refuse the expectations defined by our gender like Heather. We can also experience the catharsis of bearing witness to the realities of female suffering and entertain the possibility of restorative justice. In this way, the horror genre—especially the immersive world of survival-horror video gaming—may continue to be influenced by religious themes and, in turn, may shape theological understandings of the conflict between the oppression and liberation of women.

As theologian Mary Malone wrote, "it is unlikely that the grip of patriarchy will ever be completely loosened, but the process of trying to create an inclusive community can bring joy and even exhilaration."[53] Ultimately, isn't that why we engage with the alternative worlds presented by horror, to enjoy and be exhilarated by the experience? For some viewers, the fantastical counterworlds of *Silent Hill* can offer a hopeful, if horrifying, alternative to the status quo.

NOTES

1. Ruether, *Womanguides*, xi.
2. Daly, *Beyond God the Father*.
3. Schur, *Labeling Women Deviant*.
4. Russell, *Authority and the Challenge of Feminist Interpretation*.
5. Ruether, *Womanguides*.
6. In *Depatriarchalizing in Biblical Interpretation*, Trible challenges the sexist interpretations of Genesis (2–3) and argues that the Creation story does not present Eve or her gender as inferior but the opposite, with the order of creation illustrating Eve's value: "she is not an afterthought; she is the culmination" (36). See also Daly, *Beyond God*, for further discussion of societal ramifications of patriarchal interpretations of Eve.
7. Ruether, *Womanguides*, 64.
8. Ibid.
9. Klopfer, *Feminist Scholarship on Women in the Bible*.
10. Daly, *Beyond God*.
11. Ibid.
12. Kissling, *Roman Catholic Fundamentalism*.
13. Howland, *Religious Fundamentalisms and the Human Rights of Women*.
14. Ruether, *Womanguides*, 112, and Russell, *Authority and the Challenge of Feminist Interpretation*. See also Milne, "Genesis from Eve's Point of View" for discussion of the creation story as one of sexual equality and liberation.
15. Daly, *Beyond God*, and Kissling, "Roman Catholic Fundamentalism."
16. See Schur, *Labeling Women*; Howland, *Religious Fundamentalisms*; Rose, *Christian Fundamentalism*; and Jordan, "Beyond Belief?"
17. Daly, *Beyond God*.
18. Ibid. See also Eller, *The Myth of Matriarchal Prehistory*.
19. Russell, "Authority and the Challenge of Feminist Interpretation"; Kissling, "Roman Catholic Fundamentalism"; and Malone, "Women in Theology."
20. Daly, *Beyond God*.
21. Kermode, *Mark Kermode's Secrets of Cinema*.
22. Kirkland, "Masculinity in Video Games: The Gendered Gameplay of Silent Hill."
23. Steinmetz, "Carceral horror: Punishment and control in Silent Hill."
24. Creed, *Horror and the Monstrous-Feminine* and Kristeva, *Powers of Horror*.
25. Directed by Luca Guadagnino (Lionsgate).
26. Both directed by Ari Aster (A24).
27. Directed by Henry Joost and Ariel Schulman (Paramount Pictures). For a fuller discussion on matriarchies in this film franchise, refer to Subissati and West, *Mother Lover: Matriarchy in The Wicker Man and Paranormal Activity 3*.
28. See Eller, *The Myth of Matriarchal Prehistory* for discussion of the contested existence of prehistoric matriarchies.
29. Pruett, *The Changing Utility of the Otherworld in the Silent Hill Series* and Kirkland, "Restless Dreams and Shattered Memories: Psychoanalysis and Silent Hill."
30. Video games created by Team Silent/Konami, *Silent Hill* (Playstation, 1999) and *Silent Hill 3* (Playstation 2, 2003) and *Silent Hill*, directed by Christophe Gans (Sony Pictures Home Entertainment and TriStar Pictures, 2006). The game *Silent Hill 2* (Team Silent/Konami, Playstation 2, 2001) is generally considered part of the original canon in terms of themes and mythology but is not included here due to its focus on psychoanalytic themes more so than religious elements.

31. It should be noted that the mythology and events in the franchise are complex and differ both between and within games, depending on player choices. For the ease of clarity, I have tried to focus analysis on common themes and canonical/"normal" events and endings.

32. Steinmetz, "Carceral horror."

33. See Pruett, "The Anthropology of Fear: Learning about Japan Through Horror Games."

34. Subisatti and West, *Achievement Unlocked: Resident Evil and Silent Hill.*

35. Daly, *Beyond God.*

36. Kirkland, *Horror Videogames and the Uncanny.*

37. Kirkland, *Masculinity in Video Games.*

38. Although *Silent Hill 2* is not included in the current discussion, the Mannequin and Abstract Daddy monsters can also be read as reflections of male abuses against women.

39. Green, "'Mother is God in the Eyes of a Child,'" 152.

40. Ibid.

41. Jordan, *Silencing Rape, Silencing Women,* 254.

42. Malone, *Women in Theology.*

43. Green, "'Mother is God in the Eyes of a Child,'" 156.

44. Ibid.

45. Ibid.

46. Ibid, 149.

47. Ibid.

48. Kirkland, *Masculinity in Video Games.*

49. Daly, *Beyond God,* 66.

50. Ruether, *Womanguides,* 112.

51. Lang, *One of Us: The Transcendent Rise of Religious Cults in Horror.*

52. Green, "'Mother is God in the Eyes of a Child,'" 159.

53. Malone, *Women in Theology,* 225.

WORKS CITED

Abdel Halim, Asma M. "Reconciling the Opposites: Equal but Subordinate." In *Religious Fundamentalisms and the Human Rights of Women*, edited by Courtney W. Howland, 203–14. New York: Palgrave Macmillan, 1999.

Creed, Barbara. "Horror and the Monstrous-Feminine: An Imaginary Abjection." In *The Dread of Difference*, edited by Barry K. Grant, 37–67. Austin, TX: University of Texas Press, 1996.

Daly, Mary. *Beyond God the Father: Toward a Philosophy of Women's Liberation.* Boston: Beacon Press, 1973.

Eller, Cynthia. *The Myth of Matriarchal Prehistory.* Boston: Beacon Press, 2000.

Green, Amy M. "'Mother is God in the Eyes of a Child': Mariology, Revelation, and Mothers in *Silent Hill*," *Journal for Cultural and Religious Theory* 14, no. 1 (Fall 2014): 143–64.

hooks, bell. *Feminist Theory: From Margin to Center.* New York: Routledge, 2015.

Howland, Courtney W. *Religious Fundamentalisms and the Human Rights of Women.* New York: Palgrave Macmillan, 1999.

Jordan, Jan. "Beyond Belief? Police, Rape and Women's Credibility." *Criminal Justice* 4, no. 1 (February 2004): 29–59.

———. "Silencing rape, silencing women." In *Handbook on Sexual Violence*, edited by Jennifer Brown and Sandra L. Westlake. Abingdon, UK: Routledge, 2012.

Kermode, Mark. *Mark Kermode's Secrets of Cinema*, Episode 5, "Horror." (Aired 14 August 2018, BBC Four UK).

Kirkland, Ewan. "Horror Videogames and the Uncanny." Paper presented at the Breaking of New Ground proceedings of DiGRA, Brunel University, London UK, 2009a. http://www.digra.org/wp-content/uploads/digital-library/09287.25453.pdf.

———. "Masculinity in Video Games: The Gendered Gameplay of *Silent Hill*." *Camera Obscura* 24, no. 2 (71) (2009b): 161–83.

———. "Restless Dreams and Shattered Memories: Psychoanalysis and *Silent Hill.*" *Research Journal on the Fantastic* III, no.1 (Spring 2015): 162–82.

Kissling, Frances. "Roman Catholic Fundamentalism: What's Sex (and Power) Got to Do with It?" In *Religious Fundamentalisms and the Human Rights of Women*, edited by Courtney W. Howland, 193–202. New York: Palgrave Macmillan, 1999.

Klopfer, Sheila. *Feminist Scholarship on Women in the Bible.* Waco, TX: The Center for Christian Ethics at Baylor University, 2013.

Kristeva, Julia. *Powers of Horror.* New York: Columbia University Press, 1982.

Lang, Alison. "One of Us: The Transcendent Rise of Religious Cults in Horror." The Black Museum Lecture Series, 2014. Accessed May 21 2019. http://theblackmuseum.com/ ?p=1076.

Littleton, C. Scott. *Understanding Shinto.* London, UK: Duncan Baird Publishers, 2002.

Malone, Mary. T. "Women in Theology." *The Furrow* 50, no. 4 (April 1999): 217–25.

Milne, Pamela. "Genesis from Eve's Point of View." *The Washington Post*, March 26, 1989. Accessed 29 May 2020. https://www.washingtonpost.com/archive/opinions/1989/03/26/ genesis-from-eves-point-of view/dc371184-1f4c-4142-ac2d-d5efee72a0da/.

Pruett, Chris. "The Anthropology of Fear: Learning About Japan Through Horror Games." *Interface: The Journal of Education, Community and Values* 4, no. 6 (2010): 1–19.

———. "The Changing Utility of the Otherworld in the Silent Hill Series." Online gaming blog horror.dreamdawn, June 12, 2011. Accessed August 19, 2019. http://horror.dreamdawn.com/?p=29211.

Rose, Susan D. "Christian Fundamentalism: Patriarchy, Sexuality, and Human Rights." In *Religious Fundamentalisms and the Human Rights of Women*, edited by Courtney W. Howland, 9–20. New York: Palgrave Macmillan, 1999.

Ruether, Rosemary Radford. *Womanguides: Readings Towards a Feminist Theology.* Toronto, Canada: Beacon Press, 1985.

Russell, Letty M. "Authority and the Challenge of Feminist Interpretation." In *Feminist Interpretation of the Bible*, edited by Letty M. Russell, 137–46. Oxford, UK: Basil Blackwell, 1985.

Satha-Anand, Suwanna. "Truth over Convention: Feminist Interpretations of Buddhism." In *Religious Fundamentalisms and the Human Rights of Women*, edited by Courtney W. Howland, 281–92. New York: Palgrave Macmillan, 1999.

Schur, Edwin M. *Labeling Women Deviant: Gender, Stigma, and Social Control.* New York: McGraw-Hill Inc., 1984.

Stanton, Elizabeth C. *The Woman's Bible.* Boston: UPNE, 1993 [1895].

Steinmetz, Kevin F. "Carceral Horror: Punishment and Control in *Silent Hill.*" *Crime Media Culture* 14, no. 4 (2018): 265–87.

Trible, Phyllis. "Depatriarchalizing in Biblical Interpretation." *Journal of the American Academy of Religion* 41, no. 1 (March 1973): 30–48.

Weber, Max. *The Sociology of Religion*, translated and edited by Ephraim Fischoff. Boston: Beacon Press, 1963.

OTHER MEDIA

The Faculty of Horror Podcast. "Episode 49. Achievement Unlocked: *Resident Evil* (2002) and *Silent Hill* (2006)." Presented by Andrea Subissati and Alexandra West. Toronto, April 18, 2017. Accessed 28 August 2019.

The Faculty of Horror Podcast. "Episode 26. Mother Lover: Matriarchy in *The Wicker Man* and *Paranormal Activity 3.*" Presented by Andrea Subissati and Alexandra West. Toronto, 2015. Accessed 28 August 2019.

Hereditary. Directed by Ari Aster. New York City: A24, 2018.

Mark Kermode's Secrets of Cinema: Horror. Presented by Mark Kermode. London: BBC Four, 2018. Accessed on BBC iPlayer 10 July 2019.

Midsommar. Directed by Ari Aster. New York City: A24, 2019.

Paranormal Activity 3. Directed by Henry Joost and Ariel Schulman. Los Angeles: Blumhouse Productions, 2011.

Silent Hill. Directed by Christophe Gans. Culver City: TriStar Pictures, 2006.

Silent Hill. Created by Team Silent. PlayStation. Tokyo: Konami, 1999.

Silent Hill 3. Created by Team Silent. PlayStation 2. Tokyo: Konami, 2003.

Suspiria. Directed by Luca Guadagnino. Santa Monica: Lionsgate, 2018.

The Wicker Man. Directed by Robin Hardy. London: British Lion Films, 1973.

Chapter Twelve

"They Say with Jason Death Comes First/He'll Make Hell a Place on Earth"

The Functions of Hell in New Line's Jason *Sequels*

Wickham Clayton

Guarda quel grande che vene,
e per dolor non par lagrime spanda:
quanto aspetto reale ancor ritene!
Quelli è Iasón

Dante (XVIII 83–86)

JASON

In *Jason Goes to Hell* (1993) Jason goes to hell. This, however, only happens at the climax of a film that spends a large amount of time considering how sending Jason to hell might be possible in light of a completely revised mythology for Jason Voorhees.

Jason is the death-defying, hockey-masked supervillain from the *Friday the 13th* franchise, for which *Jason Goes to Hell* is the ninth filmic installment. The following two films, *Jason X* (2000) and *Freddy vs. Jason* (2003),[1] begin with Jason (played by Kane Hodder in *Jason Goes to Hell* and *Jason X*, and Ken Kirzinger in *Freddy vs. Jason*) in a state of (presumed) postmortem torment, whether the revised mythology of *Jason Goes to Hell* is retained or not (it is not). In the above epigraph, Dante Alighieri surprisingly enough isn't referring to Jason Voorhees, but Jason leader of the Argonauts from Greek mythology:

"Look at that imposing one approaching,
who does not shed a single tear of pain:
what majesty he still maintains down there!
He is Jason [. . .]"[2]

However, one can imagine the magisterial strength of the acquirer of the golden fleece of King Aeëtes of Colchis and historical philanderer in hell as potentially not dissimilar to the dark unflappability of cinema's popular serial murderer and devoted son.

Although hell is relegated to a single bookend in each film, titular in one case, it becomes a significant narrative and characterological undertow in these three movies.[3] Within the *Friday the 13th* film series, distributed and sometimes produced by Paramount Pictures, Jason was originally a young boy, whose drowning led his mother, Pamela Voorhees, to kill the counselors at Camp Crystal Lake, both at the time of his drowning, and decades later when the camp attempts to reopen. Pamela is discovered and killed, and Jason, somehow still surviving in the lake, witnesses his mother's death and gets revenge on anyone within an unspecified radius of Crystal Lake, even following some high school students to Manhattan. At the end of each film, Jason is dispatched and either disappears to return in the following film, or is resurrected somehow in the next movie, returning to life each time. *Jason Goes to Hell*, the first film in the franchise to be produced by New Line Cinema, marking a distinctly different direction stylistically and narratively in the overarching story,[4] attempts to explain this phenomenon, depicting Jason's spirit as a demon worm which can change bodies. The film meanwhile troubleshoots how to work around these resurrections and send him to hell. *Jason X* assumes there is some sort of hellish experience in Jason's mind while his corporeal body survives to kill for a couple of centuries, ultimately in space, and repeating the mythology in a humorously absurd setting. *Freddy vs. Jason* on the other hand, sees Freddy Krueger from the *A Nightmare on Elm Street* series also in hell but having domain over Jason's soul, resurrecting him to support the revival of his own memory, which then gives him power over death as well.

While hell is the goal of *Jason Goes to Hell*, and the starting point for *Jason X* and *Freddy vs. Jason*, hell itself takes up little narrative and discursive screen time across all three. However, through analyzing the aesthetic and narrative construction and depiction of hell in these films, along with considering theological discussions surrounding the nature of hell, its geographies, and its torments, I aim to show how these films reflect religious and theoretical models of hell in Abrahamic traditions. Furthermore, I aim to pinpoint which historical and denominational conceptions of hell are especially relevant in these models. In doing so, I will argue that, in spite of an assumption of, and in some cases a demonstration of, a lack of awareness of theological scholarship and history in considering hell, the way hell is represented (and Jason within them) does connect to some widely accepted cultural understandings. In these films, when we see hell, we uncomplicatedly "read" hell. Hell, in these movies, is a place with vague, largely ambiguous, and shifting (depending on the creative team for each film) topography, dimensions, and purpose. For hell to be of particular use in these films, hell must in some way relate to broad mythological concepts and cultural understandings of this place of postmortem torment.

Establishing such a cultural and mythological background is not entirely necessary to a narratological analysis of the use of hell in New Line's *Jason* movies. However, researching scholarship on hell does reveal not only the way hell links these movies to conceptions of religion both ancient and contemporary but how this conception of hell then impacts storytelling, particularly commercial storytelling. Furthermore, it provides an opportunity to consider how hell is integrated into these movies on individual bases as well as part of an overarching and sometimes inconsistent narrative, while also playing on the anxieties around contemporary mythologies.[5]

Karrà Shimabukuro writes of "functional aesthetics," developed out of Bordwell's expression of directorial authorship. In writing about the *A Nightmare on Elm Street* films, she aims to solidify a way of thinking of a series or a franchise as a slightly shifting aesthetic, which progresses through different authors with similar fundamental elements of form. This breaks down the concept of directorial authorship throughout a serialized narrative, where the form is borrowed from previous entries which then becomes the function of the narrative(s). Shimabukuro writes that, if we take Bordwell's concept that film techniques allow an approach to authorship and apply it to a franchise or series "in order to look at what narrative is written by the series as a whole, and what elements contribute to this 'writing,' it is possible to examine the ways in which the narrative is built across a series, expanding Bordwell's concept that 'a film's stylistic texture is pervasive, uninterrupted from first moment to last' to include a series."[6]

Shimabukuro's identification of this concept doesn't entirely apply to *Jason Goes to Hell*, which mainly retains only the iconography of the hockey mask and the location of Camp Crystal Lake. As we will see, at the very least the makers of *Jason Goes to Hell* were trying to take the series in a new direction. Even the narrative patterns and structures change between the Paramount *Friday* movies and the New Line *Jason* movies. According to J. A. Kerswell, "New Line Cinema acquired the rights to the *Friday the 13th* franchise—with an eye on the inevitable *Freddy vs. Jason* monster mash that eventually came 10 years later—and attempted to breath [sic] new life into it with *Jason Goes to Hell: The Final Friday* (1993)."[7] However, hell is an element which, once introduced, becomes part of the series's functional aesthetics through the next two films linked to this franchise. And surprisingly, with the different sensibilities, there is some small consistency in depiction stylistically, largely because of popular cultural conceptions of hell.

HELL

Jason Goes to Hell: The Final Friday was uneasily received. According to Kerswell, "The results were decidedly mixed, with an ill-advised body-hopping storyline."[8] However, hell was central to the film's inception. According to director Adam Marcus, "Dean [Lorey, screenwriter] and I thought of Jason as hell's assassin."[9] This film begins with Jason (Kane Hodder) as the subject of a surprisingly incoherent sting operation, which ends with his body decimated by heavy firepower. Jason's body is delivered to the coroner (Richard Gant), who eats Jason's still beating black heart and becomes possessed by Jason's spirit. This spirit transfers from person to person in the form of a demon worm with teeth, which is vomited out of each person's mouth and enters the orifice of its choice of the next possessee. One thing leads to another and we discover Jason *is* the worm, and the only way to send him to hell is for a blood relative to stab him with a special dagger.

This happens over the course of approximately ninety minutes, and in the climax, Jason regains his original form by possessing the body of a blood relative. He is restored by "magic evil spirits," which take the form of whitish-orange light. Jason is stabbed by another blood relative with said special dagger, and the "spirits" leave the body, which director Adam Marcus explains as such:

> Now the magic evil spirits that we saw that entered the body, now they're all leaving. Um, and I don't know where the magic spirits are going. They're going to, like, Heaven or something, I don't . . . I . . . I don't know what's happening here. We just thought it was cool. There was no logic behind this.[10]

Whatever significance or unifying coherence the aesthetic conception of hell and spirits may have within the film, by Marcus's own admission here, this is unlikely to be in any way planned. However, it is clear that the sequence is designed to register as both supernatural, as well as embodying some religious or mythological conception of the afterlife and the world outside of our own.

The ground opens with white light streaming downward from above (presumably God?), and demon hands reach up from the ground and pull him underneath. After a brief conclusion with the romantic leads, the coda sees a dog unearth Jason's hockey mask from the dirt before running away. As a final shock, the knife-gloved hand of Freddy Krueger, from the *A Nightmare on Elm Street* series, comes out of the ground, grabs the mask, and pulls it underneath.

The imagery behind the opening credits of *Jason X* is the only place the movie suggests any connection with or link to hell. We see the credits appear over images of flames, cavernous rings and circles descending into a flaming pit, with images of hostile faces, researchers, and scientists looking at the camera, largely superimposed over the fiery valley. Eventually, the camera pulls back to reveal all this imagery occurring within Jason's (Hodder) eye. The opening credits sequence suggests Jason has escaped hell or is experiencing a different form of it than the end of *Jason Goes to Hell* would suggest. The fact that the imagery appears within Jason's eye suggests the torments of hell are not physical, but psychological. However, this isn't clarified or addressed in the film.

Freddy vs. Jason, however, is firmly positioned on the premise that both Jason (Ken Kirzinger) and Freddy (Robert Englund) are in hell—Freddy having been sent there at the end of *Freddy's Dead: The Final Nightmare* (1991). According to coscreenwriter Damian Shannon, "We decided that the story should start right from the last scene of *Jason Goes to Hell*—the point where Freddy grabs Jason's mask. We asked ourselves what that meant— why was Freddy grabbing the mask? We felt we needed to understand what the friction was between these two guys."[11] The film begins with Freddy as our narrator, trapped in hell, but his torment is one of legacy—the residents of Elm Street have forgotten him, and he must be remembered to become powerful again. Freddy, apparently with the power to resurrect the dead, brings back Jason to kill in his absence, so that local residents hopefully make the cognitive link between dead teenagers and Freddy Krueger. This is the extent of the explanation we are given, and thus hell is narratively stricken from both franchises.

There is seemingly little here to discuss, but what is here connects in clear, if potentially unintended, ways to theological scholarship on hell, with some creative license. Key elements of these depictions and references in the *Jason* movies connect, in some cases directly to scripture, and in others, to ideas rooted in the history of literature and the theology of hell and damned spirits. As stated, each film uses hell as a part of narrative continuity, but each movie uses a different conception and representation of what hell is to serve its narrative function. Here, I will look at a range of theological approaches and ideas surrounding hell, particularly discourses around what hell is (both geographically and conceptually), the souls that populate it, hell's torments, and its ultimate longevity.

Paul O'Callaghan has contributed an extremely useful survey of the historical development of theological scholarship around hell, and I will be leaning on his work quite a bit. O'Callaghan describes "hell" as "the doctrine of eternal condemnation"[12] and that it "is based on two of the most sublime and liberating truths of the Christian faith: that God is a faithful, loving God, and that humans are truly free."[13] And finally coming to my first point,

O'Callaghan writes that "The three most common expressions in the New Testament (regarding hell) are [. . .] 'furnace of fire,' the 'worm that does not die,' and the 'gnashing of teeth.'"[14]

While "furnace of fire" suggests the widespread idea, which I will later address, that hell is a place of flames and fire, and "gnashing of teeth" suggests pain and torment, "the worm that does not die"—a very striking inclusion considering the film under discussion—is not as commonly referred to in popular references to the Christian framework of hell. However, it acts as a key punctuation in Mark 9, following a series of references to hell fire in order to reinforce what happens to the sinner, and the supernaturality of the fire. In the King James Version, we see descriptions of torment interrupted by this reference to the worm:

> [43]And if thy hand offend thee, cut it off: it is better for thee to enter into life maimed, than having two hands to go into hell, into the fire that never shall be quenched;
> [44]Where their worm dieth not, and the fire is not quenched.
> [45]And if thy foot offend thee, cut if off: it is better for thee to enter halt into life, than having two feet to be cast into hell, into the fire that never shall be quenched:
> [46]Where their worm dieth not, and the fire is not quenched.
> [47] And if thine eye offend thee, pluck it out: it is better for thee to enter into the kingdom of God with one eye, than having two eyes to be cast into hell fire:
> [48]Where their worm dieth not, and the fire is not quenched. [15]

A strange turn of phrase that may or may not be liberally translated from the original sources. I use the King James Version, as it is a canonical contribution to Anglophone literature and culture, but multiple translations use similar versions of this turn of phrase suggesting a consistency, and although a casual reading through context clues seems to suggest the "worm" here should be interpreted as a person's soul or spirit, Joel Marcus's commentary is more complex in interpretation.

Marcus usefully provides both the original Greek[16] as well as a further interpretation. According to Marcus, "The worms, presumably, are eating the bodies of their victims."[17] Marcus furthermore suggests that Mark 9:50, beginning with the phrase "Salt is good," provides an antidote to the tortures of hellfire, as salt kills worms. Furthermore, the worm consuming our insides is a way of providing a multidimensional torture: "The image is a particularly horrific one, conjoining torture from within (the worm that devours one's insides) with torment from without (fire), but it is difficult to know how literally it is meant to be taken in the present passage, since the entire context is hyperbolic."[18] Marcus's interpretation is sound and based on extensive research and study, but this interpretation is not done without qualification and prevarication. The phrase is so vague and oblique that, for my purposes, it seems reasonable to presume that a reader *could* interpret "the worm that does not die" to be a spirit that will not expire in the midst of eternal tortures: In hell you'll be punished, and you can't escape it through death. The "salt" of verse 50 could be the escape we need to avoid the eternality of torment.

O'Callaghan suggests "the worm that will not die" holds greater significance to the part of the person that is tortured for eternity. And while O'Callaghan writes that "the language used in Scripture to speak of matters eschatological is openly metaphorical,"[19] *Jason Goes to Hell* literalizes this. Jason's soul, his spirit, is embodied in this film as a worm that will not die. Jason's body can be destroyed, but his murderousness continues through whoever this disgusting demon worm inhabits. And the use of this worm in a film that clearly establishes expectations for a journey to hell, a place with unquenchable fire, may be coincidental.[20] In the absence of proof that the creative team behind *Jason Goes to Hell* was making deliberate reference to this passage from the Bible, we have to assume for the time being that this is either an inherited and unwitting connection taken from the texts from which they took inspiration, or it is a coincidence. However, if this is coincidence, it is a wonderful and fun one.

Screenwriter Dean Lorey explains the narrative decision to show a form of spirit apart from Jason's corporeal body: "Throughout these films Jason always gets killed in different ways and he keeps coming back, but the reasons are never explained. So we decided that we'd create a mythology that explains the history of Jason and explains how this could be happening."[21] And although "the worm that will not die" may not be an accessible reference for the intended audience for the film, its connections to the biblical text may go some way to reclaiming and reasserting literary and metaphorical conceptions long-lost culturally.

While the use of the demon worm—Jason's murderous soul—may be the only place where *Jason Goes to Hell* literally depicts a portion of the Bible, theological scholarship and religiously inspired literature becomes useful in understanding how these conceptions of hell might have been considered as relevant depictions in a movie with a hoped-for wide viewership. The way hell is shown must "ring true" to an audience familiar with popular culture, which likely means an audience unfamiliar with interpretations in biblical scholarship. Historical explorations of the way hell has developed as a theological concept is useful in helping us to understand where this popular model for hell comes from and why this might even be especially relevant to such a horror film.

Terje Oestigaard identifies five phases of the development of hell in the history of Christian theology: the Deluge (a large flood), Sheol (underground), Gehenna (valley of torment), the fiery torture chamber, and the absence of God.[22] Oestigaard argues that humans, Christians particularly, took minor references in the Bible to hell, Satan, and so forth, and developed an afterlife punishment that connected to their real-life experience of the pain and corporeal punishment witnessed during witch burnings. This torment they saw firsthand became a way to reinforce the punishment awaiting sinners.[23] Ultimately, according to Oestigaard, "The traditional view of the Christian hell is retributive. The doors of hell are locked from the inside rather than from the outside, and the penalty suffered in hell is in accordance with the nature of the sins committed."[24]

Tarald Rasmussen expands on the development of this belief in fiery torment in Late Medieval theology and into the Reformation. According to Rasmussen, hell in Late Medieval Christian theology is an exceptionally scary destination, and at the time it was believed most people were more likely to be sent to purgatory than hell.[25] This description is fitting for the way it is depicted in horror—a scary film needs a scary place for scary people. This aids the representation of hell in these films as it is particularly ominous and a suitable place for a frightening, undefeatable murderer such as Jason Voorhees. This is not a place for teens who die smoking pot and fucking. The severity of this hell seems too grandiose for many of the people Jason kills.

This stands distinctly apart from Rasmussen's description of Martin Luther's concepts of hell.[26] According to Rasmussen:

> As a consequence of Luther's critique of indulgence and of the use of the sacrament of penance, purgatory was removed from the theology and the religious life of the Protestants. The dualism of heaven and hell of the Gospels was restored, and the involvement of the church with the details of the afterlife was abolished. Through this rearrangement of the topography of life after death, hell gained a new importance—though not in the sense that it became a central topic in Reformation theology and preaching. Sin is a much more fundamental concept than hell as a possible consequence of sin, and the main focus is on salvation of sin, not on the threats of hell. So it is rather the *function of hell* within the discourse of sin, salvation and damnation that changes fundamentally within the Reformation, and not so much the rhetoric of hell as a theological topic in general.[27]

So while hell is still a terrifying and ominous place, in these films, the crimes of the victims pale in contrast to those of Jason, the ultimate killer and threat. This suggests, appropriately enough, that the hell we see, in alignment with the brutality we witness, is theologically linked to a Late Medieval paradigm. In other words, only a person committing sins as rampantly egregious as Freddy Krueger or Jason Voorhees would be sent to hell.

However, the fear of hell extant in Reformation theology is significant to communicating terror. Christopher Scott McClure focuses on the way hell is presented in Thomas Hobbes's *Leviathan* (published in 1651), which he argues is surprisingly overlooked. In McClure's evaluation, "This oversight is surprising, however, because the fear of violent death is the foundation of Hobbes's political thought and Hobbes clearly states that the fear of hell is greater than the fear of violent death and that citizens are often more afraid to sin than of breaking civil laws."[28] As viewers of horror films we are presumably asked to at least consider hell as potentially scary. Wherever Jason is, that's where we don't want to be, and our cultural understanding of hell, and the narrative surrounding it contributes to this. And broadly, there are common understandings of what hell entails.

Fire, torment, and eternity are central to this contemporary understanding of hell. As stated by O'Callaghan, the New Testament frequently refers to fiery torment. The writings of St. Augustine were undeniably influential to Christian theology and in some corners remain so. Ric Machuga discusses Augustine's *City of God*, written in the early fifth century, and its discussion of hell. According to Machuga, "The three essential characteristics of hell according to Augustine are: (1) God will send the *majority* of people to hell, (2) where they will *suffer* terrible pain, and (3) once in hell their punishment is *everlasting*."[29] Furthermore, "Chapters 2 through 9 of Book 21 of *The City of God* are an attempt to explain how fire and worms can eternally afflict the bodies of the damned without eventually consuming them and bring their suffering to an end."[30] While Augustine's view is different from Late Medieval views on who will go to hell, which I will come to later, pain is significant to this characterization of hell, as is fire as a source of pain.

We therefore repeatedly see fire depicted, at least in *Jason Goes to Hell* and *Jason X*. The promotional material for *Jason Goes to Hell*, including the poster and DVD cover, features the demon worm against a backdrop of flames. Among the spirits swirling and leaving Jason's body, we see a bright light from heaven. The light is blinding, and the swirling spirits look like flames. Furthermore, the sequence where Jason's mask is pulled under by Freddy's glove is bathed in red light which evokes a sense of heat. *Freddy vs. Jason* does not directly bother with a particular visualization of a hell in flames, but much of the afterlife world that we see is located around Freddy's boiler room, certainly hot, and all steeped in red, either using lights or filters.

Even more relevant is the construction of the hellish landscape we see in the opening of *Jason X*. We see flames and a rocky underground pit, with paths marking out different levels of depth around the edges. We see circles in hell. This imagery evokes the construction of hell made popular in Dante Alighieri's poem *The Divine Comedy*, the first part being devoted to Dante's journey through hell, entitled *Inferno* (1971/2003), originally written in the early fourteenth century. While Dante's hell is not consistently a flaming pit—in fact in Cantos XXXIII and XXXIV we see demons lodged in ice, leading toward Lucifer at the center—the title itself proclaims a place defined by its fiery torment. *Inferno* lays out a geography for hell that is structured around various descending layers, levels, and circles, each with separate torments for those guilty of different sins. This geography is visually evident in *Jason X*'s opening, which incorporates hell as a form of continuity between instalments.

Dante's *Inferno* is a particularly illustrative literary and cultural touchstone for depictions of hell. Dante's descriptions of torments and the sinners experiencing them are vivid and explicit. Sinners of rage and wrath, particularly relevant to the character of Jason, experience torments deemed relevant to their sins:

> And I, intent on looking as we passed,
> saw muddy people moving in that marsh,
> all naked, with their faces scarred by rage.
> They fought each other, not with hands alone,
> but struck with head and chest and feet as well,
> with teeth they tore each other limb from limb.[31]

The hands of demons pulling Jason underground suggest such fighting among the rage-filled in hell, and perhaps the climax of *Freddy vs. Jason* is another iteration of this. However, those committing violence against others are subjected to further pain:

> But now look down the valley. Coming closer
> you will see the river of blood that boils the souls
> of those who through their violence injured others.[32]

Not a flaming pit here, but blood so hot it boils the violent sinners. Jason is no stranger to blood and the name "slasher," given to the subgenre of horror film that the *Friday the 13th* films were instrumental in defining, is suggestive of a bloody wound inflicted by killers. According to O'Callaghan, for those condemned to hell, "their immoral actions introduce an objective disorder within the cosmos that demands the reestablishment and resituation of the whole of reality. Hell is precisely the crystallization and final expression of the unrepentant sinner's innermost conviction: that of wishing to exist and act as if nothing else existed and acted, or better, as if everything else that existed fell under his exclusive, despotic dominion."[33] This feels particularly significant to violent sinners, to slasher villains.

While Dante's vision of hell is one tailored to provide different torments to different kinds of sinners, we have seen that Late Medieval theology suggests that hell is reserved for only the worst sinners. Scholarship continues to debate who goes to hell and what torments they suffer. Therefore, it will be helpful to engage with some of these theological discourses around those condemned, and what scholarship says about its eternality, especially since Jason keeps coming back from it.

In contrast to Augustine's assertion that condemnation is eternal, certain theological ideas suggest quite the opposite. O'Callaghan refers to the work of Origen: "Eventually all sinners will be purified of the sins they freely committed, he said, and will be saved: this is usually called the doctrine of the *apokatastasis*, or universal reconciliation."[34] Machuga even problematizes Augustine's interpretation of hell. According to him, the fire of hell is purifying, and exists to accomplish that purification, so there must be a point where the object of the flame is ultimately purified. Machuga writes, "A *qualitatively* eternal fire is one that is not quenched until it achieves this purifying purpose."[35]

However, the manner of this fire has been subjected to other forms of consideration. Harvey D. Egan, S.J. argues, "Hell is the paradox that God, Christ (who died and rose even for the damned), the saints, and creation itself continue to love eternally even the condemned, and that this constitutes their torment."[36] Furthermore, Egan writes, "I hold the position that the postmortem encounter of the damned with Christ the "judging fire," the "purest fire," who died and rose for them—and loves them still—is an aspect of the suffering of the lost."[37] Egan later writes, "Rejected love is experienced as wrath [. . .] What should be a fire that transforms and glorifies everything in the divine milieu transmogrifies the damned into mystical slag, the 'outer darkness' of the divine milieu."[38] With the Bible referring to Christ as a form of fire, running contrary to some contemporary beliefs that hell is the absence of God's love, as stated by Oestigaard, Egan is firm in asserting that God's love is experienced as painful fire by those who are in a psychological form organized to reject this love. Egan works to resolve the paradox of God as loving, yet a God that condemns a person to eternal torment. In this view, the bright light shining down on Jason from above aligns with Egan's interpretation—it's God's love which Jason experiences as abhorrent. However, these characterizations of hell the place also connect with a consideration of the character of hell's residents.

Joseph Corabi's writing is particularly illuminative when it comes to considering what type of person is destined for hell. Corabi writes about the Settled Character Theory of hell which he describes as follows:

> God does not condemn people to hell to exact some sort of objectively required penalty for sin, but rather because their psychological profiles are fitted for hell, they have made free choices leading them to their psychological profiles (in the long run), and God respects both the existence and the natural consequences of free choices of this sort.[39]

One part of this in particular is what Corabi calls the Fittingness thesis: "Hell is the naturally fitting outcome for someone who is psychologically 'closed-down.'"[40] This certainly seems a fitting idea in relation to Jason, a character with no character arc or development. If ever there were someone with a firmly established unmovable psychology suitable to hell, Jason is he.

Significantly, though, *Jason X* and *Freddy vs. Jason* depict Jason experiencing a psychological torment, with his corporeal body still intact. This is further supported by contemporary Vatican dictate. According to Oestigaard, "Pope John Paul II officially redefined hell on July 28, 1999. According to this redefinition, hell is the "absence of God," and the images of physical pain and fiery torture should be understood as metaphors of the psychological pain it is to live apart from God's love."[41] Whether or not Jason is experiencing God's absence, his experience of hell in *Jason X* is certainly internal, and in *Freddy vs. Jason* he is reduced to nothing but psychological experience. We see his smoldering body, and Freddy has the power to affect Jason's psychological experience, resulting in physical resurrection.

While much of this is drawing on Christian theological scholarship, I'd like to note that these ideas surrounding hell are not limited to Christianity. Some extend, sometimes uncertainly, to the other key Abrahamic religions. O'Callaghan is careful to point out that ideas surrounding hell tend to be limited to Christianity and not to its Abrahamic roots, as "among the Jews the idea of *post-mortem* retribution for sinners was uncommon."[42] However, he stresses that "the Israelites feared that a doctrine of punishment after death could facilitate the development of cult toward the dead, and they wished to avoid this on account of the danger of idolatry."[43] Perhaps considering the popularity of the *Friday the 13th* films throughout the 1980s and even continuing until now, the Israelites might have been onto something.

On the other hand, O'Callaghan continues: "It gradually became clear to (Job) that God will vindicate the just and punish sinners, but not necessarily in this life, but rather, after death."[44] Furthermore, "a kind of evolution may be observed in the Old Testament teaching about the "underworld," or *she'ol*. In effect, *she'ol*, which has many elements in common with the Greek *hades,* is considered in earlier biblical texts as being identical for all the dead, whether just or unjust. Gradually, however, different "levels" emerged within *she'ol*."[45] This does demonstrate that, while different interpretations of Jewish thought disagree on the existence of an afterlife, postmortem retribution wasn't completely ruled out. The reference to different "levels" in *she'ol* also helps reinforce Dante's construction of hell.

The Jewish connection to the afterlife as it relates to Christian theology is nicely summarized by Phillip Jenkins, who writes, "Throughout the gospels, Jesus often speaks of the fates reserved for the virtuous and the wicked. Not every Jew at the time shared those views, and the influential faction of the Sadducees even denied the afterlife. Even so, early Christians were firmly rooted in the Jewish beliefs of the time: Death was assuredly not the end."[46]

While Judaism may not comfortably link to belief in damnation for sinners after death, Islam more firmly builds upon the concept of hell understood in Christianity. According to Einar Thomassen[47] there are several names for hell in the Qur'an: Jahannam, *al-saʿīr, al-jaḥīm, al-laẓā.* He notes that Jahannam is a derivation of the Hebrew *Gê Hinnôm,* the valley where the wicked are subjected to fiery torments, while the other three terms are descriptions of specific kinds of fire. Furthermore, Thomassen writes that "Skin sensation and digestion thus seem to be the two favourite themes in the Qur'an's description of the infernal torments. However, the psychological terrors are at least as painful as the corporeal torments."[48] We certainly, in these films, get a sense of psychological terror and possible physical pain. The demon worm also links to digestion, but in a slightly more confused configuration.

There are also further clear components to situate the understanding of hell structurally, "It is clear, moreover, that hell is a prison: the people there have chains around their necks [. . .], and they are fettered by hooks of iron."[49] This is certainly echoed in the containment of Jason at the start of *Jason X*—he is restrained and suspended by chains and hooks in the research facility. Thomassen further argues that several sources suggest that hell in Islam may not be eternal.[50] Jon Hoover, in his study of hell in the work of Islamic theologian Ibn Qayyim al-Jawziyya, student of Ibn Taymiyya, notes that, "The Fire is a great remedy that purifies and reforms even unbelievers and associators. Ibn al-Qayyim elaborates these arguments far more fully than does his master, but he hesitates [. . .] to adopt them unequivocally as his own. Instead, he leaves the duration of the Fire to God's will."[51] Islam does not necessarily posit hell as an eternal punishment. Furthermore, while hell in Islam doesn't have quite as defined a geography as in Dante's hell, there are still distinct levels, for unbelievers and sinners of different sorts.

Although I do not have time to review all belief systems, and many would not have quite the same level of overlap as the Abrahamic religions, it is clear that there are multiple religious reference points to aid the widespread cultural dissemination of hell we see in the New Line *Jason* films. Furthermore, this cultural dissemination is useful in the films' shorthand delivery (*very* shorthand) of what hell is and how it might function within the world of this franchise, no matter how inconsistent the narratives are. So while this may not necessarily be a well-researched or deeply intended rendering of theological scholarship in film, these points show that multiple cultural paradigms would be able to view these films and register these particular brief moments as hell.

JASON APPEARS TO GO TO HELL

The *Friday the 13th* films create a villain who is the embodiment of mythology. Jason is a relentless villain who continues to reanimate, no matter how many times he is seemingly killed. But at all times, it is not certain whether Jason is returning from the dead, or, as in the Monty Python sketch, is "just resting." At the start of *Jason Goes to Hell*, when he is blown apart by bullets, bombs, and missiles, his death is still in question in spite of Jason being a corporeal mess. By the end, however, we have seen Jason pulled into the underworld. He is subjected to a mythology bigger than him, with a significant amount of precedent attached to it.

Therefore, the openings of *Jason X* and *Freddy vs. Jason* reinforce Jason's mythological status because he has escaped, emerged from this grand, impenetrable pit of despair, which, at the end of *Jason Goes to Hell*, appears larger than even him. Jason doesn't just escape death. That's a dawdle. He pulls himself out of hell, albeit one we see contained within his own mind, which is ultimately consistent with the Paramount *Friday* movies. If hell is in Jason's mind, a concept which has its own theological precedent, his return from the dead is both old hat and has spiritual connotations. However, I'd strongly discourage drawing parallels between Jason and Christ, as at best it could be a deeply misguided point of interpretation, and at worst would result in another essay by me.

If you are willing to read these films as inspired by or directly referencing the Bible and theological scholarship, you would not be unsupported, but you wouldn't be strongly supported either. Rather, the significance here is that this scholarship demonstrates that hell is a fluid, highly contested concept with a range of beliefs, even within specific religions, on its pains, place, populous, and permanence. However, there are traditions which are firmly acknowledged, even if not believed, within the Abrahamic religions and literary evocations of them, which aid in easy conveyance of a sense of hell. Lights, demons, flames, torture, and fear are all imagined in these brief aesthetic and narrative suggestions of hell, and that is the definition of economical storytelling.

To conclude on a slightly optimistic note, though, certain approaches to Christian theology signify hope for Jason in whatever state he appears. According to David R. Law, who considers the implications surrounding Christ's descent into hell before ascending to heaven in the days following his crucifixion, "The notion of Christ's descent into hell expresses the insight that the gospel is offered to all human beings—not only those who are alive but those who are dead. No one, not even the denizens of hell, is excluded from Christ's redemptive work."[52]

This is good news for Jason. In fact, even going to hell has been a form of resurrection for a fictional figure who was thought dead commercially; reworking Jason's mythology, blending it with facets of multiple mythologies that mean so much to audiences of many backgrounds allows him to be a part of a universe much bigger than the filmic one he previously inhabited. And as a result, far from allowing Jason to be dead and buried (or indeed *damned*), the introduction of hell, qualitatively good or bad, gave New Line Cinemas a bit of power behind the desire to get more fuel for this franchise.

Ultimately, my suggestion is that the aesthetic and conceptual construction of hell, and possibly coincidentally the explanation of the supernatural, invincible nature of Jason, ties the viewer more firmly to the mystical. We know Jason refuses to die, and being dragged to hell almost definitively suggests there will be no end to him. It may seem a strange creative decision, but at least there is some faithfulness to its execution.

NOTES

1. All of these films were distributed by New Line Cinema in a change of property rights between studios.

2. Dante, *The Divine Comedy: Inferno*, trans. Mark Musa (London: Penguin Books, 1971/2003), 235.

3. In the previous eight films, all of which are distributed by Paramount Pictures, hell is only mentioned as a means of metaphorical or poetic referencing as opposed to a real place Jason has been or will go. Hell is also ignored in the twelfth film, *Friday the 13th* (2009), which is a form of remake or reboot (both terms have arguable relevance) of the first few films in the series and is a coproduction between Paramount and New Line.

4. Both *Jason X* and *Freddy vs. Jason* were produced by New Line as well, with the remake *Friday the 13th* (2009) being a Paramount/New Line coproduction.

5. While this appears to be a fairly logical approach within the burgeoning field of research on religion and theology in relation to horror film, there is surprisingly little to build upon with regard to this specific franchise. Although there is a growing amount of research on the *Friday the 13th* series, the material that does exist fails to make much mention, or even apply any real significance to the inclusion of hell as an important location in the overarching narrative or mythos. In other words, looking to the limited research on *Friday the 13th* is not really of much help here.

6. Karrà Shimabukuro, "I Framed Freddy: Functional Aesthetics in the *A Nightmare on Elm Street* Series," in *Style and Form in the Hollywood Slasher Film*, ed. Wickham Clayton (London: Palgrave Macmillan, 2016), 51–66. Includes David Bordwell, *Figures Traced in Light: On Cinematic Staging*, (London: University of California Press, 2005), 36.

7. J. A. Kerswell, *The Teenage Slasher Movie Book, 2nd Revised and Expanded Edition*, (Mount Joy, PA: CompanionHouse Books, 2010/2018), 165.

8. Ibid.

9. Adam Marcus, *Jason Goes to Hell*, DVD commentary, (New Line Home Video, 1993).

10. Ibid.

11. Damian Shannon, quoted in Peter M. Bracke, *Crystal Lake Memories: The Complete History of* Friday the 13th, (London: Titan Books, 2005), 271.

12. Paul O'Callaghan, *Christ our Hope: An Introduction to Eschatology*, (Washington, DC: Catholic University of America Press, 2012), 189.

13. Ibid.

14. O'Callaghan, *Christ our Hope*, 193.

15. While the phrase "where their worm never dies" is repeated multiple times in the King James Version in 9:44 and 46 as well as 48, most modern translations do not include verses 44 and 46, as they are not present in the earliest extant manuscripts. M. Eugene Boring explains the issue succinctly in *Mark: A Commentary* (Atlanta: Westminster John Knox, 2006), 279: "Though present in later MSS [manuscripts], it is virtually certain they represent a scribal addition made to conform to v. 48."

16. *"hopou ho skōlēx autōn ou teleutā kai to pyr ou sbennytai"* Joel Marcus, *Mark 8–16*, (London: Yale University Press, 2009), 692.

17. Ibid.

18. Marcus, *Mark 8–16*, 698.

19. O'Callaghan, *Christ our Hope*, 194.

20. It is entirely possible this is coincidence. According to Grove, "(screenwriter Dean) Lorey and Marcus were criticised for liberally borrowing ideas from the superb 1987 horror film *The Hidden*" (201). Furthermore, the worm design bears close similarities to the sex parasite in David Cronenberg's *They Came from Within* (1975). There is certainly horror film precedent for this sort of depiction.

21. Dean Lorey, quoted in Bracke, *Crystal Lake Memories,* 221.

22. Terje Oestigaard, "The Materiality of Hell: The Christian Hell in a World Religion Context" *Material Religion* 5, no. 3 (2015): 317–18.

23. Oestigaard, "Materiality of Hell," 322–25.

24. Oestigaard, "Materiality of Hell," 314–15

25. Tarald Rasmussen, "Hell Disarmed?: The Function of Hell in Reformation Spirituality," *Numen* 56, nos. 2/3 (2009): 371.

26. For reference, Martin Luther is a key figure in the early sixteenth-century Reformation, when Western Christianity fractured into those who adhered to the leadership of the centralized Catholic Church, and protestants—those who protested the hierarchical structure of that church.

27. Rasmussen, "Hell Disarmed?" 372–73.

28. Christopher Scott McClure, "Hell and Anxiety in Hobbes's *Leviathan*," *The Review of Politics* 73 (2011): 2.

29. Ric Machuga, *Three Theological Mistakes: How to Correct Enlightenment Assumptions About God, Miracles, and Free Will*, (Eugene, OR: Cascade Books, 2015), 225.

30. Machuga, *Three Theological Mistakes*, 226–27.

31. Dante, *Inferno*, VII.109–114.

32. Dante, *Inferno*, XII.46–48.

33. O'Callaghan, *Christ our Hope*, 206.

34. O'Callaghan, *Christ our Hope*, 195.

35. Machuga, *Three Theological Mistakes*, 243.

36. Harvey D. Egan, S.J., "Hell: The Mystery of Eternal Love and Eternal Obduracy," *Theological Studies* 75, no. 1 (2014): 66.

37. Egan, "Hell," 68.

38. Egan, "Hell," 73.

39. Joseph Corabi, "Hell and Character," *Religious Studies* 47 (2011): 234.

40. Corabi, "Hell and Character," 235–36.

41. Oestigaard, "Materiality of Hell," 319.

42. O'Callaghan, *Christ our Hope*, 190. Emphasis in the original.

43. O'Callaghan, *Christ our Hope*, 190–91.

44. O'Callaghan, *Christ our Hope*, 191.

45. Ibid.

46. Phillip Jenkins, "The Afterlife Evolution: Jewish Attitudes about Heaven and Hell Shaped Early Christian Theology," *U.S. Catholic* (June 2018): 26.

47. Einar Thomassen, "Islamic Hell," *Numen* 56, nos. 2/3 (2009): 403.

48. Thomassen, "Islamic Hell," 404.

49. Ibid.

50. Thomassen, "Islamic Hell," 413.

51. Jon Hoover, "Islamic Universalism: Ibn Qayyim al-Jawziyya's Salafī Deliberations on the Duration of Hell Fire," *The Muslim World* 99, no. 1 (2009): 197.

52. David R. Law, "Descent into Hell, Ascension, and Luther's Doctrine of Ubiquitarianism," *Theology* 107, no. 838 (2004): 254.

WORKS CITED

Bordwell, David. *Figures Traced in Light: On Cinematic Staging*. Berkeley, CA: University of California Press, 2005.

Boring, M. Eugene. *Mark: A Commentary*. Louisville, KY: Westminster John Knox Press, 2006.

Bracke, Peter M. *Crystal Lake Memories: The Complete History of* Friday the 13th. London: Titan Books, 2005.

Corabi, Joseph. "Hell and Character." *Religious Studies* 47 (2011): 233–44.

Dante. *The Divine Comedy Volume 1: Inferno*. Translated by Mark Musa. London: Penguin Books, 1971/2003.

Egan, Harvey D., S.J. "Hell: The Mystery of Eternal Love and Eternal Obduracy." *Theological Studies* 75.1 (2014): 52–73.

Grove, David. *Making Friday the 13th: The Legend of Camp Blood*. Godalming, England: Fab Press, 2005.

Hoover, Jon. "Islamic Universalism: Ibn Qayyim al-Jawziyya's Salafī Deliberations on the Duration of Hell Fire." *The Muslim World* 99.1 (2009): 181–201.

Jenkins, Phillip. "The Afterlife Evolution: Jewish Attitudes about Heaven and Hell Shaped Early Christian Theology." *U.S. Catholic* (June 2018): 25–27.

Kerswell, J. A. *The Teenage Slasher Movie Book, 2nd Revised and Expanded Edition*. Mount Joy, PA: CompanionHouse Books, 2010/2018.

Law, David R. "Descent into Hell, Ascension, and Luther's Doctrine of Ubiquitarianism." *Theology* 107.838 (2004): 250–56.

Machuga, Ric. *Three Theological Mistakes: How to Correct Enlightenment Assumptions about God, Miracles, and Free Will*. Eugene, OR: Cascade Books, 2015.

Marcus, Joel. *Mark 8–16*. London: Yale University Press, 2009.

McClure, Christopher Scott. "Hell and Anxiety in Hobbes's *Leviathan*." *The Review of Politics* 73 (2011): 1–27.

O'Callaghan, Paul. *Christ Our Hope: An Introduction to Eschatology*. Washington, DC: Catholic University of America Press, 2012.

Oestigaard, Terje. "The Materiality of Hell: The Christian Hell in a World Religion Context." *Material Religion* 5.3 (2015): 312–31.

Rasmussen, Tarald. "Hell Disarmed?: The Function of Hell in Reformation Spirituality." *Numen* 56.2/3 (2009): 366–84.

Shimabukuro, Karrà. "I Framed Freddy: Functional Aesthetics in the *A Nightmare on Elm Street* Series." In *Style and Form in the Hollywood Slasher Film*, edited by Wickham Clayton, 51–66. London: Palgrave Macmillan, 2016.

Thomassen, Einar. "Islamic Hell." *Numen* 56.2/3 (2009): 401–16.

FILMOGRAPHY

Freddy vs. Jason. Directed by Ronny Yu. Burbank, CA: New Line Cinema, 2003.

Friday the 13th. Directed by Marcus Nispel. Burbank, CA: Paramount/New Line Cinema, 2009.

The Hidden. Directed by Jack Sholder. Burbank, CA: New Line Cinema, 1987.

Jason Goes to Hell: The Final Friday. Directed by Adam Marcus. Burbank, CA: New Line Cinema, 1993.

DVD Commentary from *Jason Goes to Hell*. Los Angeles: Automat Pictures, New Line Home Entertainment, Inc., 2002.

Jason X. Directed by Jim Isaacs. Burbank, CA: New Line Cinema, 2002.

Index

About the Contributors

Mark Richard Adams received his doctorate at Brunel University for his study into audiences and production, and the fan-producers of *Doctor Who*. He has a master's in cult film and television, also from Brunel. His publications include a chapter on "Clive Barker's Queer Monsters" in *Clive Barker: Dark Imaginer* and a further chapter on *Hellraiser* in *The Palgrave Handbook of Contemporary Gothic.*

Alyssa J. Beall is a teaching assistant professor at West Virginia University in the program for religious studies and the Department of Philosophy. Her teaching and research centers on religion and popular culture, particularly science fiction and horror. Her additional research interests include study abroad pedagogy, and she frequently leads short-term student programs to Asia, Europe, and the Middle East.

Amy Beddows is a psychotherapist working primarily with victim-survivors of sexual abuse. She is a PhD student researching victim blame at the Child and Woman Abuse Studies Unit (CWASU) at London Metropolitan University. Amy has a special interest in media representations of gendered violence and has written academic pieces on the portrayal of victim-survivors in the horror genre. She also writes fiction under a pen name. She currently lives in Leicester, UK with an astronomer.

Wickham Clayton is a lecturer in film production at the University for the Creative Arts in Farnham, UK. He is author of *See!Hear!Cut!Kill!: Experiencing* Friday the 13th (2020), editor of *The Bible Onscreen in the New Millennium: New Heart and New Spirit* (2020), and *Style and Form in the Hollywood Slasher Film* (2015), and coeditor of *Screening Twi-*

light: Critical Approaches to a Cinematic Phenomenon (2014 with Sarah Harman). Wickham's research primarily focuses on film form, genre, adaptation, and postmodernism.

Douglas E. Cowan is professor of religious studies and social development studies at Renison University College. He is the author of more than sixty articles and ten books, including *Sacred Terror: Religion and Horror on the Silver Screen*; *Sacred Space: The Quest for Transcendence in Science Fiction Film and Television*; *America's Dark Theologian: The Religious Imagination of Stephen King*; and *Magic, Monsters, and Make-Believe Heroes: How Myth and Religion Shape Fantasy Culture*. He is currently completing *Bodies Out of Place: Sex, Horror, and the Religious Imagination*. He lives in Waterloo, Canada.

Brandon R. Grafius is associate professor of biblical studies at Ecumenical Theological Seminary. His publications include a handbook on the film *The Witch* in the Devil's Advocates series (2020) and *Reading the Bible with Horror* (Lexington Books/Fortress Academic, 2019), which was nominated for the Grawemeyer Award in Religion. He is coediting, with John W. Morehead, *The Oxford Handbook of Biblical Monsters*.

Michael Asher Hammett is a doctoral candidate at Columbia University in the Religion Department in the History of Christianity track. His dissertation research focuses on late medieval and early modern Christian demonological interpretations of transformation of people into animals. Michael holds a BA in history from Duke University, a MLitt in reformation studies from the University of St Andrews, a MA in religion from Columbia University, and a MPhil in religion from Columbia University. He is also an adjunct lecturer in religion at Hunter College.

Jack Hunter is an anthropologist exploring the borderlands of religion, ecology, and the paranormal. He is a tutor with the Sophia Centre for the Study of Cosmology in Culture and an honorary research fellow with the Alister Hardy Religious Experience Research Centre, both at University of Wales Trinity Saint David. He is the editor of *Damned Facts* (2016) and *Greening the Paranormal* (2019) and the author of *Engaging the Anomalous* (2018) and *Spirits, Gods and Magic* (2020). You can find out more about his research at www.jack-hunter.webstarts.com.

Jessi Knippel is an academic, writer, and artist who lives in the promised land of Southern California with her partner and child. She holds a BA in theatre and in religious studies, two MA's in the intersections of religion and media/art, and is currently working on an interdisciplinary PhD in religion, gender studies, and media at Claremont Graduate School. Her research includes post/ex-evangelicals, evangelicalism in the United States, new religious movements, deviant sex cults, syncretism and folk practices in religion, as well as pop culture and religion.

John W. Morehead is an academic researcher and writer specializing in new religious movements, religion and popular culture, and interreligious conflict. His writing includes a chapter on Matrixism for *The Brill Handbook of Hyper-real Religions*; entries on Paganism for *The Handbook of Religion*; and he has been the coeditor and editor of volumes on religion and pop culture including *The Undead and Theology, Joss Whedon and Religion, The Supernatural Cinema of Guillermo del Toro, Fantastic Fan Cultures and the Sacred,* and *The Paranormal and Popular Culture.* He serves as a coeditor for the double-blind, peer-reviewed online *Journal of Gods and Monsters*, and is coediting, with Brandon R. Grafius, *The Oxford Handbook of Biblical Monsters.* He blogs at www.TheoFantastique.com.

Karrà Shimabukuro is an assistant professor at Elizabeth City State University. Her research focuses on elements from medieval and early modern literature that are carried forward in popular culture and how they represent a particular historical and cultural moment. Her most recent work analyzes the role of the devil in the culture wars, and his connection to *The Last Temptation of Christ* and *The Passion of the Christ* in "The Devil and The Culture Wars: Demonizing Controversy in *The Last Temptation of Christ* and *The Passion of the Christ*" in *The Bible Onscreen in the New Millennium,* 2019.

Kevin J. Wetmore, Jr. is a professor at Loyola Marymount University. He is the author of a dozen books, including *Post-9/11 Horror in American Cinema, The Theology of Battlestar Galactica,* and *Back from the Dead: Reading Remakes of Romero's Zombie Films as Markers of their Times.* He is also the editor of over a dozen books, including the Bram Stoker Award–nominated *Uncovering Stranger Things* and *Catholic Theatre and Drama: Critical Essays.* He has written over one hundred articles and book chapters on everything from Godzilla to possession films to Christianity on the Japanese stage.

Steve A. Wiggins is the author of *Holy Horror: The Bible and Fear in Movies* (2018) and *Nightmares with the Bible: The Good Book and Its Cinematic Demons* (Lexington Books/Fortress Academic, 2021).

Joshua Wise is an independent scholar and resident theologian for an Episcopal church. He works mainly on Christian eschatology and the dialogue between theology and popular culture. He is the author of the book *No*

Avatars Allowed: Theological Reflections on Video Games and the editor of the book *Past the Sky's Rim: The Elder Scrolls and Theology*. He also runs the All Ports Open podcasting network where he discusses theology and gaming every week on the podcast No Avatars Allowed.